LAKER GIRL

LAKER GIRL

Jeanie Buss with Steve Springer

TRIUMPH
BOOKS

To my mom and dad: I can never return all you have done for me. I love you.

To my siblings: thanks for sharing your love and lives with me.

To my girlfriends: thanks for keeping me laughing.

To my Boobah: thanks for inspiring me every day with your love and affection.

Copyright © 2010 by Jeanie Buss and Steve Springer

No part of this publication may be reproduced, stored in a retrieval system, or transmitted in any form by any means, electronic, mechanical, photocopying, or otherwise, without the prior written permission of the publisher, Triumph Books, 542 South Dearborn Street, Suite 750, Chicago, Illinois 60605.

Triumph Books and colophon are registered trademarks of Random House, Inc.

Library of Congress Cataloging-in-Publication Data

Buss, Jeanie, 1961–
  Laker girl / Jeanie Buss with Steve Springer.
    p. cm.
  ISBN 978-1-60078-511-5
  1. Buss, Jeanie, 1961– 2. Basketball—Management. 3. Sports personnel—Biography. 4. Fathers and daughters—Biography. 5. Los Angeles Lakers (Basketball team) 6. Buss, Jerry. 7. Jackson, Phil. I. Springer, Steve, 1945– II. Title.
  GV884.B87A3 2010
  796.323092—dc22
  [B]

2010034238

This book is available in quantity at special discounts for your group or organization. For further information, contact:

Triumph Books
542 South Dearborn Street
Suite 750
Chicago, Illinois 60605
(312) 939–3330
Fax (312) 663–3557
www.triumphbooks.com

Printed in U.S.A.
ISBN: 978-1-60078-511-5
Design by Patricia Frey
Photos courtesy of the author unless otherwise indicated

CONTENTS

FOREWORD

In 1999, the NBA had its league meetings in Vancouver, British Columbia. Attending was my first official duty as the Lakers' new basketball coach.

In June, I had made the journey to Los Angeles to be introduced and had gone through the flurry of the press gauntlet, but these meetings officially kicked off the new season.

At the end of the first day, Jeanie Buss, the Lakers' VP in charge of business affairs, hosted a dinner.

We had an exchange at that first meeting that was very cordial but relatively brief. I asked her if I could get her a drink and then brought my staff over to meet her when I delivered her vodka gimlet. She was engaging.

The next day, I left at noon after a coaches meeting to catch a plane back to L.A. I was still in the process of moving and getting settled and had a lot of loose ends I wanted to tie up before we started our training camp in Santa Barbara the following week.

When I got to the gate at the airport, however, there was a delay due to weather.

Seated there, waiting for the next flight, were Jeanie and her assistant. I joined them and we proceeded to have a very interesting conversation about the organization. I realized Jeanie was, first and foremost, very dedicated to the success of the Lakers. She had taken her position as a genetic gift, but she had earned the respect of those she worked with through dedication and hard work. We talked for almost an hour before boarding the plane.

As the first-class passengers were called, I asked if she was going to board the plane, but she said she flew coach, explaining that flying first class wasn't necessary and that the Lakers didn't need the added expense. Let's just say that was the beginning of something special.

Jeanie treasures the Lakers and the fans that love the team. She protects and promotes this very successful organization as if it were a Rembrandt painting, making sure it gets the best showing possible.

When Twitter became a media source of information, Jeanie was on it, giving "her people," the Lakers fans, the inside scoop on the games and the players.

This book will take readers behind the scenes of the Lakers' world and show how Jeanie goes about getting things done in this storied franchise.

I have often been at odds with her about her dedication to "getting the job done" when she gets up at 5:00 AM to do a TV interview after a late-night game, or when she flies across the country for a one-day meeting in New York. She is a trooper, knows what her passion is, and knows what is best for this team she's taken to her heart.

After the last game of the 2009–10 season, when we were pressed to the limit to win a seventh game against the Boston Celtics in the NBA Finals, a *Sports Illustrated* writer was garnering stories about me winning my 11th championship as a coach. Jeanie was his target for a "What was the best…" story. Was this championship or that one the most memorable? Which one did I or she particularly favor?

Jeanie quickly passed the questions on to my daughter Chelsea. Jeanie deflects attention or personal credit quite deftly, and graciously chooses to step out of the limelight. She has not written this book for her own aggrandizement, but to let her fans and the Lakers fans know what her work entails and to give them an inside look at her team, the Los Angeles Lakers.

—Phil Jackson

INTRODUCTION

I AM OFTEN ASKED WHAT IT IS LIKE TO BE THE DAUGHTER OF Dr. Jerry Buss, owner of the Los Angeles Lakers and a man who has given me the prestigious title of executive vice president of business operations. The short answer is, it's pretty darn good. The long answer is this book.

Writing this book presented me with an opportunity to demystify what goes on behind the velvet rope that surrounds our business. *Laker Girl* is a journal of the 2009–10 Lakers season; alternating with the monthly entries are chapters detailing my life story to give you some perspective on how I came to view the world.

It is also important for me to introduce you to the love of my life, a man who also happens to be the head coach of the team my dad owns. Insert your own "don't fish off the company pier" jokes here, but it is no joke. Phil Jackson, one of the most successful coaches in NBA history, is also my boyfriend.

I knew even before the season began that this would be a year to remember. The Lakers were the defending NBA champions, meaning the entire league would be giving us their best shot each and every night. We had added Ron Artest, a talented but enigmatic player who had the potential to be a great asset or a major distraction. And with Phil in the final year of his contract, there was a very real possibility that the window for this particular Lakers team was about to close.

I hope that even if you don't know who I am, have never heard of Phil Jackson, or don't even know who the Lakers are—hard as that would be to believe—I still might have piqued your interest. This is the story of a family business in which the owner's daughter is dating her father's star employee. No matter what the business is, who wouldn't be interested in that?

LAKER GIRL

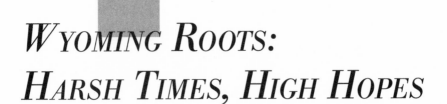

WYOMING ROOTS:
HARSH TIMES, HIGH HOPES

I NEVER FAIL TO MARVEL AT HOW BLESSED I HAVE BEEN IN MY life or how unlikely this all seemed at one time, considering where my dad started his life.

His parents, Jessie and Lydus, divorced when he was just a year old in 1934.

My dad lived with my grandmother in Evanston, Wyoming, where she worked as a waitress and scrubbed floors. With the Great Depression devastating much of the country, it was a rough existence. My dad remembers standing in food lines in sometimes brutally cold weather at the age of four, gunnysack in hand.

If there was no heat in the house, shredded paper might substitute for kindling wood.

When he was nine, my dad got his first glimpse of a bright, new world where snow was for skiing and heat was for sunbathing. My grandmother took him to Los Angeles where she got a job as an accountant at a greeting card company.

My dad would have been thrilled to stay there, but three years later, he found himself back in Wyoming after his mother married Cecil Orville Brown. Brown was also from Wyoming and back they went, settling in Kemmerer, where Brown purchased a plumbing store.

His stepfather soon put a shovel in my dad's hands and informed him that he would be getting up at 4:30 in the morning to dig ditches sufficiently large enough to hold plumbing pipes before heading off to school.

After school, there was football practice. After that, odd jobs to make a few dollars. And somewhere in there, my dad had to fit in his homework.

Adding more misery to the long hours and the backbreaking work was the weather. For much of the year, when my dad poked his head out the door for his predawn labor he was hit in the face with temperatures that sometimes dropped as low as 15 degrees below zero.

Even at that age, however, my dad was already thinking about how to generate revenue streams, although his first streams wouldn't even qualify as a trickle.

Still, for a 13-year-old living in Kemmerer in the darkest days of World War II, two dollars a day was a good start.

That's what my dad earned at the Kemmerer Hotel for a five-hour, after-school shift as a bellhop. A more accurate title would be bellhop/ shoeshine boy/janitor.

Around that time, the entrepreneur the sports world would come to know was also emerging as my dad started his first business.

He sold stamps through the mail. After purchasing the merchandise wholesale, he squeezed out a profit that fell short—sometimes far short— of a dollar per stamp. His profit for a whole month would be about the same as his daily earnings at the hotel: two dollars.

But my dad was driven by the desire to buy clothes or other essentials he wasn't getting at home.

Beyond the practical considerations, he harbored the dream of his ultimate possession: a car.

By the time he was 15, my dad put away that dream, his shovel, and his shoeshine kit and got a real job, even though that meant quitting school.

He left home before his senior year of high school and became a "gandy dancer" for the railroad.

There wasn't any dancing involved, just a lot of sweating. My dad and hundreds of other laborers would head out into vast, lonely stretches of Wyoming on handcars, powering themselves along the tracks by furiously pumping a lever up and down.

Upon arriving at an area where the rails were in need of repair or reinforcement, they would go to work.

Work was an eight-hour day. With overtime, it could be a 14-hour day, and working for "Mile-a-Day" Mike McGuire, as my dad did, it usually turned out to be closer to 14 hours than eight.

After three months of that, school didn't look so bad.

My dad returned to the classroom, but he might not have stayed there long, had it not been for Walt Garrett.

Mention Walt's name around STAPLES Center, or anywhere in L.A. for that matter, and you'll undoubtedly get nothing but blank stares.

But if it wasn't for him, people in L.A. may never have heard of Dr. Jerry Buss. And I certainly wouldn't be wearing a Lakers championship ring and hanging out with people like Jeremy Piven, Michelle Kwan, and David Beckham.

Walt was the first man to really believe in my dad, to tell him that he didn't belong in a frozen ditch or on a handcar in the middle of nowhere.

With your brilliant mind and your grasp of science, Walt told him, you belong on the road to a university.

Walt, a science teacher at Kemmerer High School, had heard that my dad had come back from the railroad for his senior year.

That pleased Walt.

He also heard, however, that my dad was back at his old job at the Kemmerer Hotel and was living there rather than going back home.

That didn't please Walt, who figured my father's grades would suffer from such an arrangement.

So Walt convinced my dad to come live with him in his apartment. The conditions were hardly ideal. My dad slept on a cot in Walt's spare bedroom.

The important thing, Walt told him, was to use the time in the apartment to hit the books. Walt kept repeating to my dad over and over like a mantra that he was a gifted student who must not let his potential slip away.

Nice to hear, but not nice enough to overcome my dad's lack of enthusiasm for school. Four more years in a classroom after high school didn't sound as appealing as moving back to California, the place he remembered so fondly. Once there, my dad figured, he would be happy with a roof over his head and a car to drive, no matter what he did for a living.

But Walt was persistent. He stayed on my father, teaching him chemistry and physics at home as well as at school. The home schooling was conducted while Walt and my dad played cards.

My dad responded, in spite of himself. By the end of his final semester, my father was doing so well in Walt's chemistry class that the student became the instructor. Walt had my dad standing in front of his classmates, teaching parts of the course.

Still, the thought of four additional years of school looming ahead turned my father off.

Instead, he found a shortcut...in the post office.

It was there that my father spotted a notice for a job as a government chemist. Education requirement: one year of college.

That didn't seem so bad.

When he brought the idea to Walt, the science teacher jumped on it. He found a science scholarship and helped my dad qualify for it. My dad was accepted at the University of Wyoming in Laramie.

Don't get too excited, my father told him. I'm only going for one year.

Walt nodded.

My father was on his way. Walt knew darn well my dad wasn't going to stop after just one year.

My dad later admitted that the fear of poverty, the memory of those bread lines, and the prospect that he could wind up in the coal mines of Kemmerer as did so many others drove him not only out of town, but to ever greater heights even after he had gained enough wealth to buy those coal mines if he had so desired.

When my dad got to the University of Wyoming, he wasn't worried about how many years he'd be there. He was more concerned with surviving day to day.

As it had been since he was standing in that bread line so many years earlier, money was the issue.

My dad may have been the boy wonder in Kemmerer, capable of teaching a chemistry class while still in high school, but that didn't buy him much more than academic credibility in Laramie. He still needed food and a place to live, essentials that weren't adequately covered by his scholarship.

He got a room at a local church by working as the janitor on the property.

He got food by working as a busboy in the college cafeteria, a job that also earned him a few dollars.

Still, his finances were so tight that he couldn't even afford textbooks, a huge handicap considering his two majors: chemistry and mathematics.

So he learned to plan ahead. Knowing his classmates wouldn't think about hitting the books until a test was looming, he borrowed those books when the test was still in the distant future, doing his studying early.

It wasn't easy. Add chemistry and math and several required classes to the burden of two jobs and there wasn't much room in the equation for sleep. My dad worked about 35 hours per week and carried 18 units in his first year at Wyoming.

It may have been a grind, but it didn't grind him down. My dad finished the year as an A student in his major.

So then what? My dad made the decision Walt Garrett had hoped for: he would stay in school for another year and get his degree. After all, he was excelling at academics and a degree would mean a more lucrative future as a higher-ranked chemist on the government scale.

There was another reason for my dad to stay at Wyoming, one Walt couldn't have anticipated. That reason was JoAnn Mueller.

JoAnn, my mother, had grown up in Boise, Idaho, but she also lived in Portland and New York City, and went to high school in Fairborn, Ohio.

Upon graduation, she wanted to purse a nursing degree at Ohio State, where many of her friends were going.

But her father Carl, divorced from her mother, insisted that JoAnn go to college in Wyoming, where he was working as a park ranger.

If I'm going to pay your tuition, Carl told her, I'd like you to go someplace that's more affordable.

Whatever reservations my mother had about going to the University of Wyoming disappeared one night two months after she arrived.

A sophomore named Jerry Buss had invited her to a dance. When he dropped her off at the end of the evening, she told her two roommates, "I just met my future husband."

A little over a year later, my dad indeed asked my mom to marry him, but he didn't have much to offer financially. The best he could do as far as a ring was concerned was a cigar band.

"Someday," he told her, "I'll get you a real ring."

She wasn't concerned with that. She was in love, and that was all that mattered.

Her father, living in Cheyenne at the time, wasn't quite so enthusiastic.

"Why do you have to get married so quick?" he asked my mom when she told him that that they wanted to get hitched within a few weeks. "I thought you wanted to be a nurse."

"Not now I don't," she said.

The father of one of my mom's friends was a justice of the peace. With five or six of my parents' friends in attendance, he performed the ceremony on December 6, 1952.

Still teenagers at 19, they had become man and wife.

I don't know how my dad even had time for my mom considering his schedule as a sophomore at Wyoming. It was even more demanding than his freshman year.

For one thing, that government job that had brought him to Wyoming in the first place had materialized. He was hired as a chemist by the U.S. Bureau of Mines. The position didn't affect his class schedule since he worked from midnight to sunrise.

To supplement his income, my dad also worked poker and pool tables relentlessly, turning the experience he had gained in his idle hours in Kemmerer into a revenue-generating operation.

There certainly weren't any idle hours in college where, determined not to give up his precious time with my mom, he sometimes gave up sleep altogether, going from job to class to the poker table.

It was the early 1950s, the Korean War was raging, and young men my dad's age were being drafted. But fortunately for him, he got a student deferment.

My dad took his new responsibilities seriously. He wanted to make enough money to have a family. And he wanted to make enough to allow my mother to stay home to take care of that family.

Once again, he looked toward education to secure his future. The boy who once balked at going to college was now focusing on graduate school.

My dad had graduated from high school at 17, and by taking a full load of classes every semester and going to summer school, he was able to graduate from Wyoming in two years, getting his degree in June of 1953.

Because he was so brilliant, my dad had scholarship offers for graduate school from many colleges, Harvard and Yale among them.

Ultimately, it was the sweet memories of his brief stay in California as a kid that won him over. That thrilled my mother, who had also dreamed of a life in California, although she had never been there.

My father was a huge fan of USC football and track and field. Consequently, he decided to go there to pursue a PhD in physical chemistry.

Once in L.A., he figured he might transfer to nearby Cal Tech, a prestigious academic institution, but he never did.

The decision made, my parents packed up their car in preparation for the trip west. My mom decided to go first to Cheyenne to say good-bye to her father. From there, she would take a train to meet my father in L.A.

My father took the car, but stopped to visit an aunt. While he was in her house, someone broke in and stole everything in the car, including the suitcases, my mother's nursing textbooks, and even her wedding dress.

My parents hadn't had much to start with. Now, they were beginning a new life together with absolutely nothing.

2

OCTOBER

October 27

LAKERS 99, CLIPPERS 92

I don't believe this. It's opening night, something I've been dreaming about and planning for months, and I'm sick.

I sure hope this isn't an omen for the season ahead. I don't want to start the year on the injured list.

Flying back from an NBA Board of Governors meeting in New York last week, I sat across the aisle from a person who coughed the entire flight. I was worried this might be the result.

After a visit to the doctor, I decided to push on with my obligations to host tonight's ring and banner ceremony even though my voice sounds a lot lower than normal because of the congestion in my chest.

Any lower and I'll sound like Phil.

Unfortunately, I'm getting used to this. I was also sick during the 2009 playoffs, probably because I was so worried about how things would turn out.

Today was actually pretty quiet. Because we've had the Lakers' schedule since July, the ticket orders and everything else people needed from me were requested and delivered a week, or even a month, in advance.

Once I got to STAPLES Center, my symptoms receded into the back of my mind as I got caught up in the festivities.

It was good to see everybody again, and also time to get back to business. It's like returning to school after summer vacation and seeing all your friends.

There's anticipation and excitement about the possibilities for the season ahead, but it is different being the defending champions because you know everybody's got their sights set on keeping you from repeating. I guess that's what makes it fun.

I had a great outfit to wear for my role as emcee of tonight's nationally televised celebration. That's the good news.

The bad news is I'll probably never be able to wear it again because then people would say, "Hey, didn't you wear that on opening night?" So I guess tonight is also a retirement ceremony for these clothes.

Was I the right person to host this presentation? With Phil being the coach, I guess it kind of worked. If we're fortunate enough to win championships when Phil is no longer on the sideline, maybe someone else in my family will represent the team.

I couldn't wait to see our championship rings. Although the process for making them began right after we won last season's title when bids went out to several ring companies, and though I had seen diagrams, models, and pictures since then, I had yet to get my hands on the finished product before tonight.

Along the way, we got feedback from my dad, our general manager Mitch Kupchak, our players, front office staff, and my two brothers, Joey and Jesse—everyone wanted to be involved. It was great to have so many eyes focused on our plans.

For this ring, however, we didn't consult Phil because he had strong input on the last ring, which is special because of its tribute to the triangle offense. No need, we figured, to repeat the same theme.

For years and years, the ring design produced by the NBA was the same. All that changed was the season and the names of the team and the players engraved on the side.

It wasn't until the 1980s, when the Lakers started winning all those championships, that things changed. It was our coach, Pat Riley, who said he'd like every ring to be unique.

The NBA used to pay for them, but when Pat proposed we design our own, we were told we would have to assume the cost.

After that, every one of our rings told its own story, taking on a unique theme that represented that particular championship.

For example, we won in 2002, and then Chick Hearn died two months later. So it was important to us that we honor him with a microphone and his trademark phrase, "slam dunk," engraved on the ring. We missed him so much. We still miss him.

On the side of the championship ring from 2000 are the words "Bling, Bling." That's because Shaquille O'Neal kept using that expression that season as he talked and talked about his goal of getting his first ring. The Larry O'Brien Trophy is also on there with a nice-sized diamond where the ball should be.

The idea of making each season's ring distinct has now spread throughout the league. A Chicago Bulls ring looks completely different from ours or those of the Boston Celtics.

There are NBA standards, including a minimum requirement in terms of diamonds (one carat) and the use of the NBA logo.

The 2009 ring holds 2.85 karats. Everything is geared toward the number 15 because that's how many championships we've won. For example, the ring is made of 15-karat gold, not the traditional 14 or 24. There are also 15 diamonds around the outside.

Each player has his face laser-etched on the side of his ring. That has never been done before. Now, that's for players only, not Phil or anybody else who gets a ring.

In the past, players have asked if they could have their numbers on their rings, or their stats, or who we faced in each round of the playoffs. But you can't fit everything on there. It's not a media guide.

Homage is paid this time around to our home court, STAPLES Center, by depicting its unique rooftop that juts out at one end. In the past, we've had a replica of the Forum on a ring, so it was time STAPLES Center got its place of honor.

I kind of wanted to go the extra mile and put the words "STAPLES Center" on the side because that's never been done and it would have started a trend.

That didn't happen, but somebody else will do it, trust me, because that's a nice perk to put into a naming-rights contract. A team could sign a 20-year deal with a sponsor with the guarantee the sponsor's name will be on the championship ring.

Of course, there's one big catch. The team has to first win a championship.

I wear the female version of the ring, which is much smaller than its male counterpart. On my finger now is the 2002 ring. It's got a big purple amethyst in a triangle surrounded by three small triangles to signify the three titles in a row. Around the big triangle, it says, "Back to Back to Back." There are 14 diamonds, with eight on the bottom to signify the championships my dad had won at the time as owner. Of the six on the top, five are for the team's titles when it was in Minneapolis, the last one representing the Lakers' other championship in L.A. when Jack Kent Cooke was the owner.

Yes, I have to admit that one is eye-catching, but that's why they call them cocktail rings. They start conversations at cocktail parties. And this is the *ultimate* cocktail party ring.

My father doesn't wear any of his rings. They are on display at STAPLES Center. Most of the men don't wear them.

Phil always pulls his latest out of his safe-deposit box during the playoffs to inspire his players, but he got tired of his 2002 ring because he had to wear it so many times before he got another one.

I think the ceremony went really well. Lisa Estrada and Tim Harris, two key members of our front office, put together an unforgettable program to honor last season's NBA champs as well as all those Lakers teams who preceded them to the top. To represent the previous nine titles we have won in L.A., we called upon Jerry West, Magic Johnson, James Worthy, Michael Cooper, Jamaal Wilkes, Norm Nixon, A.C. Green, Rick Fox, and Robert Horry to join us.

The Lakers have been so fortunate, and I am grateful for that.

In addressing the crowd, Magic singled out my dad for praise. Up in his suite, my dad did the Richard Nixon victory sign in response. And the fans loved it.

Then there were the rings themselves. It's not only how they look, but how they are presented. When you open the box, the ring, enhanced by two small lights, spins around.

Talk about bling! This is the most showstopping ring ever. The only thing missing is having "I Love L.A." playing when you open the box.

It was a special, memorable night.

Sick? Who said I was sick?

October 28

This time, my cold won.

I had planned on being on a plane this morning, heading east to Minneapolis where the Timberwolves will open their season tonight against the New Jersey Nets. It will be Minnesota's first game under its new coach, a guy by the name of Kurt Rambis.

Instead of rooting him on in person, I stayed home on my doctor's advice. I really wanted to go to support Kurt. Phil and I feel so close to him and his wife Linda, a Lakers executive and one of my closest friends.

Oh well, at least I know I'll be able to see Kurt when his team plays the Lakers here in L.A. But then, I won't be able to cheer him on.

I WAS EXAMINING SOME PHOTOS from last night's ring ceremony and one looked like a wedding picture.

My wedding.

The ring I'm presenting to Phil in the picture is, of course, his championship ring. But to me it appears that we are getting married. NBA commissioner David Stern is in the background between us as if he is officiating the ceremony, and the championship trophy looms above us like an altar.

I posted the shot on my Twitter account as our fake wedding photo since there won't be a real one with Phil.

A championship ring is not a bad second prize. Especially since this is the ninth one for me.

October 29

Tomorrow night should be interesting.

Seated in front of me will be David Beckham and his wife Victoria, or as she is known in the pop world, Posh Spice. Seated beside me will be Australia's answer to that celebrity couple, recording star Chantelle Delaney and her husband, former Australian rules football player Jess Sinclair.

I told Chantelle they sounded like the Beckhams and she said that is exactly what the media in her country calls them. Well, they are all going to come face to face tomorrow night.

Chantelle is hoping to move to L.A. to take on another career challenge.

This job gives me an opportunity to meet fans from all over the world and all walks of life. All paths, it seems, cross here at Lakers games.

Sitting with me in my regular spot in the first row off the floor across the court from the Lakers bench is never a sure thing. For example, if Chantelle and Jess had asked for tickets on opening night, it would not have been possible. I didn't have any extra seats because Robert Horry, who took part in the ring ceremony, was sitting with me.

I never know where these ticket appeals are going to come from. In the case of my new Australian friends, the request originated with a PR person who posted it on the Lakers' website.

Those in search of seats also go to my dad, Mitch Kupchak, Linda Rambis, Tim Harris, our business operations senior vice president, and John Black, our public relations vice president. We all take care of people…when we can.

There is no set procedure. We could hire a person solely to handle ticket requests, and not only would that person be working all day, every day, but we'd probably need to hire nine more people to adequately handle the load.

So I don't encourage people to just pick up the phone and try to reach me.

In the case of Chantelle and Jess, the request was taken off our website by an intern, who passed it on to a superior, who then decided it should come to my attention.

As you can see, when it comes to tickets, it's really not that easy to get to me.

OUR PARTNERS AT ANSCHUTZ ENTERTAINMENT Group (AEG) never cease to amaze me. The company owned by Phil Anschutz and headed by Tim Leiweke is the reason the Lakers are not still playing at the Forum. The $400 million investment Mr. Anschutz made to build the Lakers' state-of-the-art home has been a turning point for the city and key to much of what the Lakers have accomplished in the last decade.

I was like so many of the native Angelenos who thought that downtown L.A. was dead. Nothing but traffic and crime. When the plan was first announced, I thought that fans would travel there for Lakers games and then leave as soon as the game was over.

That could not be further from reality. As a matter of fact, L.A. now has a true center at the heart of the city and a focal point for the community. The film and television industry have begun incorporating shots of STAPLES Center whenever they're doing a montage of Southern California. I am now a believer.

It took the vision of someone like Mr. Anschutz to see the possibilities and a facilitator like Tim Leiweke to pull it off. In addition to building

STAPLES Center, Mr. Anschutz also purchased a 30 percent stake in the Lakers. The investment has paid off on both levels as STAPLES Center is one of the premier venues in the world and the Lakers have competed in seven NBA Finals since relocating from Inglewood.

It has been what they refer to in business school as a win-win situation.

October 30

Mavericks 94, Lakers 80

When we get home from a game, Phil usually wants to talk about it, but not tonight. He was really wound up with tension, so disappointed in the execution of the defense, so concerned, so agitated.

Normally, I use my camera for "Jeanie Vision," which appears on the Lakers' website. I talk to Phil on the way to the game and then I talk to him afterward at home. For the postgame session, I wait until he's out of his suit. I usually want to give him extra time to think so he'll have a different take than he has immediately afterward in his postgame press conference. Sometimes, his perspective has changed after a reflective drive home.

But tonight was just so uncomfortable. This is the Phil the world never sees. I couldn't get him to focus. He wouldn't answer questions. I didn't know if he wasn't listening to me or if he was just ignoring me.

He changed the channels on the TV again and again before finally putting the remote down and answering a question I had asked five minutes earlier.

I put away the camera and just let him deal with it in his own way.

His way was to go back to the remote and watch highlights on *SportsCenter*.

We both know the problem with the Lakers. The team is not at full strength physically. We don't have one of our pillars, Pau Gasol, who is still out because of a strained hamstring.

Ron Artest, while he has fit in smoothly with the guys, is not shooting well. That also disrupts our team as he tries to find his rhythm.

The result: an unexpected loss.

Finally talking to me, Phil gave credit to the Mavericks. He doesn't just say that stuff for the benefit of the media. He believes it. He talked about their excellent game plan and how they stuck to it. He complimented them on being well prepared.

All that said, however, he also reflected on his own team's difficulties.

When we go to bed after a defeat, it is never a restful night. Phil tosses and turns. I can't tell you how many times he's elbowed me like he's going up for a rebound. I should probably wear a whistle to bed.

At heart, Phil is still a player, and sometimes, especially after a disappointing effort by his team, he seems to be a player again in his dreams.

The other night, he told me his alarm clock went off and he incorporated it into a shot-clock dream. He was upset because he didn't get the shot off in time.

But a night like this, after a loss like this, is the worst. In Phil's anguished sleep, he stole my pillow right out from under my head while I was asleep because he thought it was the ball. When I told him in the morning what he had done, he was pretty proud of himself.

No apologies, and none needed.

October 31

Phil was up early, eager to get to practice. His frustration after last night's game had been replaced with resolve.

I asked him what time he thought he'd be home and he said, "Late." That meant closer to 2:00 PM than 1:00 PM. It was going to be a long practice. When Phil isn't satisfied with his team, he doesn't hold anything back. That's why he's good.

When Phil got home, late as he had predicted, I asked him, "Did you torture them today? I know you were angry."

He said, "Yeah, I made them watch the tape of last night's game."

And he's going to have another tape waiting for them when they arrive for Sunday's game against the Atlanta Hawks. Phil doesn't want his players getting comfortable sitting on a loss. So he's going to have a video made that will make the players feel they are being criticized for their last performance.

Which they are.

Phil wants them eager to get on the court and play the right way. They are going to need to fire themselves up and be feisty because Atlanta is not a natural rival for us. We only see the Hawks twice a year, so it's easy to kind of ignore them as opposed to a conference opponent against whom the competitive feelings come more naturally.

Every loss comes back to haunt you because they are hard to erase. Now we've already been dealt our first one, and a home loss at that.

These games can pile up quickly. You can see what's going on with Cleveland. Last year, the Cavs were dominant at home, going 39–2, but this season, they lost their home opener. That shows you how fast you can get behind.

We've got a really heavy home schedule early in the season, so if we don't get on a roll soon, we are going to dig ourselves a hole.

Having said that, I have to concede that, in the last two seasons, this team has really seemed to jell in that long January-February stretch when we are away from home much of the time. So there's certainly no reason to panic just yet.

Except Boston is already 3–0.

I know we are spoiled here, and nothing reminds me of that quicker than thinking of Kurt in Minnesota. He's not worried about the home court in the playoffs. He's just hoping to *make* the playoffs.

Phil called him to find out how it's going after two games, and Kurt called back while we were at dinner.

Phil told him how impressed he was with the way the Timberwolves ran the triangle offense the previous night against Cleveland, especially in the second quarter.

"I was tempted to show it to our team," Phil said, "so they could see how well the triangle can be executed."

That was a nice thing for Phil to say to Kurt.

Phil really misses him.

Kurt picked up a lot from Phil, from Pat Riley, from Del Harris, from all the coaches he worked with. But Kurt told Phil what he really learned from him is that you've got to have a system in place; that way, when the pressure's on, the players always have the system to fall back on, no matter what. It's a base to build upon.

The hard part is getting players committed to it. Kurt watched Phil stick to his philosophy and be stubborn when he had to be. The triangle offense, Phil says, is an equal-opportunity offense. As guys start realizing how good they can look in the triangle, they buy into it more and more.

Kurt's a good teacher in his own right. He's very patient, making sure not to put too much on his young team's collective shoulders.

MONOPOLY:
PLAYING FOR KEEPS

CALIFORNIA WAS STILL THE GOLDEN STATE IN THE 1950s, BUT not for my parents. Not at first.

When my father arrived in L.A., he moved into an apartment on the USC campus and my mother joined him a few months later. Then they moved to an off-campus apartment and settled down to a life of scrimping and saving.

While my dad pursued his studies at USC, my mother, her dreams of a nursing career no longer practical, went to work as a bank teller to help get my father through school. They both worked really hard to realize their dream of creating a family.

A big night for them was to play board games at home or have people over. They couldn't afford much else.

My dad kept them on a strict budget. For example, he would have my mother buy chocolate milk instead of regular milk because it was two cents cheaper.

Their total food budget for the month was $80.

Once, walking down the street, my parents found a $5 bill. To them, it was like winning an all-expenses-paid trip to Las Vegas.

What did they do with it? My father kept two dollars, gave my mother two dollars, and saved the remaining dollar for food.

While it was rough at the time and despite all the wealth they have enjoyed in the ensuing years, both my parents say they look back fondly on those early days of matrimony when they were forced to live from paycheck to paycheck.

After my father got his doctorate from USC, he was offered a teaching position at the college that paid $450 per month. Instead, he accepted more than double that amount at Arthur D. Little, an international management consulting firm.

The biggest drawback was that the company was in Boston.

They had assured my father that they would soon transfer him back to the West Coast. When that didn't happen because the advent of commercial jet travel had made the need for offices on both coasts unnecessary, my dad transferred himself, returning to L.A. where he landed a position with the Douglas Aircraft Company.

It was the dawn of the space age, and my dad was going to be involved in rocket development.

I can't say exactly what he did because some of his work was classified.

It was 1958, my brother Johnny had been born two years earlier, and three more kids would soon follow. My father's dream of becoming a professor was fading away, a consequence of his growing financial obligations.

Another dream, however, was coming into focus, a dream bolstered by a friendship my dad forged with a co-worker, Frank Mariani.

Like my dad, Frank, who had grown up in a poor Boston neighborhood, was anxious to supplement his income. My dad was making $700 a month, Frank $500.

They agreed that the best route to their mutual goal was through rich Southern California land. They would form a real estate company.

What assets did they have to bring to the table? Modest ones, to be sure. My dad, used to living on a tight budget, tightened it even more. He and Frank would save $83.33 each from their monthly paycheck for one year with the goal of raising $1,000 apiece.

A third partner and Frank's roommate, Ted Ward, would also come up with $1,000. When they had $3,000, they figured it would be enough for a down payment on a $25,000 duplex.

It was the meager beginning of Mariani-Buss, a financial empire that would alter the landscape of both Southern California and the sports world.

Without so much as a clump of dirt to its name, Mariani-Buss started to grow.

With two of Mariani's brothers and a sixth investor each coming up with $1,000 of their own, the group, named Cal-Ven Inc., obtained a 14-unit building in West Los Angeles in 1959.

Purchase price: $105,000.

There were to be no vacant units. If one opened up, a member of the investment group would occupy it and pay the rent. And there were to be no repair bills. The investors would do all the repairs themselves.

The most famous story about those early days involved an apartment my dad and Frank were painting. It was at the end of a long day after they had finished their day jobs, and they were anxious to go home.

So they had little patience when they found a hole in one of the walls. Neither man was sure how to fill it.

It wasn't rocket science. That was the problem. They *were* rocket scientists.

Finally, my dad came up with the solution. He took off the dirty T-shirt he was wearing and stuffed it into the hole.

If that building is still standing, my dad's dirty old T-shirt, a great souvenir, might still be behind the wall of someone's apartment.

A year later, Cal-Ven, its number of investors doubled, bought a second property, a 16-unit building in Cheviot Hills, with a down payment of $18,000. Then a third building was added, purchased for $150,000.

With another mouth to feed thanks to the birth of my brother Jimmy in 1959, the money was attractive. The family was getting too big for $80-per-month food budgets.

But my dad still wasn't ready to turn his back on a career in science. In 1960, he went to work for TRW doing research in physics.

In 1962, my dad and Frank formed a second real estate company, Dyna Real (dynamic realty) Inc.

Real estate became a family operation. My grandmother Jessie was the company bookkeeper and my dad's stepbrother Jimmy was the maintenance man. With Jimmy on the job, walls were no longer stuffed with T-shirts.

Still determined to juggle two careers, my dad quit TRW after two years and became a guest lecturer at his alma mater, USC.

By 1963, however, he could no longer deny the reality of his realty business. He was making $80,000 per month. It was time to focus fully on his future.

My dad had never wanted my mom to work. So when his real estate business started to take off, he had her quit her job at the bank.

After that, my mom always had a Cadillac. My dad was always buying her Cadillacs. I remember her in those cars, beautiful and always the coolest mom in the neighborhood.

What my dad bought her that probably meant the most was the ring. He had promised her back when he couldn't afford to put anything on her finger that he would make it up to her one day.

Sure enough, with the money coming in, my dad purchased the most amazing wedding ring. Absolutely flawless. It was three-plus karats, emerald cut.

He told my mom he was going to make something of himself, and he always lived up to his word.

At times, it seemed like my dad and Frank could do no wrong. Under one of their properties, oil was discovered. On the surface, the Southern California real estate market was booming.

By the age of 34, my dad had made his first million.

As any businessman knows, however, no boom is immune to a subsequent bust. A recession in the late 1960s caused my father, Frank, and their investors to feel the sting of a financial setback.

They began to diversify, buying resorts in places like Palm Springs and Mammoth, and going out of state to buy property in Arizona and Nevada. When another recession followed in the early 1970s, my dad and Frank kept buying, gambling that real estate values would inevitably bounce back.

Eventually they did, and my dad and Frank were big beneficiaries. For example, eight properties they owned on Wilshire Boulevard increased to nearly 10 times their purchase value over a three-year period.

By 1979, Mariani-Buss had 200 properties, owned 1,000 houses, employed 400 people, and had holdings worth around $350 million.

It was an empire bathed in the green glow of money, but it was about to take on two other colors: purple and gold.

I WAS BORN ON SEPTEMBER 26, 1961, at Saint John's Hospital in Santa Monica, back when my dad's real estate empire was still just a blueprint in his mind.

But as I grew, so did the family fortune. The third child behind Johnny and Jimmy with Janie to follow two years later, I fortunately missed the days of restricted food budgets for my mother and late-night handyman chores for my dad.

The first home I remember was a beautiful, ranch-style house in the Rustic Canyon area of Pacific Palisades. The home was built by actor James Arness, known to television viewers in the 1950s, '60s, and '70s as Marshal Matt Dillon on *Gunsmoke*.

Before that, we lived in a house on Warren Avenue somewhere in the city. I've never driven over there to see it as an adult, but I plan to someday.

I was three or four when we moved into the Pacific Palisades house, and the thing that still sticks in my mind was the large oak tree in the front.

I didn't know until recently that tree was the reason we were able to buy that home. The revelation came at a luncheon in November 2009 given by the Pacific Palisades Chamber of Commerce and attended by several former Miss Palisades. A winner of that honor myself in 1979, I was asked to speak.

Also at that luncheon was actor Peter Graves. Knowing he had lived in the Palisades since the 1960s, I told him I had grown up in the old James Arness house.

Peter replied, "Oh, James loved that house so much, but when his son fell out of the tree, he just couldn't stay there anymore."

Turns out James' son, Rolf Aurness, suffered a severely fractured skull when he tumbled out of the tree and onto the concrete below at the age of nine. He did recover and went on to become a world surfing champion, winning the title in Australia in 1970.

I told Peter, "I know that tree. I have a scar on my leg from climbing it."

What I didn't know until Peter passed away four months later, but learned while reading his bio, was that he and James Arness were brothers.

I had no idea the house was for sale because of that damn oak tree in the front yard. It was a kid magnet. We all loved to climb it, but if you lost your footing, you fell right onto the cement driveway.

Our house was the gathering place for my brothers' friends. We had this big backyard where they could play football, so everybody came over.

I spent a lot of time at a park near our house and at the homes of several kids in the neighborhood. My parents had brought back a cowbell from a trip to Switzerland, so when my mother wanted me or my siblings to come home, she would ring it. You could hear that bell as far as four or five houses in either direction.

When I think of my mom in those years, I think of the sweetest person I knew. Everybody in the neighborhood loved her. She always had a smile and an even temper. She was always fun. And for me and my friends, she was the ultimate den mother.

She is a smart woman. I don't think she could have kept up with my dad if she hadn't been. Her intelligence was a big attraction for my dad when he first met her.

He couldn't have made the money he did nor built the empire he ran without my mom's input and support. She was always there for him. He could count on her to create a loving home for their children.

I so admire my parents' relationship because they worked together as partners then and still do to this day.

OURS WAS A HOUSEHOLD THAT ALWAYS revolved around sports.

Purple and gold may be the dominant colors running through my life now, but in my earliest memories, it was cardinal and gold.

When I was a kid, all sports seemed to revolve around the USC Trojans. They had lured my dad to their campus to pursue his graduate studies, and he passed that passion on to me. The letters *USC* were stamped on my mind before I knew what going to college meant.

Everything in our house was cardinal and gold. No surprise there. There were Trojan pillows and USC drinking glasses. All the tchotchkes that come with supporting your team could be found in every room.

My dad would take the whole family to all the home USC football games at the Coliseum and even some road games. We went everywhere, from Baton Rouge to Iowa City.

I remember bringing my stuffed animals and my Barbie dolls to the games to amuse myself.

It wasn't just football. It was USC everything. My dad would take us to Trojans basketball games, track and field competition, and whatever else was in season.

He also mixed in some Dodgers games. We grew up knowing our family outings were centered around sports.

And that included the ponies. Whether I was watching horse racing or riding horses myself, they were also a big part of my childhood.

Between the ages of 10 and 12, I went through my horseback-riding phase. I never had a horse of my own, but I loved to ride them, especially buckskin horses, those with pale coloring and a black mane, because that's what Little Joe rode on *Bonanza*. I was so excited when my dad gave me and my sister riding lessons.

My parents owned thoroughbreds, mostly horses that ran at Del Mar.

We would spend our summers there and go to the "Where the turf meets the surf" racetrack every day. As soon as school was out, our parents had us in the car, driving south on the 405 freeway.

My sister and I would run around the racetrack. We would sneak into the backfield or roam the stables where we could be with the horses all day, petting them when we could get close enough. Some of the jockeys were nice enough to give us extra goggles.

There wasn't a lot of security in those days. All my mom would say is, "Be back by the ninth race."

We met jockeys like Willie Shoemaker and Jerry Lambert. We got to see horses like Seattle Slew. We were flies on the wall for that whole era of horse racing.

To make money, my sister Janie and I would go to the ticket sellers in the booth and ask if they wanted something to eat or drink. We were their junior waitresses.

When we were home, the big thing in our house was Monopoly. My dad loved the game. He loved it so much that he named many of his apartment buildings after the board game's properties. He owned a St. James Place, a Park Place, and a Boardwalk.

I learned about real estate by playing Monopoly. I loved getting houses on my property and then turning them into hotels.

My dad could play the game without a board. He would remember every piece and every move and what everybody owned and how much money each person had. All he ever needed you to do was roll the dice. He knew every inch of that board.

BOTH OF MY GRANDFATHERS DIED before I was born. I had both of my grandmothers in my life growing up, but they both passed away before I turned 14, so I missed out on having them during my high school years.

They were very different. My mom's mom, Lois, was the perfect homemaker. She sewed. She cooked. Back in those days, having home economics skills was really important. Nowadays, courses in those areas don't even exist in some schools, and I kind of miss that.

But Lois wasn't just a homemaker. During World War II, she was a Rosie the Riveter. She went to Portland to work on the construction of battleships and other vessels used by our navy. With many of the men gone to the front, women took their place in the workforce. I love hearing those stories about her and really admired her for assuming that role.

What I remember most about my dad's mom, Jessie, was all the places she took me. She couldn't manage four kids, but she always said, "I'll take one. I'll take Jeanie." So I got to stay at her house and go out to dinner with her a lot.

One restaurant she took me to that I never forgot was a place on Montana Avenue in Santa Monica called The Broken Drum. It had a blinking neon sign that alternated between the restaurant name and the phrase "You Can't Beat It."

Being a kid, it took me a while to get the joke, but once I did, I thought it was the funniest thing I had ever heard. Of course, being a child, I hadn't heard much.

They always treated me special there, always putting a few extra cherries in my Shirley Temple.

My grandmother would also take me quite often to Benihana. She was a lot of fun.

I loved spending weekends at her house in Santa Monica. It was on one of my dad's properties. She had a special cabinet reserved for my toys. I couldn't take them home with me, but that made them all the more special because playing with them was part of being with Grandma.

Now at Phil's house I have a toy chest for his grandkids. Phil has six grandkids, ranging in age from four years down to four months. All three of his daughters got married within two years, and all of them have started families. When the kids come over, they know these are the toys for Grandpa's house. They also don't get to take them home.

I had such a fond memory of that rule, so I re-created it.

My dad put my grandmother to work at his real estate office because he wanted to be around her, which I thought was very cute. She was the apple of my dad's eye.

I had two grandmothers who were both very strong in their own way. From homemaking with Grandma Lois to the social skills I gleaned from Grandma Jessie, I learned so much from them that serves me well to this day. I just wish I could have had more time with them.

Growing up, I also liked to be around my brothers because they had friends who were cute. When everybody would come over to play football, my sister and I would hang around to watch. In those days, I identified my family with the Brady Bunch.

My sister and I were complete pests to our brothers. When Johnny got his driver's license and a car, we would beg him to take us to Disneyland.

"You have a car. Let's go," I would say, over and over and over again. "That's what you do if you have a car. You go to Disneyland whenever you want."

As a 10-year-old, that seemed perfectly logical to me.

Like most kids, we always got into the spirit of Halloween. All four of us would take our pillow sacks and go around the neighborhood trick-or-treating. I was a ballerina or a princess, the usual for a little girl. Like most kids, we would figure out which houses gave the best candy and try to sneak over there a second time.

Unlike most kids, however, we lived on the same street as the guy who played Lurch (Ted Cassidy) on the TV show *The Addams Family*. To us, of course, his was the most frightening house. The image of him answering the door, to this very day, gets me scared. It took me years to finally get up enough courage to go to his front door. Until then, when we reached his house, I would just run home.

When we returned with our individual bags of candy, my dad would gather us around and say, "Okay, to make it fair, you are going to split your candy with me."

So we got half the candy and my dad got half the candy. Not until I was older did I realize, *Wait a minute, he got half of four shares, adding up to two full shares, and all I got was a half.*

When I was younger, that didn't really dawn on me. I thought it was a good deal.

IT WASN'T ALL FUN and games, though.

There were problems between my parents while I was still in elementary school. As I got a little older, those problems became more evident to me. We still had our trips to the Coliseum and Del Mar and our marathon Monopoly games, but my dad was absent from the house for longer and longer periods. When I asked about it, all my mother would ever say was, "He's at the office."

He seemed to be at the office a lot, day and night.

When I would go over to my friends' houses, their dads would be home. It didn't make sense to me. I would say to my friends, "Shouldn't your dad be at the office? That's where all dads are. At the office."

My dad would come home on weekends and spend a lot of time with me and my siblings, but it wasn't as much time as my friends' dads seemed to spend with them.

What I didn't know was that my dad had moved out and was living a separate life. Back then, parents felt the top priority was to protect their kids in situations like that. Spare them the pain rather than tell them the truth. I think my parents were just doing what they thought was best for us. Rather than explain the situation, they shielded us from the concept of divorce and the pain that it can generate in a child.

Nowadays, the more accepted approach is to be honest and tell kids the truth, so they are not waiting for the other shoe to drop. It can be harmful to leave them totally in the dark. They tend to internalize everything.

I remember kids would tease me when I was 10 and 11, asking, "Where's your dad? Where's your dad?"

I didn't ask my mother why he was at the "office" more and more. We didn't have that conversation.

I didn't want to be embarrassed by admitting to my friends that I didn't know where my dad was. I thought if I said that, they would laugh at me.

Instead, I took what I thought was the easy way out. I simply said, "He's dead."

NOVEMBER

November 1

"I don't know where to start," my dad said when he called me the other day. "I have known this couple for years, really nice people. They are from Orange County and have four daughters, all blondes, 18 to 24 years old, each one more beautiful than the last.

"I was meeting them for our usual lunch today, but only the woman showed up. She told me her husband had walked out on her after 26 years of marriage. She is left with nothing and doesn't know what she is going to do."

All I could say was, "Dad, that is so sad."

"They asked me if I could help them," he said. "What they want is their own reality show because the mother thinks that could be a way for her to earn a living."

I told my father that, considering the daughters' ages, they would be very appealing to the reality-show audience.

My dad told them, "I don't know anything about reality TV, but Jeanie knows Ryan Seacrest."

Which brings us to this phone call.

"I was hoping you could help me get them to Ryan," my dad said. "Why don't you meet them before Sunday's game and we can go from there."

After meeting with the family, I can certainly agree with my dad about their beauty. But as for getting them together with Ryan, I wasn't so sure about that because he is the busiest guy in Hollywood.

Not to worry. Turns out Ryan Seacrest is at tonight's game, sitting right near me. Unbelievable good fortune, since he doesn't make it to a lot of games.

"Will you go up to my father's suite with me to meet these sisters?" I asked him. "I thought my dad was exaggerating about their beauty, but that's not the case. He has always had a good eye for talent."

"You don't have to convince me," Ryan said. "I have a lot of respect for your dad's opinion about women."

I took Ryan up after the first quarter and he thought the girls were adorable.

They were in shock to meet him. Whether anything comes of this, I don't know, but I definitely came through. They asked, and within an hour I produced Ryan Seacrest.

November 2

The Lakers are leaving for their first road trip, with back-to-back games in Oklahoma City and Houston tomorrow and Wednesday.

Phil wants me to take him to the airport, which is kind of a hassle for me. I'd say 90 percent of the guys just leave their cars there because they have secure parking where they catch the charter flight.

But I know that for Phil, it's more than just a matter of where to leave his car. He needs my support, the feeling that I'm there for him. So I'll take him.

Of course, that means I'll also have to pick him up when the Lakers return. And it will be late at night. At least, by design, we live 10 minutes from LAX.

One thing I don't have to worry about is helping Phil pack. He is a good dresser, definitely stylish, with a feel for what looks good on him, what works for him.

Beyond the clothes, though, we don't always agree. I like him clean shaven with his hair longer. Sometimes he listens, sometimes he doesn't.

November 3/4

LAKERS 101, THUNDER 98 (OT)/LAKERS 103, ROCKETS 102 (OT)

There was unexpected drama surrounding the Lakers in Oklahoma City, but a potential problem had been resolved by the time I heard about it.

Phil called me from the team bus to tell me Kobe Bryant was having flu-like symptoms, but had been cleared to play by a doctor.

Strict procedures have been put in place by the NBA because of the H1N1 virus. Players with flu symptoms are to be kept away from their teammates until it is determined whether or not they are contagious. Hopefully, that will keep the virus from spreading throughout the league.

I usually talk to Phil three times a day when he's on the road. He'll first check in during the morning. Then, he'll call before he leaves for the game or from the bus.

Finally, Phil calls me after the game while he's sitting on the bus waiting for the players. It takes them a lot longer to come out, of course, because they have to shower and dress. Phil has been after them to get out of the locker room faster.

Usually, if I want to talk about the game, I have to pull it out of Phil, win or lose. He wants to hear about everything I've done that day. Literally. Like, "After lunch, did you go back to the office?" He just wants to talk about anything other than the game.

Good or bad, he wants to put it aside and take his mind off basketball, if only for a while.

I have to be insistent. "No, no, no," I'll say, "I'm not going there. I want to talk about what just happened on the court."

After the Houston game, I wanted to know about Andrew Bynum, who hurt his elbow. How bad was it? When are you going to know if he'll miss any time?

It seems like I always have to drag Phil's focus back onto the game, and then he'll talk about it.

I usually end up working late when the team is away. That's when I can get a lot of stuff done, avoiding interruptions by the ever-present ticket orders.

Then, I watch the games alone at home, checking game stats on my computer and fan posts on Twitter. Sometimes, if the game is tight, I'll call a girlfriend and we'll sit on the phone and share the stress.

The Lakers won in overtime in Oklahoma City, but all I could think about was how tired they were going to be because they were not going to get into Houston until very late.

Phil has a tough time sleeping on the road as it is. It's often hard for him to get comfortable in hotel beds. Even when he does, trying to come down from a game, with his adrenaline still flowing, can be difficult.

While the Lakers battled in Houston, I was flipping back and forth between our game and the Boston game because the Celtics were in Minnesota.

That game had such meaning for the fans there because it was Kevin Garnett's homecoming and a chance to beat one of the premier teams in the league.

The Timberwolves were ahead at halftime and the game was tied at the end of three quarters.

Down 92–90 in the fourth, Minnesota had the last possession of the game but missed the final shot. It was so disappointing.

I flipped back to our game against Houston, which ended up similarly close except the Lakers won. Another night of highs and lows in a long NBA season.

Once the season kicks into gear, it's NBA basketball for me all the time. Thank you NBA League Pass.

With the overtime again delaying the Lakers' flight, Phil landed late Wednesday night, but at least he got a ride home from assistant coach Frank Hamblen and his wife Uta.

Thank goodness he hitched a ride, because it was 2:00 AM by the time Phil walked in.

Not that I knew it at the time. I was asleep.

November 5

With an off night upon us, Phil wanted to stay home and prepare dinner himself. It's no sacrifice on his part. He likes to cook. Sometimes, he does the shopping, too. It's like a hobby for him, something that relaxes him.

Tonight, he made pasta, sauce, and garlic bread.

I don't make any menu suggestions. I'm just happy he is a part-time chef. Otherwise, I'd never have a home-cooked meal.

We watched the Bulls-Cavs game. He was pulling for Chicago and I was for Cleveland. Phil still has an affinity for the Bulls. He likes a lot of their players, though I can't mention any of them because I'd probably get him in trouble for tampering.

My rooting interest? I pull for the home team to win, but the Cavs are struggling on their home court, ultimately losing the game 86–85.

Here it was, a free night, and we were watching the NBA. During the baseball season, we watch that too, especially when the playoffs start.

If there is a good hockey game, we'll turn that on as well.

Actually, hockey is one of our favorite sports. Phil likes the game and really understands it. Not surprising since he played amateur hockey. This season, he's a big Kings fan.

When the Anaheim Mighty Ducks won the Stanley Cup, Phil followed them throughout the playoffs and was impressed. He felt they had perfect teamwork, enabling them to be more than the sum of their parts.

When we have exhausted the sports schedule, we will watch *Dexter*, *The Office*, *Curb Your Enthusiasm*, or *Dancing with the Stars*.

We particularly like *Dexter* this season because John Lithgow is a close friend of Phil's. He is cast in that show as a psychopathic killer. When John's character was committing one of his crimes, Phil paused the TV and said, "I don't know if I can watch this. This is really disturbing."

November 6
LAKERS 114, GRIZZLIES 98

Today is Lamar Odom's 30th birthday. I'm happy he is able to celebrate with his new wife, and that all the uncertainty about his wedding and his new contract is behind him.

For two weeks, we had been hearing rumors that Lamar was going to marry Khloe Kardashian. It seemed like there was a different rumor every day. The wedding's on. The wedding's off. Yes, it's in Vegas. No, the whole thing is a hoax.

We didn't receive the invitation until the Friday afternoon before the Sunday event. It was such a beautiful invitation that I saved it.

Phil and I don't have a big social schedule because so much of our time is dictated by the NBA calendar. Fortunately, we were free that Sunday, September 27.

I wanted to go because I love weddings. Phil, however, I wasn't so sure about. When we were invited to Shaquille O'Neal's wedding, Phil said he wasn't going. Nothing personal. He just didn't feel comfortable, in his role as coach, attending a player's wedding. So I went and Phil stayed home.

The issue didn't come up in Kobe's case because he had a small, private wedding.

To my surprise, Phil said we had to go to this wedding. Lamar is so important to him that Phil wanted to support him in every way possible.

The wedding was at the Beverly Hills home of Irving Azoff, a longtime Lakers floor-seat ticket holder, manager of bands like The Eagles, and now the head of Live Nation Entertainment.

When we got there, the paparazzi were lined up in force outside, a sight Phil never likes to see. When you checked in, you had to sign a release because the wedding was being filmed for a television show. If you didn't agree to be on camera, you wouldn't be allowed in.

Once we made it through the photographers and the paperwork, we found ourselves in a beautiful setting in the backyard.

Pretty much the entire Lakers team was there. So was my dad, and celebrities like Ryan Seacrest, Alan Thicke, and Chelsea Handler. In all, I'm guessing, there were somewhere between 250 and 300 guests.

The ceremony was tastefully done, not at all like the tabloids made it out to be.

Khloe wore a beautiful dress, and the complementary color for her and the bridesmaids was lavender. I took that as a nod to Lakers purple. Lamar had a Lamar-type outfit, a tuxedo with white piping on the seams. It was really cool, but like nothing I had ever seen before.

The maids of honor were Khloe's sisters Kourtney, who is pregnant, and Kim. There were also two best men, Gennaro De Gregorio and Jamie Sangouthai.

We couldn't hear the vows because of the helicopters flying overhead.

The reception was on the tennis court in a tented area fixed up to look like a club, complete with chandeliers, wood-paneled walls, and white carpet.

The tables were all different sizes and shapes. Some were high and had bar stools. Some were rectangles. Some were round. Very interesting. There was a grand piano in the center next to the dance floor.

Kobe and Vanessa sat at the head table with Khloe and Lamar and the rest of the wedding party.

Babyface, a recording artist who gives me chills, sang "You Are So Beautiful."

Adding the perfect touch for Lamar, who loves his candy, were the bowls of it all around the room, everywhere you looked. I stuffed a couple of Starbursts into my purse so I could have a treat on the way home.

At the reception, Phil checked out which of his players were consuming alcohol since training camp was about to start. The problem with being the date of the coach is that he is the party pooper. Nobody can have fun when he's around.

When the music started, Phil was ready to leave.

"Come on, can't we stay and dance?" I asked.

"No," he said, "we've got to go."

So I didn't get a chance to go for the bouquet.

We again ran into the paparazzi when we got outside. They were yelling at Phil, "When are you going to marry Jeanie? When are you going to marry Jeanie?"

They are always looking for a reaction.

Phil didn't think it was funny. He was actually kind of speechless.

So I answered for him, saying, "Look, I got over it. You people need to get over it, too. He is never going to marry me."

November 7

Last night's game was very emotional for those of us in the Lakers family, from the scorer's table to the locker room.

Especially the scorer's table.

This is the first season in 49 years that John Radcliffe's smiling face has been missing from that spot at a Lakers home game.

Our official scorekeeper, John started at the Sports Arena in our second season in L.A. and moved with us to the Great Western Forum and then STAPLES Center.

He decided to retire at the end of last season, but we told him we wanted him back for at least one game this season to honor him.

Unfortunately, that never came to pass. John died of heart failure on September 22 at the age of 73.

But our plans to honor this man, who spent 29 years in his full-time position as a coach and then athletics director at Torrance High School, went forward last night. John was truly a man for all seasons, coaching baseball, softball, football, track and field, and volleyball at Torrance.

We unveiled a plaque last night officially naming the spot where the timekeeper and other support personnel sit the John Radcliffe Scorer's Table.

His wife Carolyn and daughter Suzanne were part of the ceremony. The Lakers were a big part of John and Carolyn's lives together.

And John was a big part of our lives. I was really touched by the players' response to the dedication, which took place during a timeout. They were all clapping.

That's understandable. John was the man the players checked in with when entering the game. He was a familiar figure they all knew, whether it was one of our players, an opposing player who then joined the Lakers, or a former Laker playing for a visiting team. John was a guy who always made it feel like home regardless of which team you were on.

Those of us in the spotlight—executives, coaches, and players—are only a part of the Lakers organization. Without people like John, the operation could not be successful.

It is heartwarming to know he will be remembered every time anyone walks by the scorer's table. It is heartbreaking that he didn't live to see himself immortalized in Lakers history.

November 8
LAKERS 104, HORNETS 88

At tonight's game, I met Maria Sharapova, one of the top tennis players in the world. She's dating a Laker.

How do I know? She was introduced to me by Sasha Vujacic's mother.

Maria is phenomenally beautiful. People will say, "That woman is cute…for a tennis player." But in Maria's case, she could be a supermodel without having any athletic skill whatsoever. She's that pretty.

PHIL AND I HAD A WONDERFUL EXPERIENCE prior to tonight's game. Si "Lam" Huynh of Prince Jewelers in Arcadia presented Phil with custom-made cufflinks containing 10 diamonds on each in the form of Xs to represent the 10 championships Phil has won. His name and the title years are engraved on the side.

As if that weren't enough, Lam presented me with a gorgeous pendant containing five amethyst stones, representing the five players on a court, surrounding a diamond-studded gold basketball. All of it was contained in a gold circle made to look like a rim.

Phil and I are so lucky to be in this position where people give us gifts that are so rare and so personal. I was touched Lam would do that.

And do it for nothing.

He refused to take money for his handiwork. He did agree to tickets for the game and dinner up in the Arena Club, but that hardly equaled the value of these pieces.

I didn't know what else to say or do. The whole experience was humbling and a bit overwhelming.

I'm under no illusions as to why I, in particular, am the recipient of such gifts. It's because of the love people have for the Lakers, because of what this brand means to them. It certainly isn't because of anything I have done.

That's why it is so important to me to be accessible to the fans, to hear their stories about how the team has affected their lives.

I kept Lam's business card and made sure to mention to Phil that Lam makes all sorts of really nice stuff and that the holidays are coming up.

It was the least I could do for Lam.

November 9

As I was leaving the office today, Linda Rambis pulled me aside.

"You got a minute?" she asked.

Phil was making dinner, but I am never in such a hurry that I don't have time for Linda.

Especially now when she needs my support. It's rough on her with her husband living in Minnesota where he is, of course, coaching the Timberwolves. Linda elected to stay behind so their daughter Ali, the youngest of their three children, can finish her senior year of high school.

Linda has also kept her job in the Lakers front office where she is invaluable in so many areas. I have to admit I'm selfish. I don't want her to leave. I don't know what I would do without her.

Linda told me she had gotten a call from a Timberwolves PR guy. The team wants to do a Kurt Rambis glasses night. The Suns did a similar thing when Kurt was in Phoenix.

But Kurt doesn't want it to turn into a promotion based on making fun of him, the guy who used to wear the goofy glasses when he played. That's not him anymore, so he won't even discuss it with the PR guy.

That's why the guy was appealing to Linda.

Good call. She gets it. She understands it would be great for the fans who have really gotten behind Kurt. He has already become a major attraction in town despite the slow start by the Wolves. In the local papers, he has been referred to as the *Minneapolis* Laker, a natural tie-in to the area's glorious basketball past.

There's also a tie-in between Kurt and the team's recent past. He replaced Kevin McHale, the two forever linked by Kevin's unforgettable foul that sent Kurt crashing to the court in the 1984 NBA Finals between the Lakers and the Celtics. It has been shown more times on more stations and in more arenas than just about any other foul in league history.

That, however, is ancient history to Kurt. He is more interested in leading Minnesota to a successful season.

Linda assured the PR people that Kurt will go along with the glasses promotion, but she told them they have to present it to him as an opportunity to raise awareness that there are people in desperate need of glasses. Make it an occasion, she said, to collect used eyeglasses to be donated to the underprivileged.

As I told Linda, I've had to use the same strategy to talk Phil into participating in fan promotions he didn't particularly want to do.

Linda is now committed to an NBA head coach. We have that in common, and need to support each other.

She ran a couple of other ideas by me. I told her they were all great and she should go back to the Timberwolves with those as well. Her experience in L.A. is going to be a real asset in Minnesota.

Am I worried about divided loyalty on Linda's part? No way. I want to see the Timberwolves do well. I want them to sell out their games and hopefully generate the same environment we are so fortunate to have here in L.A.

In no way would that diminish the Lakers. We are not competitive with the Timberwolves in selling tickets. They're two different markets. If they sell one ticket there, that doesn't mean we sell one less ticket here.

Others would see it differently. Believe me, there are executives in this highly competitive league who would have a heart attack just thinking about helping another team in any way, shape, or form.

November 11

A Laker Girls reality show?

Why not? The highs and lows our dancers go through would be familiar to viewers of many other reality shows, but in our case, it's real, not contrived. There are exhausting workouts, stiff competition, and spectacular dance routines, as some aspirants get the thumbs up to stick around and others get a thumbs down.

As good as the idea of the show is, I'm not about to take credit for it. That goes to Paula Abdul, still the most famous Laker Girl of them all.

That may come as a surprise to those in the younger generation who know her only from *American Idol*.

Having left that show, Paula would be ideally suited to produce another talent show, this one based on her roots in purple and gold. So when she asked me if I'd help pitch the idea, I gladly agreed.

We had a meeting yesterday at VH1. It seemed to go really well, but I've been through too many of these situations in regard to projects surrounding my own life to get too excited too early. Just because you have a good meeting doesn't necessarily mean it will lead to anything.

I sure hope it does. This show would be eye-opening.

Fans only see the Laker Girls out on the court dancing the night away, but never get to go behind the curtain to see the grueling steps they have to take to get to the STAPLES Center floor.

There are so many talent shows where a winner is crowned. But then what? Unless they are celebrities or become celebrities as a result of the show, they seem to disappear after their 15 minutes of fame.

On a Laker Girl reality show, the fun would be just beginning. The winners would go through an entire season in front of the viewing audience. They've got a job, but who is going to make the most of it? Who is going to rise and become a star?

The Laker Girls made Paula a star, and she made the most of it. It was primarily Paula who took girls who had been cheerleaders at USC or

UCLA, but didn't necessarily have a dance background, and taught them how to perform and choreographed the routines.

Then one night, back when the Jackson family was still together, Jermaine Jackson was attending a game and asked, "Who choreographs the Laker Girls?"

When he was told it was Paula, Jermaine hired her. She choreographed the Jacksons' 1984 "Torture" video and also worked with performers ranging from the Rolling Stones to Dolly Parton to ZZ Top.

Paula is also a singer and has been No. 1 on both the singles and albums charts.

She has won Grammys, Emmys, and People's Choice Awards, and has a star on the Hollywood Walk of Fame.

But perhaps none of that would have happened had influential people not seen her in action at Lakers games, a potentially great stepping-stone to success.

Yet, in all the seasons since then, with all the Laker Girls who have performed on our famous hardwood, we haven't seen another girl use the opportunity as successfully.

Maybe if Paula was involved again, she could inspire another Laker Girl to rise to the heights she attained, to use that exposure to launch another spectacular career.

The Laker Girls set the bar for NBA dance squads, and over time, every team has created its own version. Paula's vision is to take it to another level.

We will have to wait to see if that level includes a reality show.

November 12

LAKERS 121, SUNS 102

The news that Byron Scott got fired by the New Orleans Hornets today caused Phil to again reflect on the precarious nature of his profession. Anytime a coach goes down, all coaches feel it.

This one came as a surprise, at least to me, because Byron's done a great job in a difficult situation. It brings to mind that old cliché that it's easier to fire one person than 12.

I'm not worried about Byron. He has a solid reputation, has been successful with two teams, and will find another NBA job if that's what he desires.

Of course, as soon as his name was severed from the Hornets organization, it was linked to our organization.

I have already had a media person email me today, writing, "I'm hearing Byron is going to be the next Lakers coach."

I wrote back to say, "I am sure, at some point, he will be in the mix, but Phil's not going anywhere. He's not hanging it up anytime soon."

It's not something I can really talk about, because who knows how long Phil is going to stay here? If he were to leave, Byron is a popular former Laker, he's been a good coach, and my dad likes coaches with experience.

Some felt Byron would have become the Lakers coach if he had waited a little longer in the spring of 2004. He took the Hornets job a mere 22 days before Phil parted ways with the Lakers. But at the time, Byron didn't know what was in store for Phil, and he had a great opportunity with New Orleans.

Now that he's left the Hornets, the speculation has begun anew.

November 14

Oh man, the Lakers looked bad last night in Denver. Not only did we lose 105–79, shooting just 34.8 percent from the field, but we scored only 23 points in the second half, the worst half in team history.

Phil didn't walk in the door until after 3:00 AM. This time, he had his car at the airport, so I didn't have to worry about how he would get home.

It has been a long two days. We played Phoenix at STAPLES Center Thursday night, a televised game on TNT. That means a late start, because we are the second game of a doubleheader, and a long game because of the additional commercial interruptions.

And that, in turn, meant a late arrival in Denver later that night. Phil texted me when they landed at 3:00 AM Mountain Time, even though he knew I was asleep. By the time he got to bed, it was 4:20.

Back-to-back games are tough enough. But one of the surest guarantees in the NBA is that a team arriving in Denver for the second game on consecutive nights is going to lose because of the combination of the late-night landing and the altitude change.

Phil can look at the schedule prior to the season and predict what he calls "scheduled losses," based on back-to-back games.

He canceled the Friday morning shootaround, but that didn't seem to make much difference.

The best word to describe Phil's feelings about Friday night's game is *disappointment*. He just can't seem to get through to his players.

They watched some of the game on the way back to L.A. last night and they could see what they did as opposed to what he had asked them to do. The light bulb finally went on.

A bit late.

Phil was so tired this morning that I let him sleep in. He canceled practice, but he still planned on going in. When I asked him why, he said, "I have to see my boy Pau."

Injured players are required to come in for treatment even when there is no practice, and Pau Gasol is suffering from a strained right hamstring that has forced him to miss all nine of our games.

Phil has great affection for Pau. He marvels at how good he is. When you are a coach, you want the best out of your players. Pau is able to give Phil that, and uses his talent in the right way. Phil has told me several times that he considers Pau the most skilled big man he has ever coached. So naturally gifted with great hands and great intellect about the game, Pau has a solid understanding of the triangle. He's a superstar, Phil said, who doesn't get the credit he deserves.

It is disappointing for Phil when he doesn't have the man he considers his basketball son out there.

When Phil got back from seeing Pau, I told him that I had listened to a call-in show after last night's game.

"The fans are mad at you," I said, "not even so much about losing, but because there was an 18–5 run by the Nuggets and you didn't try to stop it with a timeout."

"They did not execute, did not do what I wanted them to do," Phil said. "Instead, they continuously did the wrong thing. So I just let them stew in it. I can't bail them out every time. They've got to listen to my instructions, and then I will have sympathy for them if it still doesn't work out."

"That argument won't satisfy the fans," I said. "They are hurt if you allow the Lakers to be embarrassed. Do you know you set the record for the lowest-scoring half in Lakers history?"

"No, I wasn't aware of that," Phil replied.

"Yeah," I said, "You don't want to be left in the record book with that one. I like the fact there are a lot of other records with your name by them, but I don't think anybody wants to be remembered for that one."

THIS AFTERNOON WASN'T THE LAST TIME today Phil saw Pau. There Pau was again tonight, popping up unexpectedly.

Since I watch all the sporting events Phil likes, I made him watch one of my favorite programs tonight, *48 Hours Mystery*.

During one of the commercial breaks, there was a promo for Monday night's episode of *CSI:Miami* featuring…Pau Gasol.

Pau stayed in Europe so long during the off-season that he missed Lamar's wedding, coming into L.A. the day before the start of training camp. That means he must have filmed his *CSI* cameo during the preseason.

When the promo came on, we hit the pause button and I said, "It's nice to see him working, but I'd rather see it on a basketball court!"

Phil said the television appearance had nothing to do with Pau's injury because he was at 100 percent the first two weeks of the preseason. It wasn't like he just showed up with the injury. They were training twice a day, they were playing in games, and when you do all that, stuff happens.

There is nothing in the players' contracts to prevent them from doing something like that as long as they live up to their responsibilities, meaning practices, games, and team appearances.

You've got to remember that in L.A., half of these guys have their own publicists. That's one of the perks of playing in this city. You are in a market where you can go on Jimmy Kimmel or Jay Leno or take guest roles on scripted shows. Jordan Farmar did *Numb3rs* on CBS with Pau. Luke Walton has been on a soap opera. I'm sure Lamar is filming *Keeping Up With the Kardashians* right now. That's normal. Those opportunities are there for players on the Lakers.

It dates back to Magic Johnson guest starring on sitcoms in the 1980s and Kareem Abdul-Jabbar being in *Airplane!* and other movies and TV shows.

From my point of view, all that publicity is good. It maintains awareness of the Lakers brand.

It also doesn't hurt us in terms of attracting players. When a free agent thinks about coming here, he looks not only at the history of our basketball achievements but also at what being a Laker did for certain players off the court. It's got to make a free agent wonder if he can put a price on all those fringe benefits.

Still, we are going to watch Pau's *CSI* episode because we are curious to see what he did and how strenuous it was.

Maybe he had a stunt double? I don't think so. How do you find a stunt double for a guy who's 7'0" and weighs 250 pounds?

As it turned out, Pau had to do some heavy lifting on the show, pulling a guy out of a car and dragging him on the ground, and he also had to re-create a car crash with him as the driver. In all, he was on the set for three days.

I don't really like to see him exert himself like that, just because you never know what could happen. It takes a lot out of a person.

After seeing the show, Phil was relentless with Pau, teasing him through the media. If Phil was really upset, he would have put his foot down before Pau did the show

But I think, in retrospect, Phil was disappointed, and maybe even a little mad. When a player doesn't make the Lakers his top priority, then something is lost as a team.

WHEN WE GO OUT TO DINNER, it's usually the early-bird special unless we are meeting other people. We stayed home Saturday night and Phil made dinner after *48 Hours Mystery* was over. There was salmon, risotto, sweet potatoes, and a glass of wine.

No more TV, no football, no sports. Just music and conversation. It was nice.

November 15
ROCKETS 101, LAKERS 91

It was reassuring to see Kareem hold a press conference tonight at STAPLES Center to talk about being diagnosed with leukemia. He is a private man who likes to keep things to himself, but I'm sure it's been difficult to keep this hidden. Hopefully, there's less pressure on him now and he can concentrate on his treatment.

The news came as a shock to me and Phil when we heard about it for the first time this week. Kareem didn't look at all run-down, so there was no reason to suspect he wasn't well.

To further educate myself, I Googled "chronic myeloid leukemia," the form of the disease that he has contracted.

It's scary, but Kareem was reassuring when he said that with the proper medication and regular blood tests, the condition can be managed.

As an organization, we went through something similar 18 years ago when Magic Johnson was found to be HIV positive. With Earvin, we didn't know what was going to happen.

My dad told me about the diagnosis just before Earvin's press conference, which I attended. My dad called my sister and both of my brothers as well.

I've only seen my dad cry twice. Once was when his mother passed away. The other was the day of that press conference. It was distressing to see him that way, but it wasn't surprising because of his relationship with Earvin, who is like a son to him.

After the press conference, I walked into the hallway that led to the Forum offices and saw my dad and Kareem embrace to share their grief.

I stepped back to allow a private moment between these two men who are not known for their displays of emotion.

My father was devastated that day. It broke my heart because he has always been the strong one for the players, the father figure. They were looking to him for strength at that time more than ever. As we all were.

When the press conference was over, my dad wanted to be with Earvin. When Earvin left, my father just wanted to be with our family.

Once Earvin went public, we were inundated with calls from all over the world. Our phone system at the Forum couldn't handle the massive volume.

In addition to the calls, there was mail. Boxes and boxes and boxes of mail.

Everybody, it seemed, had a cure for HIV and wanted to share it.

Most of the opinions centered around food, or blamed pollution in the environment. Some said this is what happens when you don't take care of yourself.

Many people couldn't understand how it had happened. It wasn't supposed to be a disease that touched professional athletes. It just didn't make sense to those people.

Along with the cures, we found some fans were enclosing money in their letters. People would send a dollar. There would be checks for $5,000.

Fans were despondent, and everybody wanted to do something, contribute in some way, or simply pray. They just had to do something.

The letters were really touching. I wish we had thought about publishing them in a book.

Earvin decided to form a foundation and use the donations to further HIV awareness.

Our focus at the time was on Earvin, as it should have been. But ultimately, we had to deal with the effect on our franchise. Losing Magic Johnson would have hurt under any circumstances, but it was even worse because there was no time to prepare for it.

Back in the late 1980s, the decision was made to purchase a new scoreboard for the Forum because the old one didn't have a video screen. The idea was to time the unveiling for the season following Kareem's retirement. It wasn't like getting a new player, certainly not one with Kareem's skill. But at least we could offer the fans a new Forum attraction.

There was nothing to compensate for the sudden loss of Earvin. Instead, our team completely changed overnight.

We had lost to the Bulls in the 1991 NBA Finals, Earvin's last season, and we never got a chance to avenge that defeat. The opportunity to see Magic go against Michael Jordan again was gone.

In the last few seasons, we have come to depend on Kareem again, this time as a coach for our young center, Andrew Bynum. Watching Andrew incorporate some of Kareem's moves, especially the sky hook, has been exciting for Lakers fans as they watch the development of the next big man in a long line of purple-and-gold superstar centers.

As Andrew matures, I see his growth on the court as an evolutionary process. He will continue to polish his skills by working with our coaching staff to present impossible matchups for other teams.

And it's not just our young players who are continuing to evolve. Kobe spent time over the summer working with Hall of Fame center Hakeem Olajuwon to learn new moves. This is a good example of periodically seeking out new inspiration and new teachers. You can't just stay with one person your entire career, because then you aren't going to expand your game. I think, based on the way Andrew is playing right now, he is proving his ability to enhance his potential.

November 16

Last night was very emotional for our players. It wasn't because they were facing Houston, but rather because they were up against a familiar face who had played an important role in last season's championship.

There was a ceremony before the game to honor Trevor Ariza for his contribution to last year's team and to present him with his ring.

I was asked if I wanted to make the presentation, but I decided it wasn't a good idea. I don't know if he'd want to accept a ring from me, representing the organization, because he wasn't re-signed after last season.

So instead, our team captains, Kobe and Derek Fisher, presented the ring. That was appropriate, less of a distraction prior to the game, and enthusiastically applauded by the fans.

When Kurt Rambis comes here, Phil is going to give him his ring. That way it will be player to player and coach to coach. I think that makes more sense.

Our fans are fond of Trevor and happy for him because he is playing well this season. You never want to break up a championship team. It's always hard.

I want to see him do well this season, just not at the Lakers' expense.

November 18

The injury bug has hit us early. Luke Walton is out for six weeks with a pinched nerve in his back, and Pau is still unable to play.

Everybody said how easy it was going to be for us at the start of the season with 17 of our first 21 games at home. People were speculating that we could get a nice cushion, but with the injuries, I don't think we are going to be able to take advantage of all this time at STAPLES Center.

It's been frustrating for Phil, but instead of focusing on those who are in the trainer's room, he is complaining about the effort of those still on the court.

I don't want to just smile and say, "Oh, honey, it will get better." But in my heart, I think it will.

Phil said practice was very lively today because Pau was back on the floor. He's not quite ready to make his season debut, but when he does, that will give us a big boost.

I REALLY APPRECIATE LAKERS FANS and I enjoy interacting with them. Sometimes, though, it gets to be a bit much.

Like the time I was getting a mammogram. I was changing into an examining gown when several nurses asked if they could take a picture with me.

"I'm getting a mammogram," I said as politely as I could. "How about if we wait until I'm dressed?"

People love the Lakers, and they feel a connection to the team through me. They want autographs, they want tickets, and they want jobs.

The first request is somewhat feasible, the last two, not so much. We try to accommodate as many donation requests for signed merchandise as possible. We schedule two autograph sessions per season, but the demand always exceeds the supply.

Tickets are limited as well, so there are never enough for all the requests. In this business, that is a good problem to have, so I should stop complaining.

I am often asked about job opportunities in our organization. Since we are a small company with just over 100 full-time employees, we don't have a lot of turnover. I recommend to those interested in the sports business to not only focus on individual teams, but also businesses connected to those teams like media companies, corporate partners, and sport venues.

November 19
LAKERS 108, BULLS 93

Pau is back.

I'm happy because of what he brings to the team, but also because of what he has done for Phil's frame of mind. With Pau playing, Phil is so much more fun to hang out with. I like having him back to his old self.

Phil had challenged Pau, asking him over and over, "When are you coming back?" And Phil told the media, "We don't expect him back until Christmas."

I think he threw that there out to motivate Pau.

The transition back was seamless. It was as if Pau had never left. What a boost to the team.

Pau missed 11 games because of a strained right hamstring, and Phil was pleased that our record was as good as it was without him playing. But clearly, we are much better with him in our lineup.

And it looks like he'll stay there. Pau reported no problems afterward with the hamstring. He said it feels good.

Since Pau was traded to the Lakers by Memphis in February of 2008, we have won more than 80 percent of our games. That is ridiculously good. Wow, what a fortunate turn of events his acquisition was for the organization.

I don't think even Phil anticipated how well it was going to work with Pau.

What made me particularly proud about that trade was that word didn't leak out until the deal was done. If it had, I guarantee you there would have been teams in our conference who would have offered a better deal just to make sure the Lakers didn't get Pau. They would have thrown money and players with expiring contracts at Memphis because it was the expiring contracts that motivated the Grizzlies to make the deal. That was what they were looking for.

Phil was not advised the trade was in the works until it went down. That's as it should be. Had the negotiations leaked out and then collapsed, Phil would have been left in an awkward position because he would still have to coach two of the players who were offered to Memphis, Kwame Brown and Javaris Crittenton. But at least he could have told them, in all honesty, he wasn't in on the decision to trade them.

I think it's a burden on a coach if he knows who might be going. It's smart for the general manager to consider that factor when deciding whether or not to include a coach in trade discussions.

Now, if you are talking about a trade that is a tough call, meaning roughly equal talent on both sides of the equation, the general manager may decide that getting input from his coach outweighs other considerations.

But in this case, although Phil did get a lot out of Kwame, clearly Pau's potential for our team was too great to pass up.

I found out about the deal from my brother Jim, probably the day before. The Lakers were on the road and I didn't say anything to Phil because it was almost too good to be true, too unbelievable to get excited about.

It's important to understand, Phil feels like he's going to war with his players. He has studied the great generals, the successful military strategists. For Phil, his players are the guys he's in the trenches with, and he will defend them to the end. When you are on the team, you are *on the team*.

He was pleased with the roster he had before the organization obtained Pau, although he was always in search of consistency from his players, especially after the Lakers were knocked out in the first round of the playoffs by Phoenix two years in a row. The first time, the Lakers were up 3–1, but failed to finish off the Suns.

Just because Phil wasn't clued in about the specific deal for Pau doesn't mean GM Mitch Kupchak and Phil are not in constant communication about the Lakers' needs in general, and specifically when someone is out for a while because of an injury.

Luke is a good example. If he is going to be unavailable for the next few weeks, do you make a move to get someone to take up his minutes?

These are issues Mitch and Phil wrestle with all the time.

November 22

LAKERS 101, THUNDER 85

Tonight was Chick Hearn Night, always one of my favorite events of the year. I love paying tribute to our legendary broadcaster who passed away in 2002 after spending 42 years as our play-by-play announcer. We celebrate his memory at the home game played closest to his birthday. On this annual night, I enjoy meeting the winners of the scholarship fund that bears his name at the University of Southern California and am always thrilled to know I've brought a smile to the face of his 92-year-old widow.

If you had the fortune to have heard Chick, you are familiar with his innovative, passionate, and sometimes hilarious Chickisms.

As the years go by, fewer and fewer people will realize how much they echo Chick when speaking about basketball and beyond.

For example, *slam dunk,* not only a classic basketball term but now a common expression in all areas of life, was coined by Chick. As were *air ball, dribble drive, ticky-tack foul, faked him into the popcorn machine,* and so many others.

My early memories of Chick weren't tied to the Lakers but to his job as host of *Bowling for Dollars.* It was his sense of humor and his ability to bring out the best in the contestants that made it more than just another TV game show.

The first Chick story most people tell when recalling *Bowling for Dollars* concerns a woman who announced that, if she won money on the program, she was going to take her family to Las Vegas.

The woman stepped up and promptly threw a gutter ball.

"You bowl like that, lady," said Chick, "you aren't even going to make it to Pomona."

When my dad bought the Lakers, one of my first thoughts was, *Wow, I get to meet Chick Hearn.*

Little did I imagine how this larger-than-life broadcasting superstar would affect my career.

I began in the family business as the general manager of the Los Angeles Strings of World Team Tennis. The old Prime Ticket network was carrying our tennis events, and when Chick said he wanted to be the announcer, he gave us instant credibility. Even the tennis players themselves were excited because they were being interviewed by Chick.

But it wasn't just tennis. Chick was very supportive of everything I have done in my career.

Still, I was always intimidated by him because he had such a commanding presence.

His widow Marge, on the other hand, is like the grandmothers I no longer have. I love listening to stories about her and "Fran" (she refers to her late husband by his given name, Francis). They met in high school and were married eight days short of 64 years.

Everything Marge says is worth listening to because she has such great insight.

When Phil was let go after the Lakers lost to Detroit in the 2004 NBA Finals, Marge was so compassionate. I felt lost without Phil, so it meant so much to me to have Marge in my corner. I didn't expect that from someone of her stature.

When you are in the middle of change, it's easy to get overwhelmed. You can't see past the pain. It was Marge who always said something to cheer me up. She's very wise that way and a valued confidant.

How many grandmothers really understand the men in the NBA, from players to coaches to owners to league executives? Marge can do that by drawing on a half-century of involvement in the game.

The winners of this year's Chick Hearn Memorial Scholarship, awarded to students at the USC Annenberg School for Communication and Journalism, are Alex Goldsmith, a senior from Santa Fe, New Mexico, and Trevor Thompson, a junior from Valencia, California. They both receive a $5,000 scholarship, an internship at Fox Sports Net, and a chance to work on a Lakers telecast.

Chick would be proud to know his memory is serving as an inspiration to the next generation of broadcasters.

November 24

LAKERS 100, KNICKS 90

The Lakers may have won tonight, but that doesn't mean Phil was pleased. He came home grumpy and dissatisfied because his bench struggled after the team had built a 25-point lead.

Phil had to put Ron Artest and Andrew Bynum back in, and he didn't like burdening his starters with additional minutes after it appeared there was nothing left but garbage time.

In general, Phil hasn't been satisfied with the way the bench has played lately.

He gets satisfaction when the team executes what it works on in practice.

Me? I look at it like, "Omigosh, another win. That's great."

Phil's contentment comes from what he sees on the court, not on the scoreboard. Most of all, he wants to see effort. There are games we've lost that don't bother him because he knows the team played to its potential.

After a STAPLES Center game, he always brings home the stat sheet and we go over it. He points things out to me about turnovers or offensive rebounds or whatever jumps out at him. He goes into detail about why this or that was a key to the game.

In preparation for tonight's game, we watched the Knicks and the Celtics play last Sunday afternoon.

After it was over, Phil hit the rewind button because he wanted to show me again and again a pick-and-roll situation where one of the Knicks didn't switch. Phil stressed in our little impromptu film session why the defense always has to be ahead of the pick.

That's Phil, always teaching even if it's just me sitting there as the only pupil.

November 26

It's Thanksgiving Day and Phil made the players practice. They played Tuesday night and he gave them Wednesday off.

"Why do you make them practice on Thanksgiving?" I asked him. "It seems like you should have made them practice yesterday and then given them today off."

"Because," he said, "most of the guys are not from Los Angeles, so they are away from home. Even if they are married and their wives are here, they are still not 'home.' So it's really important for them to think of the team as their family. This being a family holiday, I want to bring them all together."

Phil traditionally forms two teams—one with the big guys and one with the smaller players—and has a Thanksgiving scrimmage. That way, some of the players have to run the offense from positions they are not familiar with. It makes them thankful for their teammates. When you are on a team of all big guys, you really miss having a guard who can handle the ball. If you are the small guys, you really miss having someone to feed inside.

It was a pretty lively game, with the Smalls beating the Bigs. Phil knows those are the kinds of things that build chemistry and camaraderie. And the players still get home in plenty of time to have a Thanksgiving dinner.

Our turkey dinner was a collaboration between Phil and his 32-year-old daughter Brooke, who lives about five minutes from us in Playa del Rey. She made the stuffing and brought everything over the night before. Phil stuffed the bird before practice and let it cook while he was gone.

Phil got home about 1:00 or 1:30, and we sat down to eat at 4:30, just before sunset. It was really pretty with the reflection from the ocean.

Phil made the turkey, the mashed potatoes, the sweet potatoes, and this really yummy dish consisting of peas and French onions with a creamy sauce. Oh, it was all so good.

My contribution was peeling and boiling the onions the night before.

My friend Stacy came over, joining Brooke, her husband Jack, and their two kids, three-year-old Jackson and one-year-old Makayla.

We spent much of the night trying to entertain the kids. Every 15 minutes, we gave them something new to do.

Phil tries to talk to the little ones like they are adults, which doesn't really go over well. Phil is the voice of authority, but to a three-year-old, he can seem scary and can, inadvertently, inspire a flow of tears.

Phil loves them. It delights him to have them around, and his bond with his grandkids will get stronger as they get older.

It was a nice evening. Often the Lakers have played on Thanksgiving, so it was wonderful to have this amount of time off.

The team leaves tomorrow for a game in Oakland on Saturday. Three of Phil's kids live in San Francisco, so Friday night, he will have another family dinner.

Ben and Charley, Phil's 30-year-old twin boys, live up there, as does his daughter Chelsea, who is 34 and expecting another child.

Phil's oldest is a 41-year-old daughter named Elizabeth who lives in Washington, D.C.

If it's a holiday, I join Phil on the road. One year, we were in Orlando for Thanksgiving. Shaq was still playing for the Lakers and had that big house there from his days with the Magic. He invited the whole team over for a catered dinner.

It was quite an experience. We had heard so much about this big, crazy house he lived in, and it proved to be just that with an indoor court, a pool, and toys everywhere.

I thought it was really a nice gesture for Shaq to invite everybody over, a pleasant alternative to eating Thanksgiving dinner in a restaurant.

Before I met Phil, I was always with the rest of the Buss family on Thanksgiving. We went to Las Vegas five years in a row before Phil came into my life. My dad would have a big suite where we gathered for dinner.

I also remember my mom spending hours cooking Thanksgiving dinner when I was a child. It was always so delicious and we used the good china, which made it even more memorable.

This Thanksgiving, my family went to Disneyland and ate in a private restaurant named Club 33, located above the Blue Bayou restaurant in New Orleans Square.

My dad knows how to make things fun.

CROWNING ACHIEVEMENTS: FROM THE PALISADES TO INGLEWOOD

DIVORCE IS PAINFUL FOR CHILDREN, AND EACH OF MY SIBLINGS took our parents' split in a different way. As a 12-year-old in the sixth grade when my parents split up, I felt I was the cause of their divorce because I thought I wasn't lovable enough to make them want to keep the family unit together.

It's hard not to think there is something wrong with you in a situation like that. At that stage of your life, you are so self-centered that you don't realize there is a bigger world beyond you.

I was like most teenagers with divorced parents, having this fantasy that they were going to get back together so we could have this happy, TV-sitcom family, and that I was going to be the one to make that happen.

I would say to myself, "Oh, Mom and Dad are going to be in the same room tonight. Maybe we will all be back together."

My mom was really good at helping me through that period, and I finally realized that it was best for my mom and dad to get divorced because they had become very different people.

They never aired those differences in front of us. There was never any yelling or screaming in our house. My parents never used me or my siblings as pawns in their divorce nor bad-mouthed each other to us. There was no manipulation of the children whatsoever to get back at each other.

Never.

I was so fortunate in that regard. Even though they weren't meant to stay together, my parents were still committed to putting the family first and have remained so to this day.

They maintained a pretty good relationship compared to so many of their peers who got divorced and never spoke to each other again.

My parents are amazing. They would have been married 60 years now if they were still together. In a way, they are still together. My mom believed in my dad when they were married and she still believes in him now.

Whenever possible, it's important to have a strong relationship with both parents, even if they are not together.

As a child of divorce, I'm very sensitive to Phil's relationship with his kids. He has been divorced twice and has children from both marriages.

I like to give Phil's kids their time with their father and not intrude. They've been really great about embracing me and including me in the group. That means a lot to me, and I always want them to feel welcome when I'm around. But their relationship with their father is special and I'm not there to interfere with that or replace their mother or monopolize his time.

AS MY TEEN YEARS BEGAN, my days on horseback ended. I guess one day, the girly side of me took over because I suddenly realized how dirty and dusty I was after riding. The dirt was even under my fingernails. Rather than spending time in the saddle, I was more interested in getting dressed up and going to the Del Mar racetrack.

I went to Pacific Palisades High School where my classmates included Forest Whitaker, who went on to become an Oscar-winning actor, former NFL quarterback Jay Schroeder, and soap opera star Elizabeth Keifer.

I was the scorekeeper for the boys' basketball team, but I also played on the girls' squad. Sort of.

I was a center, but I was so bad that I was still on the junior varsity team as a senior. I worked so hard that the coach let me stay on until graduation. Or maybe he just felt sorry for me because I was so horrible.

Either way, it was fine with me because I got to mentor the 10th graders. As a result, I had this great basketball experience in high school, making me a fan of the sport long before my dad bought the Lakers.

I'll never forget the time I got elbowed in the left breast during a game. I started yelling, "Coach, coach, take me out!"

He yelled back, "What do you want me to do, get you a sling?"

In my senior year, I was nominated for homecoming queen, but I lost. I was not popular in high school.

Looking for a chance to make up for my poor showing, I saw a notice for a Miss Palisades contest. Because it wasn't associated with the high school, it was an opportunity for me to enter a beauty contest that wouldn't be based on popularity.

So I signed up, even though my parents thought I was crazy to do it.

The competition included an interview with the judges. My interview was the highlight for me because one of the judges was Adam West, who played Batman in one of my favorite TV shows growing up.

It turned out to be a really good experience because I learned valuable lessons about poise, how to make eye contact, and how to conduct serious conversations with adults, all important skills for a teenager in terms of personal growth.

Three outfits were required for the competition: a swimsuit, a casual outfit, and an evening gown. My gown was the dress I had bought for my upcoming prom. I wore it in a beauty contest and then to the prom, the ultimate dress. I still have it.

For me, the most significant part was that I won, especially because so many people doubted me. Becoming Miss Palisades gave me a lot of confidence and made me realize that you can't just listen to others, because if I had, I never would have entered the contest.

Some of the girls I competed against had also been in the homecoming queen competition. So for me, it negated that whole high school popularity thing, which can be hard on a girl's confidence.

I learned I could set a goal and achieve it, which was wonderful for my self-esteem.

I take pride in the fact that I will always be Miss Palisades of 1979. Nobody else will ever have that particular title. I compare it to the Lakers winning a championship because no other team will ever be the 2009 NBA champions.

As Miss Palisades, I was required to go to events like the opening of a bank wearing my crown and holding those giant scissors they use for ribbon cuttings. I was also in the Palisades Fourth of July parade.

My role was to serve as an ambassador and to mingle with the public.

Being very shy at the time, those obligations brought me out of my shell, and although I didn't know it then, they prepared me for my career as a high-profile member of the Lakers organization.

My dad was at my high school graduation, but he was unable to come to my crowning as Miss Palisades. I did talk him into judging the contest when I passed my crown on the following year.

My memories of those years have recently been rekindled because I went to my 30-year high school reunion, which I was fortunate enough to have a role in planning.

I LIVED WITH MY MOM UNTIL I graduated from high school. We were like best friends. I loved spending time with her, but I longed for more time with my dad.

There was no routine as far as seeing him. He would have somebody pick me up when he was available.

I would always be taken to a spot that seemed glamorous to a teenager. My dad owned hotels in Palm Springs and San Diego. He also had a boat and was still going to Del Mar for the races.

He saw each of his kids individually because our schedules were all different. My sister had her horses, and Johnny and Jimmy had their sports and other hobbies.

Sometimes I would go out with him and a woman he was dating, and I would think, *Couldn't she just be quiet for 30 minutes so I could have a conversation with my father?*

I was envious when he spent time with someone else. It didn't matter who the date was. I didn't want to share my dad with anybody.

But I never resented the girls themselves. They weren't trying to be my mom.

I had started meeting those girls when I was about 14. They were usually like 20 or 21 and treated me like a little sister. It was cool hanging out with them during the weekends I visited my dad...as long as he reserved some time just for me.

I never looked upon it as being disloyal to my mother because by then, she was also dating. Nothing could break the bond of a mother and a daughter.

At that point, my mother was also traveling a lot. She went to the 1976 Olympics in Montreal. She went to Europe. She wasn't just sitting around. She was enjoying herself.

The older her kids got, the more she was able to live her own life, but she was always there for us.

When I reached my late teens and my dad's girlfriends were closer to me in age, we would go shopping together. They would do my hair, give me makeup tips, and all that kind of stuff.

They would never pump me for information about him. Never. They respected him and spoiled me.

In the summer of 1979 following graduation, I moved in with my father. I finally got the chance to have the closeness with him that I had wanted for so long.

I'm still friends with a lot of the girls from that time period. They are all still beautiful and many are successful career women.

My dad is a romantic. He wanted to fall in love. He hoped each girl might be the special one he had been looking for.

As I got much older than the women he was dating, however, it wasn't the same for me.

I JOINED MY DAD AT A MOMENTOUS TIME in his life. In May of that year, he, Frank Mariani, and their group of investors had just purchased the Forum, the Lakers, the Kings hockey team, and the 13,000-acre Raljon Ranch in the Sierras for $67.5 million from Jack Kent Cooke.

The deal broke down as follows: Forum ($33.5 million), Lakers ($16 million), Kings ($8 million), and the ranch ($10 million).

In all, there were nine pieces of property spread over three states.

My dad's lifelong love of sports had resulted in the addition of yet another title to the chemist/aerospace engineer/college lecturer/real estate baron. He was now also the owner and operator of a sports empire.

While this was certainly my father's biggest venture into sports, it wasn't his first. In the early 1970s, he and his attorney, Jerry Fine, put in $25,000 apiece to buy the Los Angeles Strings of World Team Tennis.

Until then, I wasn't even aware that my dad was interested in being a sports owner. I had never heard him talk about buying a team in those days. It was always about real estate.

The WTT was a concept designed to take advantage of the increasing popularity of both team sports and tennis. There would be a little of everything for the tennis fan: men's and women's singles, and doubles and mixed doubles.

Even then, my dad already had the idea that what the sports world needed was a little sizzle, best supplied by the entertainment world. For the first match ever played by the Strings, held at the L.A. Sports Arena in 1974, my dad asked one of his limited partners to serve as master of ceremonies, a guy by the name of Johnny Carson.

Stars or no stars, however, the idea of team tennis was slow to catch on in L.A., where there are so many options for the sports fan. The Strings lost $200,000 the first year and $1 million the second year.

By then, Jerry Fine had bailed out, but my dad wasn't going anywhere. To him, this was the first rung on a ladder that could lead to the purchase of a team in a major sport, and he wanted to use the opportunity to learn how to make the climb.

To attract the players he wanted on the court and the number of fans he wanted in the stands, my dad knew he was going to have to offer better surroundings than the L.A. Sports Arena, which was already beginning to show its age even though it was barely 15 years old.

So he did what Jack Kent Cooke had done. He packed up his act and headed south, striking a deal with Cooke to use the Forum. It was an ideal situation for both men since the Strings' matches were in the off-season for both of Cooke's teams, the Lakers and the Kings.

It was also an opportunity for my dad to start a business relationship with the man who had the power to grant him access to the world of his dreams.

So the Strings began playing at the Forum in 1976. In 1978, the team won its first WTT title. But the Strings' championship also gave them a dubious honor. It was not only their first, but the WTT's last. Plagued by financial difficulties with other teams—despite the fact my dad had made generous loans to troubled owners—the WTT folded.

But only temporarily. It would be resurrected several years later in a shortened format.

While my dad hated to see his first link to sports broken, he could console himself with the knowledge he had kept his eyes on a bigger prize.

It had become known in the L.A. sports community that Cooke, faced with a costly divorce, was thinking about cashing in the Southern California portion of his sports empire. He would retain majority ownership of the Washington Redskins.

My dad had inquired about teams in the NFL, Major League Baseball, and the American Basketball Association. But suddenly, Cooke appeared to be my father's best hope for breaking into big-time sports.

Cooke had already abandoned L.A. physically, moving to Las Vegas. But every few weeks, he would call my dad and invite him to fly over and talk.

And talk they did, through 1977, 1978, and into the spring of 1979. Then finally, my dad got the call he had been waiting for.

"Are you ready?" asked Cooke.

My father, whose goal had once been to get courtside seats for Lakers games, now had a chance to own the court itself and all that went with it.

The terms of Cooke's split from his wife had been set. He was going to pay out $41 million, a California record for a divorce settlement.

Already living on a 51-acre estate in Virginia, Cooke agreed to sell the Lakers, the Kings, and the Forum to my dad, but it wasn't easy. Deals of that magnitude never are. But to my father, it was just another game of Monopoly, just like all those games we had played over all those years in Pacific Palisades.

Only this time, the pieces were real. And so was the money.

It was a lot more complicated than swapping Boardwalk for Park Place and Marvin Gardens. My dad had to raise a lot of cash, and the Chrysler Building in New York and property in three other East Coast states were put into the mix. When it was all done, there were enough escrow papers to fill a library and enough lawyers to fill the Forum.

The *New York Times* called it "the largest single financial transaction in the history of professional sports," but also "the most confusing, complex transaction in the history of sports."

My dad had become a major player in L.A. I was graduating from high school at just the right time. I was as determined as ever to be involved in the family business. But it looked like that business was no longer going to be primarily real estate. Instead of contractors and bulldozers, we'd be dealing with athletes and Zambonis.

A purchase price of $16 million might seem like a bargain for the Lakers, whose value is now estimated to be more than $600 million. But it represented a nice profit for Cooke, who purchased the team from Bob Short for $5,175,000 in 1965.

Short had been negotiating at the time with Dodgers owner Walter O'Malley, who envisioned a new home for the Lakers in Chavez Ravine alongside Dodger Stadium.

When Short told O'Malley about Cooke's offer, the Dodgers owner's response, according to Short in the book *Winnin' Times*, was, "Hell, you gotta sell. That's a tremendous amount of money for 10 pairs of tennis shoes."

I remember my dad telling me that when he first arrived at the Forum after concluding his deal, an amusing thought went through his head.

Surveying the large arena, imagining his teams playing there, he thought, *I just purchased this landmark building for all this money, and they don't even give me the keys to the place?*

Of course, he knew full well he didn't need an actual key to get into the Forum. He also knew what he had bought was the key to the future of our family.

MY DAD HAD STARTED DROPPING HINTS to me and my siblings about the purchase two or three months earlier.

He would say things like, "What rock group would you most like to see?"

I'd say, "The Rolling Stones."

Back then, my dad had a terrace box at the Forum, the closest thing to a suite in that arena, which we could use for any event.

"What if I could get you in the front row?" my dad asked. "Would that be fun?"

"Yeah, that would be great," I said.

"And what if I told you that you would be able to sit on the stage?"

"How would that be possible?"

"I can't tell you just yet, but I'm working on it."

He would tease us like that.

Finally, my dad told us what was about to happen a few days before the sale, but I still couldn't comprehend how incredible it was going to be.

I had become aware of how big the Lakers were a year earlier. They were in the playoffs in 1978 against Seattle, and a guy I was dating in high school wanted to go to what turned out to be the only home game the Lakers would have in that brief postseason. They would be eliminated in a best-of-three, first-round series.

I asked my dad if I could get tickets. Claire Rothman, the general manager of the Forum and a woman I would later work with and come to greatly admire, got us the best seats I had ever had, right in the center of the court a few rows back.

My boyfriend, enamored with the Lakers, couldn't believe where we were sitting. I was enamored with the whole scene because I suddenly realized how huge the Lakers were in this town.

I knew who Kareem Abdul-Jabbar was. But other than that, I probably knew more about Ann Meyers, the legendary female basketball player, than who was on the Lakers at that time. I wasn't the least bit interested in going to a hockey game. So the Lakers and the concerts were the big deal to me.

There was a press conference at the Forum to announce my dad's purchase. What I remember most was that Ryan O'Neal was there and the Forum was set up for boxing. That's because Ryan was filming a boxing movie there with Barbra Streisand called *The Main Event*.

My head was spinning as I met Ryan and mingled with all those famous people.

I saw sportscaster Stu Nahan, a familiar TV face, interviewing my dad. The whole thing was surreal.

I GUESS I ALWAYS KNEW I was going to go to USC because of my love for the Trojans, handed down from my father.

After all those Saturday afternoons at USC football games, I couldn't imagine myself going anywhere else. It would have been too weird.

I did allow the thought of going back East to briefly enter my mind, but it left just as quickly because I knew I couldn't handle the weather.

My sister went to USC for a year, and my younger brother Joey later graduated from there. Johnny and Jimmy took classes there as well.

When I was in high school, I would visit my dad at his house in Bel Air. That's where I lived over the summer following graduation.

Set to enter USC in the fall, I was going to move back home with my mom in the Palisades.

One day, with the time for college drawing near, I burst out in tears.

"Why are you crying?" my father asked.

"Because I've had so much fun staying here this summer," I replied.

"Well," he said, "why don't you just stay while you go to college?"

"That would be great," I said. "I would love it."

"But if you're going to stay," he told me, "then I'm going to have to buy a bigger house."

And that's what he did. He bought Pickfair, one of the most famous mansions in the world.

DECEMBER

December 1

In the early 1980s, I dated a defenseman for the Los Angeles Kings named Jay Wells.

When his contract was up, he said to me, "Is there any way you could find out what the other defensemen on the team make?"

"You don't know? You've got to be kidding me," I said.

"No, we are not allowed to know," he said.

I was flabbergasted.

"It's not surprising that it's kept secret," Jay explained. "When I go in to negotiate for a new contract, if I can say, so-and-so is making $60,000 and so-and-so is making $100,000, and I play more minutes than the $60,000 guy but less than the $100,000 guy, then I've made a pretty reasonable case for getting $80,000. That's not something management wants."

"Since you NHL players have a union, it should be sharing that information with you," I said. "No way should you be in the dark. No way should you have to accept the general manager's salary figures just because you have nowhere else to go to learn the truth."

That concept was hard for me to accept, so I got Jay the information he wanted.

That conversation is on my mind because I attended a Board of Governors meeting in New York last week at which we discussed our labor negotiations. The current collective bargaining agreement is scheduled to expire at the end of the 2010–11 season.

I understand if there is mistrust amongst some of our players because they've heard stories about the old days when the professional athletes were deceived or simply lied to about the teams' finances, leaving them forced to take what they could get.

But in this day and age, the players are our partners. There are no secrets. There is no hidden money. There is no way we could get around the players, much less the IRS. That is not the way we operate. This is the age of information. It's all out there.

It's just a shame there has to be this feeling of disconnect between the owners and the players. It worries me and leaves me uncertain about the future.

The players should know that we are working for the good of the league. For example, if we had two teams that were experiencing financial problems, we wouldn't want to see them fold. I have been involved in too many minor leagues where that happened, and it is devastating for everyone.

Having 30 teams is a benefit for the players because it means more jobs, and it's a benefit for the NBA because it means a larger television footprint and therefore more fans.

I hope the players understand that these negotiations are not just about that next contract. It's also about where they are going to be employed after their playing days are over. Hopefully, they will become part of the NBA family by getting jobs in broadcasting, scouting, coaching, or the front office.

And yes, even ownership. Michael Jordan owns a team, and Magic Johnson owns part of the Lakers. Eventually, other guys are going to be owners.

Shutting down the league for any reason—the unavoidable consequence if the negotiations fail—hurts all of these opportunities for everybody. It takes us backward.

So we've got to find a way to work this out, to make sure everybody shares in the wealth. That's the way it should be.

These are those who might speculate that if some teams are struggling, it's only because there is a bad economy right now, but that's really not the case. Some teams have been losing money since the last collective bargaining agreement was signed.

A work stoppage would not be good for anybody. Instead, the economics have to be fixed. Then everybody's piece of the pie will get bigger.

I want the league to be around 50 and 100 years from now. That will be our legacy.

December 4

LAKERS 108, HEAT 107

A couple of Lakers are making headlines, but unfortunately it's not because of what they are doing on the court, but rather what they are saying to the media.

Sasha Vujacic has been complaining about playing time, and Ron Artest has decided to reveal he drank cognac in the locker room at halftime when he played for the Bulls a decade ago.

Phil's reaction to the two remarks was quite different.

He is very disappointed in Sasha's behavior. Phil has the team practice on Thanksgiving Day because he considers the Lakers a family. Well, you don't treat your family like this.

Sasha and Phil are butting heads right now. They are not on the same page.

Every player has to understand that the Lakers aren't all about them. Sasha is too worried about his individual performance. He's concerned that less playing time is affecting his stats.

Playing time is not a right, it's a privilege. Maybe Sasha has lost sight of that.

This is a teachable moment for Phil.

These players are all competitive and they are battling for playing time every day. I get that. I understand the chemistry that goes on between the players better than I do the Xs and Os.

During the game, I have a great view sitting directly across from the bench on the other side of the court. Anything I see from there relating to body language, chemistry, or a lack thereof, I relay to Phil after the game in case he missed it.

As for Ron, I'm sure Phil will have a conversation with him, but he is not concerned about Ron's remarks at all.

Phil sees it from a different perspective. He understands that when people mature, they analyze things they did when they were younger and look at their motivation for some of the mistakes they made.

For Ron, it was important for people in L.A. to know he's now a different guy than the player who went into the stands and fought with a fan when he was with the Indiana Pacers, or drank liquor, as he claims, at halftime of Bulls games.

In order to convince fans that he's changed, he had to exorcise the mistakes of the past by exposing them, talking about them, asking for forgiveness, and putting them behind him.

Phil has had absolutely no problems with Ron since he has been here. And he is certainly not concerned that Ron is going to start sneaking in cognac at halftime.

Phil knows Ron's work ethic. He's never doubted him. As a matter of fact, Phil has wanted to coach him for the last couple of years.

Phil says that when people try to compare Ron and Dennis Rodman, they are misguided. The two are completely different.

Dennis had to blow off steam, Phil said. He had to know how to manage Dennis' ups and downs. Ron is very consistent. Yes, he's a character, a unique kind of guy, but he doesn't have the highs and lows that Dennis had.

Phil says he could sense when Dennis needed a break. In order to keep him focused, Phil had to relax the leash a little bit.

Sometimes players need a guys' night out or an especially challenging practice or just a day off to chill out. Phil has an excellent feel for that. He is good at managing personalities, reading people, understanding their backgrounds, and figuring out who they are.

Phil's view of tonight's game was a little different from that of Lakers fans. All they were talking about, understandably, was Kobe's off-balance, buzzer-beating, 27-foot bank shot just beyond the reach of Dwyane Wade to win the game.

Phil was, of course, happy the team won, but his joy was tempered by the fact they had a nine-point lead with just under six and half minutes to play and had to depend on Kobe's spectacular game winner to pull out the victory.

December 5

I spent the afternoon at a Barnes & Noble signing copies of the Lakers' 50th anniversary book.

One woman told me her son grew up in L.A. but now lives in Sweden, so she was sending him the book for the holidays. It touches me to think that, despite being separated by thousands of miles, a mother and son can still have a shared experience as Lakers fans.

Those are the moments that remind me this franchise is bigger than any one of its players, coaches, or owners.

This team brings families and whole communities encompassing all age groups together, and that phenomenon should be treasured and protected.

I WORRY ABOUT LINDA RAMBIS. While we have the best record in the league at 15–3 and have won eight in a row, Minnesota, coached by her husband Kurt, was 2–17 on the season, including a 15-game losing streak, prior to tonight.

It's really weighing on Kurt. He's frustrated, and there's nothing Linda can do to help.

She came over tonight, we had a beer, and Phil did what he could to cheer her up. I love that side of Phil. We have all seen his success in relating to talented athletes, but he can also empathize with a wife who is concerned about her husband.

There's not a lot he can draw on as a head coach in terms of experiencing what Kurt is going through. Fortunately, Phil hasn't had those kinds of problems in his career.

But he was an assistant coach on the 1980–81 New Jersey Nets, a team that lost 14 in a row and 19 of 20, so Phil knows what a locker room can feel like when the players are feeling the weight of such a bad stretch.

Linda asked Phil what he would say to his guys, if he were Kurt, to keep them motivated. After all, you can't realistically talk about the possibility of winning a championship with a team that has won only two games one week into December. What carrot can a coach offer those guys?

Phil was honest.

"There are designated timeouts at certain points of each quarter," Phil told Linda. "I guess I would start with that. I would tell the players to just try to win that segment, get them used to taking the game in sets of minutes. Try for small victories. Don't let the burden of the big picture freeze you.

"You certainly don't want to say, 'We've got no chance of winning this game.'"

As a matter of fact, Phil texted that advice to Kurt yesterday after the Timberwolves had lost to New Orleans.

Phil himself does something similar, albeit on a larger scale: he breaks down the entire season into weekly increments. The Lakers will have two, three, or four games in a week, and Phil will let the players know, via the blackboard in the locker room, what he expects in terms of results.

Are there back-to-back games? Are there tough opponents? Is there a long home stand or a difficult road trip? Whatever it is, Phil sets the goal for that week. Maybe it's 3–1. Maybe it's 4–0. No matter what, it's realistic.

Phil then suggested that we should turn on the TV because Minnesota was playing Utah.

No, no, both Linda and I insisted, that game is tomorrow night.

Phil shrugged, but when Linda left, he flipped on the set and, sure enough, there were the Timberwolves and the Jazz.

There were only 10 seconds to play, but that was enough for us to see Minnesota leave the court with a 108–101 victory. Kurt got a standing ovation from the hometown crowd.

I couldn't wait to call Linda with the good news. Driving home, she didn't answer, but she'll have a great voice mail waiting for her.

Later tonight, Kurt texted Phil to thank him for the advice. He said he took it to heart and the team responded.

Hopefully, Kurt and his players will be able to build on that.

December 9

LAKERS 101, JAZZ 77

There was a frightening incident last night for Kobe Bryant and his family.

A SWAT team was called in to respond to a home-invasion robbery in the gated community of Pelican Ridge in the Newport Coast section of Newport Beach.

When I heard about it on the radio this morning, three suspects had been arrested, but two were still at large, possibly armed.

The two words that jumped out at me from the broadcast were *Pelican Ridge*. That's Kobe's neighborhood. The report also said the area was being locked down while they searched for the at-large suspects. I went to alert Phil, who was in the shower, that Kobe might not be able to get to the morning shootaround.

Kobe indeed missed practice.

When media members asked Phil when he found out Kobe might be absent, he said, "Well, I was in the shower and Jeanie walked in."

All of sudden, the story became "Jeanie's in the shower with Phil." It was huge on Twitter. People are teasing me and making all sorts of comments.

When Phil got home, I said, "Why did you have to explain the story like that? Why couldn't you just say, 'I learned about it this morning before I left the house'? Why did you have to bring in the shower visual?"

Phil just laughed it off. He thought it was funny.

There was nothing funny about it for Kobe, of course. He didn't want to talk about it. Understandably so. Kobe is very protective of his family.

December 10

After several months of sitting on the sideline watching the Timberwolves struggle on the court, Kurt Rambis got to watch a game tonight for the pure enjoyment of it.

In town for tomorrow's Lakers-Timberwolves game, Kurt saw his daughter Ali play for her Mira Costa High School volleyball team.

It figures to be a little different tomorrow when Kurt's 3–19 Timberwolves play the 17–3 Lakers.

As Phil's key assistant coach for several seasons, Kurt knows the Lakers better than anyone in the league, so he knows where the weak spots are. But let's face it, when it comes to the Lakers and weak spots, there aren't many to find.

Since Kevin Love came back after sitting out 18 games because of a broken hand, the Timberwolves have been more competitive. Maybe there's a light at the end of the tunnel.

But are they going to make the playoffs? Probably not, because they've dug themselves a pretty deep hole in the standings.

Since Linda sits next to me at games, I asked her how we were going to deal with our opposing interests tomorrow night. She said we are going to clap for every basket in the game.

Linda couldn't wait for Kurt to get home. She has chosen to remain in L.A. rather than join her husband in Minneapolis in order to allow Ali to stay at Mira Costa for her senior year.

Besides, Linda said, if she were to move to Minneapolis, she would be alone half the time while Kurt traveled with the team.

I'm thrilled because it keeps Linda in our executive offices where she juggles so many projects for us, including all the marketing and promotion for the preseason games.

We've been together since I was a student at USC and she was then Linda Zafrani, working in ticket sales at the Forum.

When Kurt joined the Lakers in 1981, Linda said to me, "That new guy on the team is cute."

I said, "Are you kidding me? The guy with the glasses? I don't think so."

Linda went with me to Philadelphia when the Lakers faced the Sixers in the 1982 NBA Finals, and that's when she and Kurt started hanging out.

Some may have thought Kurt didn't fit in with the fast-breaking Lakers of the Showtime era, but they were mistaken. He was athletic, he could move, he could rebound, and he could certainly hustle.

Kurt and Linda got married in Las Vegas during the All-Star break in 1985. Michael Cooper, Mitch Kupchak, and a lot of others attended, and that was a testament to Kurt and Linda's popularity. Who decides to get married with 48 hours' notice and has 85 people jump on a plane to go to the wedding?

When Kurt was signed as a free agent by the Charlotte Hornets in 1988, Linda went with him. It was really devastating for me. I lost the person with whom I had worked so closely for so long. Being in the office and at games wasn't the same for me after that.

Kurt went from Charlotte to Phoenix to Sacramento, but after all that, he and Linda ended up coming back to L.A. where he was again a player, briefly a head coach, worked in the front office, and then spent seven seasons as an assistant coach under Phil. So I was able to convince Linda to come back to the organization as well.

It's ironic Kurt wound up going to Minnesota because it was Linda who was invaluable in making our tribute to the Minneapolis Lakers in 2002 so special.

I remember having been stopped on numerous occasions by Lakers fans asking me, "Will you please tell your dad that there should be a Minneapolis Lakers banner on the wall? We should acknowledge those five titles they won. Those are Lakers championships."

My dad made the decision that, once we moved to STAPLES Center, it would be time to unite the two parts of the franchise.

So when the move was made, he told me, "It's time now, and I want to do it right."

I got the message. Let's do something meaningful while making sure it doesn't backfire on us. It means a lot to our fans and we don't want the ceremony to come across as hollow or shallow.

We decided to not only pay tribute to the five Minneapolis NBA champions, but also to the six men from those teams—players George Mikan, Slater Martin, Jim Pollard, Vern Mikkelsen, and Clyde Lovellette, and coach John Kundla—who were later voted into the Hall of Fame. We would raise one banner for the championships and one for the jerseys of the Hall of Famers.

Acceptance into the Hall has been a requirement for a Laker to have his jersey retired. We made an exception when Magic retired so suddenly because we knew there was no question he would go into the Hall of Fame after the mandatory five-year waiting period was over.

Everyone involved—Linda, John Black, Tim Harris, and Lisa Estrada—did a great job in making that night for the Minneapolis Lakers memorable.

John always keeps the former players connected, and Linda coordinated the whole thing, making sure everyone involved was in the loop. No small task.

Mikan, the first of the Lakers' superstar centers, had lost a leg due to diabetes, making travel difficult, especially at age 77. But he wanted to be here, and he was.

He died three years later, but I was comforted by the fact he lived long enough to see his era honored in Los Angeles.

In planning the presentation, I thought about the key element that was missing when these Minneapolis players were originally honored for winning championships: the rings.

They have become such a meaningful part of any title in any sport. Players don't talk about winning a banner or winning a pennant. They talk about winning a ring. I know what the rings mean to our players, yet these Minneapolis champions missed out on that. They never had a memento of their own.

So, I decided to give them all rings. That would be only fitting.

And when it came to the fitting, who did I call on? Linda, of course.

She got all the ring sizes through the spouses or the children, but told them to keep it a secret so the players would be surprised.

And boy, were they ever.

All Lakers players, current and former, share a mutual camaraderie and respect. That was obvious to anyone who was present for the ceremony. It was all I could have hoped for.

December 11
LAKERS 104, TIMBERWOLVES 92

I knew, sooner or later, the gossip writers would try to create drama among the Lakers wives. It has turned out to be sooner. Here we are in December and they are already at it, obviously inspired by the arrival of a high-profile Lakers spouse, Khloe Kardashian.

A totally inaccurate Internet report, headlined "Khloe Joins the Laker Bitches," claims that Lamar's new wife feels disrespected by the other team wives and that she doesn't get along with Kobe's wife, Vanessa.

It's all nonsense. There are no issues between Khloe and Vanessa or any other Lakers wife. Khloe has fit in really well. Yes, if Khloe were to come in here and disrupt the chemistry, that would indeed be a story. There are those who want that story to happen so badly, they are trying to create it.

I've been around this team for a good part of my life and I have to admit, there have been instances where wives didn't get along, but that is not the case here. The chemistry on this team is genuine.

And the relationship between Lamar and Khloe seems sweet and solid. I told Phil that I've never seen Lamar like this. It's nice that he has become so open and vulnerable.

"I've seen Lamar like that before," Phil said, "but he doesn't show that side of himself very often. The way he has responded to her shows me that he really cares about her."

So even Phil got caught up in the romance. Not that it inspired him to bring up the subject of marriage.

On Lamar's birthday last month, Khloe and her mom, Kris Jenner, sat with me. Khloe couldn't be more charming or popular. Our fans were screaming her name and waving at her, and she accommodated them by posing for pictures and signing autographs.

Khloe is just learning about the game of basketball, kind of getting up to speed on how Lakers games work. It's a new world to her.

I don't want to overwhelm her with information. All she wants is to be a supportive wife. A lot of times, it's not about the basketball. It's about being at the games and supporting what your husband is trying to do.

I think Khloe's real challenge starts now as the Lakers depart on their first of several long road trips. That part can be hard on a new relationship, because you get into a nice rhythm with so many home games. Then they go away and you have to adjust. Then they come back and you have to adjust again.

I'm sure Lamar is going to miss her a lot when they hit the road for these long stretches over the next few months.

So many people email me to say they hope Lamar and Khloe stay together. I think they will, no matter what the gossipmongers say or write or how many paparazzi hound them.

WHEN THERE HAVE BEEN PROBLEMS among the wives in the past, it's often because two guys are competing for the same position or the same minutes. That can cause a lot of tension among the spouses.

But our wives on this current team are really good about talking things out, seeing a problem before it develops, and dealing with it. Derek Fisher is particularly adept at monitoring where the team is emotionally at any point.

I've tried to do my part. Over the years, when a new player comes to our team and he and his wife are looking for a place to live, a pediatrician, or where to send their kids to school, I have been called in to drive the welcome wagon. That's absolutely fine with me. I'm comfortable in a role like that.

Tonight, I again had the reins of the welcome wagon in my hand for our annual holiday party for Lakers wives and the wives of the NBA Development League's Los Angeles D-Fenders. It's nice to bring everyone together like this once a year.

We have more married guys on the team than we have had in previous seasons, but because we have a young team, there are still not a lot of wives.

Girlfriends are invited too, so it becomes a different kind of event, a chance to meet some of the newer members of our ever-expanding family.

AFTER TONIGHT'S VICTORY, everyone was talking about our 11-game winning streak, the longest active streak in the league. Something like this seems to take on a life of its own.

When I think of a Lakers winning streak, I think of 33 in a row, the all-time record set by the 1971–72 Lakers. I never cease to be amazed by that unequaled feat and what it must have been like to be a part of that team.

The record for most wins in a season is 72, set by the 1995–96 Chicago Bulls, coached by some guy named Phil Jackson.

Their longest winning streak was 18 games, and they had only one other double-digit streak that season, winning 13 in a row.

You would have thought with a 72-win season, there would have been some sort of crazy streak to rival the Lakers' mark. Instead, Phil's Bulls maintained a really balanced season.

December 16
LAKERS 107, BUCKS 106 (OT)

It's been a tough summer and fall because of the serious health problems of the third resident of the house I share with Phil: my seven-year-old, 10-pound female maltese.

I named her Princess, but Phil decided she needed to be a little bit tougher, so he calls her Cujo. That has given her a split personality, reflected in her extended name, Princess Cujo.

She is an alpha dog, which means she tries to dominate everyone around her. Everyone, that is, except Phil. She definitely dominates me, and I am devoted to her.

I refer to her in public as Princess rather than Cujo because I don't want people to be afraid of her. "Princess" implies an animal that is sweet and good-natured. Phil's kids, on the other hand, call her Cujo because she has tried to dominate them, too.

Princess Cujo got very sick this year with a blood disease. I went from the exhilaration of the Lakers' victory parade in June to the anxiety caused by watching my dog suddenly licking dirt. I had never seen that before. I couldn't understand it.

But I was so distracted by all the championship events and parties and having so many people in from out of town that I didn't take her to the vet right away.

By the time I did, the vet told me I had to take Cujo immediately to a critical care veterinarian hospital in Culver City where she would undergo an emergency blood transfusion. She had no color because her red blood cell count had dwindled to almost nothing.

The licking of dirt was a reaction to a lack of healthy red cells. It's a good thing for all dog owners to remember. If your animal starts eating dirt, it's not just a quirky habit. There is something serious going on.

I had trouble taking in what I was hearing from the vet.

"What are you telling me?" I asked. "That she could die?"

"You've got to get her there right now," he said. "How long will it take you?"

Not long after I heard that.

Cujo had contracted IMHA (immune mediated hemolytic anemia), a disease in which the body's immune system kills its own red blood cells.

My dog underwent five blood transfusions. I never knew transfusions were performed on dogs. For Cujo, the procedure bought her the necessary time to allow the medication she was administered to work.

She was in the hospital for 10 days the first time and had to go back three or four more times that summer.

It was a really tough experience for me because she is the center of my life outside of basketball and work. I didn't realize until Cujo got sick how much she connects me to the rest of the world, how much joy she brings to my life. I wouldn't know my neighbors if I didn't spend time outside walking my dog, and I wouldn't know all the other dog owners in the area. When Cujo was hospitalized, I stopped walking and lost my connection to my community.

Phil was at his summer home in Montana for much of the time, so I felt extremely alone, sad, and heartbroken.

At her worst, Cujo was like a helpless blob. The illness sucked her energy and made her bloated. It was really uncomfortable for her to breathe, so all she did was pant. It was hard to watch her go through that, especially agonizing for me because I was the one giving her the medication that was causing severe side effects.

Cujo made it through thanks to the blood transfusions, steroids, and the immune suppressant drugs also used by people who have undergone organ-transplant operations.

The IMHA went into remission, but the treatment damaged Cujo's pancreas, causing her to become diabetic. At least she is no longer in danger of dying.

I learned of the diabetes on yet another trip to the hospital, so care of Cujo basically consumed my entire off-season.

I am nursing her through her latest illness by hand-feeding her food I have prepared from scratch. I have never cooked for myself or other people, but now I own a cookbook for dogs.

Cujo's health issues have forced me to change my routine. I normally spend time in the summer with Phil in Montana, but I could only manage a two-day visit this year.

I have also had to juggle things around at home in order to be there for Cujo. She requires insulin injections twice daily on a set schedule. The only other person I feel comfortable asking to help out is Linda Rambis. But now, all of a sudden, her life is changed because she is going back and forth to Minnesota to be with Kurt.

I'm certainly not complaining. Cujo is alive and has quality to her life again, and I am grateful for that.

December 21

I wasn't pleased with Phil's comments to the media Saturday in New Jersey, and I told him so when he returned late Sunday after the Detroit game.

Asked if his return next season is tied to how the Lakers finish this season, Phil said, "You have people cutting costs all around the league. That's a big part of it. I think coaches' salaries are going to take a cut too along the way. So then, they may not even want to hire me. They want to save some money."

Someone asked him if he would take a pay cut.

Phil told the reporter, "Why, would you?"

I know he was trying to be humorous, but I told him, "I don't think, in this economy, your comments are funny. Given what's happening with newspapers, a lot of the media guys you were talking to have had to take pay cuts or give up their jobs or switch to lesser-paying jobs or just freelance. A majority of Americans have struggled or taken pay cuts. It was an insensitive remark and makes you sound like you are not grateful for all that you have. You make a lot of money. You do a great job, but still, it's a lot of money. My dad has taken real good care of you. You are the highest-paid coach in the league."

Phil said, "Well, I didn't mean it like that. I meant it to be funny."

He doesn't have to listen to my advice. Phil is a grown man who does what he wants to do, but I was pretty passionate about this. I thought he sounded like he lives in a bubble, like he doesn't know what's going on in the world. He was kind of taken aback by my concerns over what he said, but he wouldn't say he was sorry. He doesn't regret things like that.

I have no idea if he is going to be the Lakers' coach next season. Anything can happen, but I like to think that if we win a championship this season, everybody will be anxious to go for the three-peat with Phil in command.

Right now, I'm just glad he's back home after a trip that became quite difficult at the end because of miserable weather conditions.

The Lakers played in East Rutherford Saturday night and were scheduled to be in Auburn Hills for a game against Detroit Sunday evening. But a huge snowstorm caused the cancellation of some flights out of New Jersey Saturday night.

Phil was really worried that they weren't going to make it out of there. That scared me.

We were texting back and forth while I was at a Christmas party.

I tweeted, "At a crazy holiday party. Don't tell Phil."

I was just kidding. There was actually nothing crazy about it, just a lot of neat stuff like imported snow and a man authentically dressed as Santa Claus. My Twitter family responded with laughs.

The Lakers made it to the airport and Phil said they were going to try to take off. When I didn't hear from him again, I figured they must have gotten airborne.

When they landed in Michigan, he texted to say it was a very turbulent flight. I don't like to think about things like that, about what could happen with an entire team on a plane.

I think the Lakers are all experienced enough to know that some days, you get a bumpy flight. Overall, they trust the pilots and have confidence they always put safety first.

I don't think Phil was ever worried they weren't going to make it once they got off the ground.

They didn't get to bed in Michigan until 5:00 AM. Phil canceled the Sunday shootaround and instead had a video meeting at 1:00 PM to get the players up and their blood circulating.

They played well enough to win, but it wasn't their best game.

In the midst of my concern over flying conditions, I eerily got an email from Carroll, Iowa, where the Minneapolis Lakers' plane went down in a cornfield in bad weather conditions. Miraculously, no one was hurt.

Next month will mark the 50th anniversary of that harrowing moment and the town is holding a commemorative celebration of that safe landing. The people there will never forget it.

Nor will the Lakers on that plane, a group that included Elgin Baylor, Hot Rod Hundley, and Tommy Hawkins.

December 25

CAVALIERS 102, LAKERS 87

Today's Christmas Day loss was awful. But to me, what was really shocking was the sight of our fans throwing foam fingers on the court. Then somebody escalated the barrage by throwing a water bottle.

I knew from my experience in crowd management that it takes just one moment for things to go from fun to frightening. I'd seen it happen at other events, but never with a Lakers crowd.

There should be no tolerance for fan behavior that could result in injury to others in the crowd or to the athletes or performers. But that's what happens when a game is highly anticipated and overly hyped and it doesn't live up to expectations for the home team. Fans get annoyed and frustrated.

Phil was certainly frustrated. He acted in a way that almost incited the fans.

As a rule, when we are giving away an item, especially a heavier one, we do it at the end of the game when the fans are on their way out. We definitely do that with the bobbleheads, for example.

My mom and dad in quintessential 1950s style: check out my mom's full skirt and my dad's higher-rise slacks. I especially love my mom's red pumps. A gorgeous couple!

Holding hands with my best friend—my mom—in Rustic Canyon Park as an eight year old. My mom looks so chic in her white suit and red turtleneck and I'm in my favorite look: pigtails.

I am just 20 years old here on the lawn at Pickfair. I loved that Kansas City Royals T-shirt because I was a fan of George Brett and all the Brett brothers.

This was taken on the night I passed my crown as Miss Pacific Palisades of 1979. My dad was a judge. I still have my sash and crown, just in case.

Preparing for one of the many events at Pickfair. The double round windows on the second floor to my left were located in my bathroom in my wing of the house.

The handsome and talented Andre Agassi is one of the kindest souls I've ever known. He suggested an insightful book to me while I was going through my divorce. He was also a huge draw anytime he played at the Forum.

I celebrated my 20th birthday with Michael Jackson after The Jacksons' fourth sold-out show of their Triumph Tour at the Forum. Michael was engaging and sweet. "Can You Feel It" was my favorite track on their Triumph album. His music was a gift to the world.

The staff of Forum Tennis. The man behind me is Lon Rosen, my friend and agent. Linda Rambis is to his left. We worked hard but we were having fun. They are all great people.

This is the 1983 L.A. Strings team photo. From left are trainer Scott Morrison, Lon Rosen, Linda Rambis, coach Lornie Kuhle, Barbara Hallquist, Larry Stefanki, Anne White, Chip Hooper, Mary Ann Landsberger, Blain Skinner, and me. Unfortunately, we didn't make the playoffs that year.

My desk at the Forum circa 1996. Funny, my desk still looks the same way: messy!

The luxury of working in a family business is that we get to share time together even while we are on the job. Standing are Johnny, Joey, Jimmy, and Janie; sitting are Jesse, my dad, and me.

Princess Cujo wasn't ready for her close-up here. She was groomed a little too close around her nose so she has a Charlie Chaplin–type mustache. But her hairdo is fabulous!

Sitting on the floor in San Antonio with my dad for Game 2 of the 2001 Western Conference Finals. The Lakers won even though Phil was ejected during the third quarter. It still stresses me out just looking at the photo. I avoid attending road playoff games now.

My dad was honored with a star on the Hollywood Walk of Fame in 2006. They said it was one of the best unveilings in their history. He is a true Los Angeles icon.

But when it comes to things like a towel, a cheer card, or a foam finger, we figure, okay, those are things that can't hurt anybody.

We are going to have to talk about what we can do to prevent this from happening again. I don't know what the answer is right now. I don't want to stop the foam finger giveaway. I don't want to assume it will happen again in the future.

Some season-ticket holders go out of town for the holidays and give away their tickets. The people who were throwing the items must have been sitting close to the floor because foam fingers don't fly very far, so I have to assume they were the recipients of the generosity of our season-seat clientele. For a lot of people, that might have been their first game.

BEFORE THE LOSS AND THE FINGER TOSS, the Lakers enjoyed a joyous ritual, courtesy of the Secret Santa.

This is another of Phil's methods of reinforcing a family atmosphere among his players. Yesterday, everybody on the team exchanged names and was required to buy a gift for the person he drew. They open the presents together in the locker room before the game.

I don't know who Phil got, but I hope he remembered to bring his gift.

Phil and his kids have a tradition of going to church on Christmas Eve around 4:00 PM. All the kids came except Elizabeth, who lives in Washington, D.C., and had her second child a few months ago.

I didn't join them because I'm not a churchgoer, so it wouldn't feel right to me. I took the quiet time to reflect on the Christmas Eves of my past.

We all hung out at the home of Phil's daughter Brooke last night, and then everybody came over to our place this morning and Phil made pancakes for the grandkids.

I saw my dad today at the game, but my mom was, as usual, with my sister in Temecula. I've gone there a couple of Christmases, but the two-hour round trip is really, really tough on me, especially when we also have a game at STAPLES Center, so I decided not to go out there this year.

We arranged for the Lexus Club in STAPLES Center to be open after the game so the Jackson and Buss families, along with our close friends the Hernandezes, could have Christmas dinner up there. I had to go home to take care of my dog.

With the game starting at 2:00 PM, it's difficult to go out with the grandkids, and you can't cook dinner because you've been gone all day.

Phil wasn't real happy when he finally came home. He figured he was going to get fined for some of the things he said about the officiating.

THIS TIME OF YEAR, I usually hear from several former players. I get Christmas cards from Karl Malone and Mark Madsen, among others.

Phil still gets a Christmas card from Shaq.

I TEXTED MY MOM LAST NIGHT to tell her that having seen so many Christmas trees and decorations this year really made me appreciate what she used to do when I was growing up. She had all these figurines around the house and really created some winter wonderlands. And the tree was always exceptional. It took a lot of work on her part.

Back at our house in Pacific Palisades, we opened our presents at night, but then we got one additional thing in the morning. So that always gave us something to look forward to when we woke up.

One of my all-time favorite presents was a puppy, a collie named Laddie. I was probably 10 that year.

I loved the food my mom would make for Christmas, crazy stuff like Swedish meatballs, potato pancakes, deviled eggs, and all kinds of other things. We were not the type of family to sit down and have a formal prime rib dinner.

After my parents divorced, the whole family didn't get together anymore for Christmas until the NBA created our new family get-together every December 25.

NOT EVERY CHRISTMAS has been a joyful occasion for me.

A couple of years ago, we played in Miami on Christmas Day and I got sick with food poisoning. Phil and the team had to leave the next morning and I was stuck in my hotel room, thinking I was literally going to die. I don't know how I got to the airport because I was so sick.

Phil is like a gigantic sore thumb, standing out wherever we go. When they recognize him, people send us meals, appetizers, dessert, and drinks on the road and even here in L.A.

It's really hard to turn stuff down. It almost feels like an insult to do so.

That particular night, we were eating out and someone sent us over some shellfish.

Phil can't eat shellfish because he has gout. I didn't want to be rude, so I ate mine and his, and I'm sure that's how I got sick.

That's one Christmas I won't forget.

December 28

SUNS 118, LAKERS 103

As it turns out, the humiliating loss to Cleveland and the embarrassing sight of Lakers fans throwing foam fingers on the court on Christmas Day was only the beginning of our troubles.

Ron Artest went home that night and wound up in the ER at UCLA Medical Center after he fell down a flight of stairs at his house, resulting in a concussion, a cut requiring stitches on the back of his head, and an injured elbow.

Ron said he was attempting to carry boxes down a flight of stairs, and there is no reason not to believe him. There was nothing to indicate he was intoxicated. Law enforcement wasn't involved.

But the idea that a healthy athlete in peak condition could be clumsy enough to fall down stairs is a worrisome thought no matter what the circumstances involved. This is a guy who should have balance and an acute awareness of his body.

Ron is an athletic guy who has probably had his bell rung before. But having belatedly learned he was actually knocked unconscious, I don't think it was wise to wait until he was awake to call the paramedics.

Unfortunately, we've seen what can happen if you don't take something like that seriously. Earlier this year, a famous actress, Natasha Richardson, died after hitting her head while skiing. Everything seemed fine at first, and then tragedy struck, so you've got to be really careful when dealing with a concussion.

Now that I know Ron lost consciousness, I can see why he can't remember exactly what happened.

Phil plans on talking to Ron about what he does remember, but they have not had that conversation yet because the Lakers have been on the road and Ron can't fly because of the concussion. I imagine, at some point, Phil wants to look Ron in the eye and get a full explanation.

It's important for Phil to connect with his players every day. When a player is apart from the team, as is the case here, it changes team chemistry.

If, indeed, there is more to this story, it will eventually come out because of the scrutiny everybody in this organization is always under.

I hope it doesn't turn out like the snowboarding incident involving Vladimir Radmanovic nearly three years ago. That was during the All-Star break and we were at the wedding of Phil's oldest daughter, Elizabeth, in Washington, D.C. Phil got a call, and after he hung up, he told us Radmanovic had slipped on some ice and separated his shoulder.

The first thing Phil's son Ben said was, "Oh, that's a snowboarding accident." Ben should know because he's a snowboarder.

Phil always tells his players, "No matter what you are doing, you've got to be careful."

I think Phil wants to make very clear to Ron that his obligation is to this team. Ron has made a commitment, he is getting paid very well to honor that commitment, but because he wasn't being careful and fell—even though it was an accident that could happen to anyone—he is now gone and that hurts the team. We miss him.

Players have to be focused. Everyone on this team is counting on everyone else. Players have to be able to believe in each other.

The fact that Ron has missed games is unacceptable no matter what the reason, unless it's because of something that happened on the basketball court.

Luke Walton's back injury becomes an even bigger issue now with Ron out. What was a short bench is now even shorter.

It was especially critical because we played a back-to-back against Cleveland and then Sacramento on the road the next night.

Phil didn't want to make the players fly on Christmas night after the Cleveland game, so he let them go home and fly to Sacramento Saturday morning. That makes for a very long day. Usually, you don't fly the same day you play.

On top of that, the Sacramento game ended up going into double overtime before the Lakers won. Then they had to get on the plane immediately afterward and fly to Phoenix where they played tonight.

Talk about unforeseen consequences: if Phil hadn't been thoughtful toward the players by letting them go home Christmas night, Ron wouldn't have gotten hurt.

Trying to make up for the loss of depth, Kobe, as hurt as he is, played an amazing game against Sacramento, staying on the court for 50 minutes. That's too much. The guy already has a broken finger. And then he hit his funny bone and his arm went numb. But he just keeps coming back. His determination is extraordinary.

PHIL DOESN'T PANIC, but he's not satisfied with the way the team is playing, especially after tonight's loss in Phoenix. I can tell by the look on his face on the telecast. He's mad at the players. He expects them to play better, injuries or no injuries.

When Phil is like that, I've had to say to him, "Don't get mad at me. I'm not one of your players."

I'll ask him a question and I can't get an answer. Hello, I'm over here. I didn't do anything wrong. The loss isn't my fault. But that's just how he gets during an NBA season.

Ron is not going to play again tomorrow against the Warriors, and it's going to make things tough because Golden State is young and they will run and run and run. And we don't have a lot of healthy legs.

7

EXPANDING MY UNIVERSE

NEARLY A CENTURY AGO, THEY WERE HOLLYWOOD'S REIGNING glamour couple, the Brad Pitt and Angelina Jolie of their era.

So when Douglas Fairbanks and Mary Pickford went house hunting in 1919, it was assumed they would select a grand mansion.

Instead, they purchased 15 acres in Beverly Hills, containing nothing more than a small hunting shack, for an estimated $35,000.

What the couple wanted was the land, and what they designed was indeed a grand mansion, which the press dubbed Pickfair, a combination of their last names. It had 22 rooms, gorgeous gardens, and a crescent-shaped, outdoor swimming pool with a sand beach. The pool, large enough and deep enough to accommodate a canoe, is thought to be the first private swimming pool in L.A.

The star power of Fairbanks and Pickford drew many of the big names of their time to their lavish parties, people like Babe Ruth, Charles Lindbergh, Charlie Chaplin, Joan Crawford, Albert Einstein, and Helen Keller.

But the music eventually died for the happy couple. Their relationship deteriorated to the point that they wound up living apart in separate wings of their sprawling estate.

After they divorced, Mary lived there with her second husband, Charles "Buddy" Rogers.

In her later years, Mary became a recluse, refusing to see anyone who visited the mansion. She would, instead, talk to them by phone from her bedroom.

She died in 1979, but Pickfair soon came alive again when my father bought it in 1980.

I first learned of his plans when he invited me to lunch at the Polo Lounge in the Beverly Hills Hotel. That meal, my dad said, would be followed by a drive out to see a house that was on the market. He said it was some old movie stars' home known as Pickfair.

I screamed. I couldn't believe it. I was going to see where Mary Pickford and Douglas Fairbanks had lived!

My father said we probably wouldn't buy Pickfair, but it might be fun to look at.

I brought my camera and made my dad take a photo of me in every room because I figured this would be my one and only chance to walk through this celebrated mansion.

The 3.2-acre grounds were as gorgeous as I had imagined them, but the inside of Pickfair was a far different story. It had been badly neglected. It just broke my heart to see the floors painted black.

The asking price for this sad relic? $10 million.

My father, who knows a thing or two about real estate, assessed what he thought the property was worth and wrote out an offer for that amount: $5.4 million.

After Mary Pickford passed away, Pickfair had been put in probate, so the bid had to be approved by a judge. He accepted the offer with the comment that he had never seen anyone pay that much for a fixer-upper.

The next thing I knew, we were moving into that historic home. I have to laugh when I think about that first day. I couldn't find the garage on the vast estate, so I wound up parking my car on the street.

Moving into that mansion dramatically changed the perception of my family. My father, who had been a familiar figure on the sports pages after buying the Lakers, the Kings, and the Forum, was suddenly a familiar figure on the society pages as well.

With a new owner, the media came up with a new name for the mansion: Buss-fare.

Living at Pickfair seemed to transform us all into Hollywood royalty.

It was a designation we took seriously. We decided to restore the house to its original glory, but it was no small task. It took two years.

As I worked at it, I became an authority on Pickfair.

The requests for media interviews about the mansion never seemed to stop.

Nor did requests by charities to hold events on the grounds. Every nonprofit event held there would easily raise $50,000 to $100,000 because people were so anxious to get on the grounds. But if we said yes to one charity, then another one would ask for an equal opportunity, and how could we say no?

Usually, we didn't.

With my newly acquired knowledge of the place, I even gave private tours of Pickfair in return for nice donations.

It was a star-studded existence. Sammy Davis Jr. lived next door (although "next door" in that neighborhood could mean quite a hike), Prince Albert of Monaco came by for a tour, and the day after the 1984 Los Angeles Olympics ended, we hosted the U.S. team.

We also hosted many foreign dignitaries because Pickfair was known around the world. Many referred to it as "The White House of the West." Everyone, it seemed, wanted to see it.

When the NBA All-Star Game was in Los Angeles in 1983, we hosted an event at Pickfair that is still held annually in other locations: a Saturday brunch for the wives of the coaches and players.

Celebrity sightings happened day and night. Once, I was pulling an all-nighter in the middle of finals. At about 4:00 AM, I heard the sound of the piano downstairs coming up through the floor of my room. I had to get up in two hours to take an exam.

I went running downstairs to find out just who in the world would be playing the piano at that hour.

It turned out to be Rick James, the famous funk singer and songwriter. Embarrassed at bursting in like that, I mumbled an apology and excused myself.

I remember Dionne Warwick singing in our yard for an event. Her voice sounded heavenly echoing in the hills of surrounding Benedict Canyon.

We also had a tennis court, so sometimes members of the L.A. Strings or other professionals would practice on our grounds. You would walk outside and find John McEnroe or Jimmy Connors hitting balls around. Just your average backyard players at Pickfair.

Linda and Kurt Rambis had their wedding reception there.

When you opened your door, you never knew who was going to be there. That was the charm of Pickfair, but it was also the burden.

It was like living in STAPLES Center or the Forum. It seemed there was always an event going on.

After a while, the loss of privacy began to wear on me. When I came down for breakfast, I couldn't be sure who was going to be in the kitchen or what deliveries were being unloaded or who was going to be blocking the driveway when I needed to get out. It seemed like people were always either breaking down equipment from an event the night before or setting up for the night ahead.

We were living in a home that seemed more like a public museum than a private residence.

I DIDN'T SPEND ALL MY TIME AT PICKFAIR. Not after I met my new boyfriend.

I would have never met him if I hadn't given in and attended my first hockey game.

When my dad first bought the Kings, I wouldn't go see them because I was afraid I might get hit by a puck.

A few years earlier, I had seen the movie *Slap Shot* and that became my impression of hockey. People go to games and get hit by pucks. It's all fights and crazy people.

So I wouldn't go to a game. Wouldn't, wouldn't, wouldn't.

My dad owned the team for six months and I still hadn't gone.

Finally, he told me, "If you go to one game, I promise you will enjoy it, and after the game, I will introduce you to all the single guys on the team."

For an 18-year-old girl, that was an offer too tempting to pass up.

It was an exciting game. The Kings not only beat the Boston Bruins but shut them out. I immediately fell in love with the sport.

Afterward, I was hanging out in the press lounge when five of the Kings showed up. One of them asked me what I did. I told him I was a student at USC. He said, "Is that United States College?"

No kidding. He didn't know what USC was. I was hooked right then. My world was so small and I thought it was the center of the universe. And here's this Canadian kid, 20 years old, and he's never even heard of USC.

His name was Jay Wells.

We started dating and I found I had a lot to learn.

One night, we were going to see The Eagles at the Forum. After just coming back from a road trip, Jay arrived at Pickfair to pick me up.

When I answered the door, I was shocked. He was completely bald.

"What happened to you?" I asked.

He simply said, "It was my turn."

The first thing I thought was, *Omigosh, is he a Hare Krishna?*

Jay explained to me that he had undergone his rookie initiation on that trip, which included shaving his head.

It was such a different world than the one I had inhabited my entire life.

It was uncharted territory for Jay as well. He had to deal with his teammates who were giving him a rough time about dating the owner's daughter, and I worried about that. But Jay didn't mind. He was a tough guy. He could stand up to anybody. He would hear things like, "Do you own the team? Are you the G.M.?" It was just good-natured ribbing.

Jay grew up on a farm in Northern Ontario about an hour and a half from Toronto. My dad couldn't understand what I could see in somebody whose background was so different from mine, so different from any other guy I had ever known.

But I found Jay refreshing. I was used to dating guys who couldn't wait to ask me if I could get them Lakers seats or concert tickets.

Not Jay. He came from such a good place.

I, on the other hand, found myself in a very uncomfortable place when I was invited to a baby shower for another player's wife. Since I was dating a member of the Kings, I was now part of the wives and girlfriends circle. I was not included because I was the owner's daughter. This was a new role for me.

The shower was being given at the home of Dave Taylor, then a player, and his wife Beth, and co-hosted by Charlotte Grahame, wife of goalie Ron Grahame.

I arrived, present in hand, and rang the doorbell. When it opened, I could see three girls crying.

"Is everything okay?" I asked.

Charlotte looked at me and said, "Your dad just traded my husband."

I dropped the present and ran, crying because I didn't know how to handle that look of anguish on Charlotte's face. It was the most awful situation to be in. I was the last person all of those women wanted to be around.

Nobody came after me. Understandably, they were more concerned with the feelings of their distraught friend than they were about how I felt.

My relationship with Jay lasted about four years, but my relationship with hockey has continued.

My dad had so much success with the Lakers, and he really wanted the Kings to emulate them. He was so frustrated when that didn't happen. My dad, the former chemist, couldn't figure out the formula for that sport.

Nor has anyone else as far as the Kings are concerned. All these years and owners later, they still haven't been able to hoist the Stanley Cup.

In the second year my dad owned the team, he told the players, "If you get at least 99 points, I will take all of you to Hawaii."

Ninety-nine points would make the Kings one of the top seeds in the playoffs. They got exactly 99 points and were matched up against the tough New York Rangers in the first round. Unfortunately, the Rangers beat the heck out of us, outscoring us 16–6 in the final two games to win the best-of-five series 3–1.

Nevertheless, my dad lived up to his word and took the entire team to Hawaii.

Jay and I got to go, too. I'll never forget how much it meant to some of those Canadian guys because they had never been to Hawaii.

EVEN AS A YOUNG GIRL, I knew I wanted to work in the family business. At that time, the business was real estate, so my goal was to be a developer.

Every summer, there was a company picnic. My parents, grandmother, and uncles were all there. I loved being a part of that. It was family, but it was also our business. It never crossed my mind to do anything else.

When the focus of our business changed to sports, I didn't change my thinking. If we had owned a dairy farm, it would not have been any different. My overriding passion was to work with my dad and everybody else in the family. That seemed like a rewarding career.

So when I entered USC, I majored in business administration, focusing on management.

In the early 1980s, I took a marketing class in which we were asked to design a campaign for an instant pudding product within the limits of an imaginary budget set by the professor.

My idea was to sign Magic Johnson as the endorser and call it "Magic Instant Pudding." The logo would be his smile and, where the teeth were, it would spell out "MAGIC."

I got an A on that project. Of course, I was lucky enough to have access to Magic, and he agreed not to name a price that would break my imaginary budget.

I bought some chocolate pudding and got Wen Roberts, then the Lakers photographer, to take a picture of Magic in his uniform taking a bite and flashing that famous smile.

"I can make pudding so fast," he said in the ad I designed, "that I can do it while I'm still in my uniform."

That class was valuable for me because even as I was learning, I was also getting on-the-job training in my dad's organization, having become the general manager of the L.A. Strings of World Team Tennis after completing my first year of college. I could apply my classroom experience to my professional career.

This was before the whole Nike phenomenon, the Gatorade phenomenon. It was at a time when sports marketing was just coming into its own. Before that, if you were an athlete and you got a deal for some free shoes, you were doing well.

Those were busy years for me, filled with responsibilities. I was not Paris Hilton or some debutante. I was a student working full-time while living at Pickfair.

It took me five years to graduate. I wasn't taking a full load because of my position with the Strings. I graduated in the spring of 1985 with a degree in business administration.

I used to have a recurring nightmare that I never graduated. In the dream, I'm told I don't have a degree. The idea of having to go back to school to get it, to be forced to get back into the routine I had as a student, frightened me.

Of course it doesn't make any sense. I have a diploma that I can look at whenever I feel the need.

I didn't make a lot of good friends in college, so I didn't feel it was necessary to walk in the graduation ceremony. Maybe that would have prevented the nightmare.

Not only did I graduate, but I have gone back to USC several times to be a guest speaker, so I feel connected to my alma mater.

Maybe the next time I'm there, I should reassure myself by checking to make sure I am listed as a graduate.

ONCE I LEFT USC, I was anxious to establish myself as an independent adult. That meant it was time to leave Pickfair and move on.

My father decided that without me around to share the experience, Pickfair no longer had the same allure. It was time for him to move on as well. So he put the house back on the market.

It was sold to singer/actress Pia Zadora and her husband, Meshulam Riklis, who decided to tear the house down and build a new mansion on the site.

Although preservationists howled in protest, the new owners said they were forced to act because of an infestation of termites.

I'm just glad I had my years at Pickfair. It was an experience I will always treasure.

JANUARY

January 1

We enjoyed a quiet New Year's Eve at home last night. With all that is going on in our lives, it was a nice respite.

Phil made pasta, we drank some champagne, and we listened to some of our favorite music.

We live right near Marina del Rey where they stage a fireworks show at midnight. So we had front-row seats.

It's been such a whirlwind with Phil's family in town for the holidays, but now they are gone, so it was just the two of us. Since it hasn't been that way for a while, we needed the time to talk, get caught up, and just chill out.

It turned out to be one of my favorite New Year's Eves because we could focus on each other.

Growing up in the Buss family, it seemed like New Year's was always about USC playing football at the Rose Bowl.

Another tradition is to get up and watch the Rose Parade, one of my favorite things to do.

I actually got to ride in the Rose Parade in 1985. I was asked to be on the Bakers Union float, but not because of my role with the Lakers. I was there to serve as an ambassador for the city of Los Angeles.

Because I had to be at the Rose Parade at 6:00 AM, my boyfriend at the time and I stayed up all night.

I was young enough to do that in those days, but I don't think I'd last now.

I rode with Jackson Bostwick, the television actor who starred in *Shazam!* as Captain Marvel. He was a nice guy and we had a lot of fun, but there was one problem. Because the cameras were all on one side, to our right, Jackson wouldn't allow me to wave with my left hand. I could only wave with my right so I wouldn't block him from the cameras.

We were perched so high up, we had to be lifted there by a cherry picker. So there I was, up there for four hours with a guy who kept telling me to get my hand out of his face.

A CARROT CAKE WAS DELIVERED to my office for the holidays from Brad Turner of the *Los Angeles Times*.

It was delicious and much appreciated because we had a house full of guests. Phil himself has eaten a piece or two over the last few days.

I told him, "See, this proves that not all members of the media are bad."

It also proves the way to gain favor with Phil is through his sweet tooth.

The cake came from the 24 Carrot Cake Company. I decided I would tweet about the store because I was grateful for the gift and because I knew—with a lot of the media people following me on Twitter—that B.T. would get harassed about it. The other media people would torture him with comments like, "Oh, you kiss ass."

That was the fun part.

PHIL HAD PRACTICE on New Year's Eve, but no shootaround today. He let the players have some time to celebrate New Year's Day. So it will be interesting to see how they come out tonight against Sacramento.

PHIL LOVES TO GO TO BOOKSTORES. We found one that was open today near our house and strolled around for about half an hour.

We spotted Tyreke Evans, a Sacramento point guard, in the store as well. I was so impressed. Here's a guy who was spending his time in a bookstore on New Year's Day, a game day.

He's a 20-year-old who is playing well enough to be a bona fide candidate for Rookie of the Year. Tyreke has really energized that Sacramento team.

I don't think he saw us, but Phil saw him.

I EVEN FOUND THE TIME TODAY to make my New Year's resolutions, as follows:

1. There is a bill in a committee of the U.S. House of Representatives called the Happy (Humans and Pets Partnered Through the Years) Act (HR 3501). It would grant a tax deduction of up to $3,500 per year for pet care expenses.

   That bill is one of the things I want to work on this year. I have tweeted about it and have received positive feedback from many people.

   When my dog was sick, it cost me more than $25,000 in vet bills to save her life. For people who do not have the good fortune to be in my financial position, a $3,500 deduction could be the difference between life and death for their beloved pet.

   Even with a healthy animal, expenses for health care can add up to thousands of dollars.

   I wonder how many more people would adopt pets if, as part of the deal, they got a financial break. It could reduce the amount of money local governments spend on animal control, so the revenue lost from the tax deduction would be made up in savings at the shelters.

   That's why they call it the Happy Act.

2. I want to go to a stand-up comedy camp. They actually have places where you can go and train to be a stand-up comedian.

   Don't get me wrong. That's not what I want to do for a living. I couldn't stand up and tell jokes. Believe me, I'm not that funny.

   But because I get asked to speak to groups so often, I want to learn to be more like a Bill Cosby, who can tell stories in an entertaining manner. I would talk about my story, what I do in the Lakers organization, and what I've done over the years in our family business, but do it with a sense of humor. Learn how to inject a punch line.

3. I want to spend more time with my 77-year-old mom.

   Because she lives in Las Vegas, I don't see her enough. I only get out there probably once or twice a year.

   She is here in Los Angeles now a lot more because this is where all her doctors are. She had colon cancer more than five years ago and had to go through chemo and radiation treatment. Fortunately, she is doing very well now and traveling more than ever.

I take her to her appointments with her doctors. It is important to me to be active in her medical care and find out what the best treatments are, the best place to go, the best doctors, the best options.

It's my way of thanking her for all she did for me and my siblings.

January 2

Phil got such a kick out of Kobe's game-winning buzzer beater against Sacramento last night, the third time this season Kobe has beaten the clock to beat the opposition.

But that still doesn't make up for Phil's disappointment over much of what he saw in the previous 47 minutes, 59 seconds. "Winning hides a lot of flaws," he said, referring to a defense that wasn't what he wanted it to be.

Phil always says that when you walk away with a victory, you tend to gloss over any problems you might have.

Phil has a lot of respect for Kobe's talent. I've asked him many times if Kobe is better than Michael Jordan was, but Phil never gives me a definitive answer.

He says they are very different players with different tools. One of the biggest differences is the size of Michael's hands. They are much larger than Kobe's.

They are similar, says Phil, in one key respect: their will to win.

Phil marvels at Kobe's will. The only person, other than Michael, who can match it is Phil himself. That's why they are such a good match. Phil understands that part of himself, the strong, willful, focused person.

It is important, Phil says, not to lose sight of the people around you when you are so fixated on a goal.

I think Kobe is good at keeping a balance between the two, striving to win but making sure his teammates feel a part of it. Michael was probably the same way.

One of the most remarkable things about Kobe is his ability to play through serious injuries like the one that is currently plaguing him, the avulsion fracture on the index finger of his shooting hand.

Most people would take six weeks to let an injury like that heal, and this guy is playing some of the best basketball of his life despite the apparent limitations imposed by the fracture. It's crazy.

Trainer Gary Vitti is putting Kobe through a painful but necessary procedure before each game to allow him to maintain control, flexibility, and the fingertip touch required to play the game. Gary winds several shoelaces tightly around the broken finger at key points to push the swelling down to the base of the finger.

Phil said that Kobe screams like nothing he has ever heard before while Gary works on him, a blood-curdling scream because of the amount of unavoidable pain Gary is causing by getting the finger functional for the game.

KOBE OBVIOUSLY TRUSTS GARY and our medical personnel, but if he didn't, we would respect his feelings.

It's important for players to feel they can seek whatever medical advice they want. We don't dictate to them what surgeries to have or not have, or when to have them. I think it would be unfair to a player for us to try to make decisions that could affect his career.

We would never say, "You must see our doctors. You are not allowed to get a second opinion."

It seems more and more players are going for second opinions, and I would never discourage that. The relationship between a doctor and a player should be a private one. If a player isn't comfortable, he deserves the right to go elsewhere.

Not to mention the fact that liability issues can come into play.

For example, some former professional football players have accused their league of improperly withholding medical information. According to the claims, doctors have run medical tests and gone to management with the results before they let the player know what's going on. I think that's a line you can't cross.

There is a right to privacy, and for those physicians who are team employees, I can see where questions of divided loyalty might arise.

Obviously, in our opinion, we have the finest doctors because these are the people we trust. And it's not just our opinion. Other teams send their players to our doctors because they are well-respected professionals.

In these economic times, some teams, in search of additional revenue, accept money from physicians in exchange for designating them as their official specialist in a given field. For an endorsement fee, a doctor can say he is the official orthopedist, dentist, eye surgeon, or whatever of this team or that, and use the team logo in his ads to generate business.

I am not comfortable with that practice. Money rather than expertise becomes the determining factor. Is this the best doctor the team can find in this particular field, or merely the one willing to pay the most money? Does any guy on the team even go to this doctor?

At the very least, full disclosure is a must. Tell the player this is the official team doctor, but this is how or why he or she was selected.

January 5
LAKERS 88, ROCKETS 79

A member of the media approached me yesterday and asked if I knew that for our game last week against Golden State, Byron Scott was a guest in my dad's suite. That was news to me.

I asked John Black, our public relations vice president, about it, and he told me they wanted to keep it under the radar. How do you keep Byron Scott being in my dad's suite under the radar? I know Byron didn't come downstairs to see everyone, which was unusual.

Usually when we have a former Laker in attendance, we put him on the video board and he does TV interviews. This whole thing doesn't make sense to me.

I was told Byron wanted to keep it low-key. Why? I don't know if I'm getting the honest answers.

Byron, an NBA coach for the last decade, is a free agent even though he is still getting paid by the Hornets, who fired him in November. He's free to talk to any team, so I would imagine he would be in the mix if Phil, who doesn't have a contract for next season, doesn't come back.

As of now, there are no discussions between Phil and the Lakers about a new contract.

Is there something going on that I don't know about? After all, *someone* invited Byron to sit there.

I've been asked about it a couple of times from people who found out Byron was here, and I don't know how to respond.

It's not just Byron. There are a lot of coaches who would love to have Phil's job, and that makes me a little apprehensive.

It's an awkward position for me to be in. If a discussion takes place on who our coach should be for next season, I don't know how much of a role I would have in that process. I hope I would be involved, at least from the business point of view. I would like to add my opinion on a coaching decision. I want the chance to offer feedback that I get from our season-ticket holders and from our broadcast partners, the people I deal with, people the basketball folks don't necessarily hear from. I think it is important to consider all viewpoints when making a decision like this.

But I know I may be too close to the situation to be involved because of my relationship with Phil. I am the poster child for not mixing business and pleasure.

I'm sure any discussions about a new coach would be between my dad, Mitch Kupchak, and my brother Jimmy. I am equally comfortable talking to my dad or my brother about our options.

As for Phil, he doesn't care.

Honestly.

For him, it's all about *this* season, about getting *this* team to where he wants it to be. He doesn't even want to think about next season. It doesn't exist in Phil's mind.

He's not happy with the team right now. Ron Artest was out because of a concussion. Now, Pau is out with another hamstring injury. There hasn't been a time this season when the team has completely satisfied Phil in terms of playing up to its potential.

Still, based on that potential, Phil thinks this Lakers team could win three or four titles in a row, but if it doesn't win this season, he would understand why the hierarchy wouldn't want him back.

I'm a big fan of Byron's, but I can't see bringing him in for next season because that would mean a radical shift to a whole new offense since he doesn't run the triangle. Byron likes to use the Princeton offense.

I have a meeting with my dad in three days. Will I ask him about Byron? I don't know.

What I do know is that at some point, Phil and the Lakers are going to separate. I want to keep everything the same. That's my nature. But the reality is there has to be a plan for the change that will inevitably take place.

What if my dad tells me that Phil is not his first choice? I know he wouldn't lie to me.

I also know that if they don't want Phil back, then he wouldn't want to come back.

That doesn't mean, however, that he doesn't want to coach at all. That is certainly not the case. He doesn't have any major health issues like he has had in the past. I think this is the best he has felt in a few years. So if he's not coaching this team, I believe he will be coaching somewhere else.

People say Phil has won 10 NBA championships and is working on No. 11 this season. Does he have a number in mind that he would be content with?

In other words, when is enough enough?

But it's not like that. It's not like Phil would immediately retire if he won his 20th championship. He would prefer to have won a championship every year he played and every year he coached. That is always his goal.

Phil would want to coach here—or someplace else—as long as he has an opportunity to win.

And remember, when Phil coaches, he doesn't win just one championship. He tends to win three in a row.

THE CONJECTURE ABOUT RON'S INJURY hasn't let up, but my dad has ignored all of it. He has been satisfied with Ron's explanation for his fall down a flight of stairs after the game on Christmas Day.

My dad demonstrated his support of Ron the first night Ron had recovered sufficiently to come to STAPLES Center as a spectator. My dad had him picked up, driven to the arena, and brought to the owner's suite, where the two men sat together.

I think that went a long way in showing how much the team is embracing Ron.

When Phil and Ron got together, Phil didn't feel the need to sit down and go over the story. Ron has already explained several times how he was injured. Phil just wanted to see Ron in person to make sure he was okay.

It's tough to be injured, especially when it is not basketball related, and I'm sure Ron was frustrated. But he has been working hard, and Phil rewarded him by starting him tonight. We needed him, so Phil stuck him out there right away.

Ron played 32 minutes, but had only seven points. He was supposed to be an integral piece of the puzzle, but he hasn't really found his rhythm in terms of contributing on offense.

Phil keeps telling Ron, "Defense is your key. Keep that focus and establish that."

The head injury shouldn't be an issue anymore. But Ron did get out of shape while recovering from the accident. That's a setback that can only be remedied by more practice time. Ron has gone through a long process to learn the offense, and the injury short-circuited that process.

PAU IS DAY-TO-DAY. When he hurt his other hamstring, he was out more than five weeks. Hopefully, it won't be that long this time, because with Luke Walton still out and Ron just coming back, it hurts to be down another guy up front.

Any healthy bodies are welcome considering our bench's performance has been less than impressive.

It couldn't come at a worse time. January is a long month for us because we have so many games on the road, 15 of our next 18.

That is, if you count the Clippers game. I find it interesting that NBA owners still haven't figured out that the Lakers and the Clippers have two more home games than any other team in the league.

Hey, I'm always looking for an edge.

January 8
Trail Blazers 107, Lakers 98

Another trip up to Portland filled with optimism.

Another trip home consumed by disappointment.

It doesn't seem to matter where the two teams sit in the standings or the relative merits of our clubs. The result is all too often the same.

We lose.

We have suffered defeat in 28 of our last 34 games in Portland. Our last victory in the Rose Garden came nearly five years ago, in February of 2005.

We are not welcome in Portland, and we feel it. That's good. It means their fans are strong.

There is a phenomenon around the league when the Lakers play on the road. There is usually a large contingent of Lakers fans in almost every city, and they make their presence known.

Not in Portland.

You don't hear Lakers fans there. They can't seem to make a difference in the Rose Garden. Portland fans should be proud of that.

I'M SURE PHIL WILL BE GRUMPY when he gets home. He often is after a loss, but he doesn't take it out on me. He doesn't kick the dog. That's not Phil.

Is he quiet after a tough defeat? Yes.

Is he distracted because he's thinking about what he is going to do about it? Yes.

Have I learned to give him his space? Absolutely.

January 13
LAKERS 100, MAVERICKS 95

Eight years after his death, the voice of Chick Hearn still echoes in our heads, but we feel fortunate to have a solid veteran like Joel Meyers now calling our TV play-by-play and a rising superstar in Spero Dedes on radio. I enjoy listening to either of them on a night like tonight when I am home and the team is on the road.

Chick did both jobs, but the days of the simulcast are history.

Spero is very talented and is probably going to end up being very good as a television play-by-play announcer or studio host or whatever he decides to do.

He has a contract with us that allows him to miss games so he can take other assignments. To us, the best assignment in the sports world is the Lakers job. So the idea that he would negotiate a contract that permits him to miss Lakers games doesn't make a lot of sense when there are people out there who would give anything to do just *one* Lakers game.

We won't be able to afford Spero if he gets to the point where he is only doing half of our games because he's working for the NFL Network or CBS or somebody else. And we can't pay him enough to make it worth his while to give up all the other TV opportunities he's going to have. Nor do we want to stand in his way.

Don't get me wrong. We hope he stays around, but we know that's probably not realistic considering how good he is and the fact that, on TV, he would have a larger audience than he does on radio.

For now, we are satisfied with the situation, but it seems inevitable that Spero is going to miss an important game or milestone.

When Joel started working for the Lakers, he was finishing up an old contract for pro football, so there were a couple of Lakers games he had to miss.

One, in particular, was a January 2006 game against Toronto that didn't appear to be of major importance. So what happened? Kobe scored 81 points.

That game, with Bill Macdonald calling the play-by-play, is in the Basketball Hall of Fame. When you hear the call of Kobe's spectacular performance, you don't hear Joel Meyers, but rather Bill Macdonald, a very able substitute. Great job by Bill, but I'm sure Joel would have preferred to have been in that seat.

It's a great example of why we feel that if you are with the Lakers, you should be *with the Lakers*. Especially when you have somebody like Kobe on the team who has the potential to break some record every night.

Chick was in the same position as Spero early in his Lakers career, a highly talented broadcaster with all sorts of offers.

In 1965, early in his fifth full season with the team, Chick was broadcasting a football game between Arkansas and Texas Tech in Fayetteville, Arkansas. Jack Kent Cooke, then the Lakers' owner, had a private jet waiting to transport Chick to Las Vegas where the Lakers were scheduled to play the Warriors that night.

It was November, and the weather was so nasty that the pilot advised Chick it wasn't safe to fly.

Chick missed that Lakers game, but no others for a long, long time. Cooke, according to Marge Hearn, Chick's widow, sat her husband down and said, "You can't keep doing this. You have to choose one job."

Marge said Chick didn't even hesitate. To him, the greatest job in the world was the Lakers job.

Chick limited his outside work after that and went on to broadcast 3,338 straight Lakers games, the streak ending only when he had to undergo open-heart surgery at the age of 85.

January 15

LAKERS 126, CLIPPERS 86

Because I didn't go to tonight's Lakers-Clippers game, I watched it on TV and was disappointed by what I saw and heard.

Not the results, of course. We won.

No, I was unhappy with the telecast because of the conjecture about the existence of a Clippers "curse" after it was announced several days ago that top draft choice Blake Griffin will undergo season-ending knee surgery for an injury he suffered in the team's last preseason game.

I would never say, nor would I want anyone in our organization to say, that a franchise has been cursed. Let's face it. Every franchise has had bad luck at some point. Does that mean every team is cursed? If you want to create a story focusing on the negative, you could make that claim.

I am going to talk to our broadcast partner about taking that approach with the Clippers.

It was our broadcast, and I don't like the idea that people think it was the Lakers saying that.

One of our favorite Lakers, Lamar Odom, is a former Clipper. He's won a championship, so he's not cursed. Ron Harper, who won a couple of championships with us and three with the Bulls, is a former Clipper. He's not cursed. So I don't buy it.

A plane carrying the Minneapolis Lakers once made an emergency landing in a cornfield. Magic was forced to retire due to HIV. Are we cursed?

To burden members of a team by saying something bad could happen to them, to make it sound like they had better beware of their future, is wrong to me. Putting too much negative energy on a person or a team is not fair.

Phil was also wrong at tonight's press conference when, asked if he believed in curses or hexes, he said, "I'm of that generation that believed in karma. If you do a good mitzvah, maybe you can eliminate some of those things. Do you think [Clipper owner Donald] Sterling's done enough mitzvahs to eliminate some of those?"

Phil said he was just trying to be funny. He wasn't.

He told me that he didn't think his comment would get blown up as big as it did. He doesn't take back what he said, but it's unfortunate that his reply became the focus. I don't think he will comment on the subject again.

January 18

LAKERS 98, MAGIC 92

Today is the 50th anniversary of an incident that almost turned into the greatest disaster in the history of U.S. professional sports: a fatal plane crash.

Unfortunately, several collegiate teams have suffered that fate. But despite the millions and millions of miles traveled by pro teams crisscrossing this country, and occasionally soaring beyond its borders, every flight has landed safely.

The closest any team has come to tragedy is the Minneapolis Lakers' flight on January 18, 1960. They were forced to settle for a cornfield in Carroll, Iowa, to end a terrifying flight through a blizzard in a rickety DC-3.

The flight originated in St. Louis, where the Lakers had played the Hawks that night.

Sleet was falling by the time the Lakers got to the airport, but according to the weather report, conditions would be considerably better en route to Minneapolis.

Three men would be in the cockpit: pilot Vern Ullman, co-pilot Harold Gifford, and trainee Jim Holznagel.

The plane, containing 19 members of the Lakers family including some wives and kids, took off at about 8:30 PM, two hours late.

It didn't take long for all aboard to regret the decision to depart. The lights soon went out, along with the heat and, of greatest concern, the plane's instruments.

It was later determined that a malfunctioning left generator had resulted in too heavy a load on the right generator, causing a power outage.

There was more bad news. The storm was getting worse.

In order to avoid the harsh weather, the plane had climbed to 17,000 feet, but without heat, the cold became so bitter that frost was forming inside on the floor and windows.

The cockpit was a truly alarming sight, as the crew had to use flashlights to see the controls. And when the five flashlights on board gave out after four hours in the air, the only device left for illumination was a faint beam from the light on an ordinary pen.

With no instruments and near zero visibility, the pilots couldn't be sure where they were. But they knew they had to land somewhere fast with their fuel running out.

Wearing goggles, the pilots dropped down to a few hundred feet and stuck their faces out the side windows to get their bearings. They spotted a highway and followed it to Carroll.

The scariest moment came when Gifford and Ullman, each trying to spot a landing area, thought the other one had control of the aircraft.

Neither did, and it briefly dipped down so low that one wing nearly brushed the treetops.

It was Holznagel who yelled out in alarm, causing Gifford to jerk the plane back up.

Gifford finally saw a water tower with what he assumed was the town's name on it. But all he could make out were the letters "LL."

Gifford joked that they must be flying into hell.

It was 1:40 AM, but the lights were coming on all over town as people were awakened by the roar of the low-flying DC-3.

"I could see there were people down there living," Gifford later said. "That's what I wanted to do, too."

After making nine passes over Carroll as they searched the landscape for a place to set down, the pilots agreed on the best of a bad bunch of options: Emma Steffes' cornfield just beyond the water tower. At least there wouldn't be any boulders, they figured, and the stalks would keep the snow from forming into mounds.

So with the landing gear in place, down they came. With the surface softened by the snow and corn, the plane bounced a couple of times, took out about 100 yards of cornfield, and came to a stop in eerie silence.

That didn't last long. When the players realized they had survived, they let out the kind of screams of joy usually reserved for the winning locker room after the NBA Finals.

Piling out into the cornfield, they started throwing snowballs at each other.

Among the rescue vehicles racing to the cornfield was the ambulance/hearse of local mortician Joe Twit. As the passengers emerged from the plane, Twit told them, "Thought I was going to have some business tonight, boys."

After the Lakers were transported to a nearby hotel, they called their families to let them know what had happened.

When one player, Larry Foust, told his wife the Lakers had crashed in an Iowa cornfield, she replied, "Call me back when you sober up."

If, heaven forbid, the Lakers had to make an emergency landing in today's information age, the whole world would know about it within minutes.

Amazingly enough, the plane was repaired, and after part of the cornfield was bulldozed to create a makeshift airstrip, it flew out of Carroll.

Less than a month later, it flew all the way to the West Coast, carrying the team to games in San Francisco and Los Angeles, its future home.

The Lakers would move to L.A. the following season.

Ullman, who passed away in 1965, along with Gifford and Holznagel, who both live in Minnesota, were the Captain Sullenbergers of their day.

I wrote a letter to Carroll mayor Jim Pedelty and the citizens of Carroll, thanking them for their heroics. It was read at a ceremony today commemorating that unforgettable night.

In September, they are going to dedicate a basketball court on the site of that old cornfield, which is now a park, and I am planning to be there for that event.

Had the team been wiped out that night, there is a chance the franchise, with owner Bob Short already struggling to find the money to keep it going, might have just folded, and the Lakers wouldn't exist today.

I'm sure L.A. would have eventually been granted an NBA team, but it wouldn't have been the Lakers. So the citizens of Carroll should take pride in the success our team has had all these years.

January 20

Tonight, the team is on the road to begin an eight-game, 12-night trip. I wonder how many players will curl up in bed with their brand-new books, courtesy of Phil.

A devoted reader all his life, Phil delights in his annual tradition of giving a book to each member of the team, selecting the start of a long, midseason trip to bestow his gift. It's something Phil has done since the beginning of his head coaching career back in Chicago 20 years ago.

Phil gave out the books today before the team left for its first stop in Cleveland.

It's an extremely meaningful exercise for Phil and he takes it very seriously. Days or even weeks before, he starts formulating in his mind which book would be the perfect match for each player.

As of yesterday, Phil hadn't bought the books, but then Pau asked him at practice if he was going to be handing them out on this trip.

That got Phil moving. In his mind, he had already organized what he wanted to do. I printed out a list of the players, and he made some final notes.

It usually takes two or three trips to different bookstores to get everything Phil wants. Because he had only one shopping day this time, Phil didn't have the luxury of going from store to store. That was fine with me because I don't like to meander.

I had a suggestion.

"Why don't you get everybody a wireless reading device like a Kindle," I said, "and start each of them off by downloading a book?"

I thought maybe they would relate to the newest trend.

"Oh no," Phil said, "you don't understand books."

It's not that Phil doesn't like the Kindle. He has one. But that's not what this is about. He wants to buy the players books that will sit on their desks or beside their beds. To Phil, there is something special about a book.

The choices he makes are always interesting. Phil has given the same book to different players over the years.

He gave Ron Artest one of his own books, *Sacred Hoops*. Phil said he chose that one because Ron is new to the team and needs to know how we do things.

One of Phil's favorite authors is Walter Mosley, so Phil picked two of Mosley's books. *Six Easy Pieces: Easy Rawlins Stories* went to Andrew Bynum. *The Right Mistake*, about an ex-convict, was selected for Lamar Odom.

I thought what Phil gave Kobe was really sweet. It's called *Montana 1948*, a novel by Larry Watson. Phil was born in 1945, so it was really about the state as he knew it growing up.

Pau got *2666*, a novel by Chilean author Roberto Bolano about unsolved murders in Mexico. It was Pau who asked about the books, but we'll see how enthusiastic he is after receiving this one. It's 898 pages.

One of Phil's other choices was *Dreams from My Father*, President Barack Obama's book, for Shannon Brown.

Kobe Bryant and Jordan Farmar have said they never read the books. Knowing that players are like that, why does Phil still give them out?

I asked him that when I first met him, and he told me they don't have to read it that day. The book may sit untouched for 20 years, but maybe when they become a father, or maybe when they retire, or maybe when they go into coaching, or maybe when they are simply curious, they will be inspired to pick it up and reflect on the choice he made for them. And if it resonates with them at that point, he will feel that his mission was accomplished.

If Phil thinks a player is coaching material or may wind up in a front office someday, he may pick a book related to that career goal.

This isn't like a homework assignment that the players have to get done. It isn't like Phil is going to pester them about reading the books. It isn't about the expectation of their reaction. It's a gift from Phil's heart, because really, what else is he ever going to give these guys? He doesn't buy them birthday presents.

Phil signs every book and adds a message. Just as he is certain they will open the book someday, he is certain they will also open their heart and read the message.

It can be a tough message for guys whose production he's not happy with, like some of our bench players.

Phil himself reads all kinds of books, from biographies and fiction to sports books, though the latter is not usually his first choice.

Books are not the only gifts Phil gives. This year, he gave my dad a jigsaw puzzle of Honolulu for Christmas. That's my dad's favorite place. He has a condo right there on the beach.

But if you have a relationship with Phil, you can be sure you are going to get a book at some point.

Phil has given my dad books, he's given my mom books, he's given his kids books, and, of course, he gives me books every year, at least a dozen in all. Recently, he seems to be giving me more and more books about dogs.

I read as much as I have time for. I have five of the books sitting on my bedside table right now.

It's a very personal thing for Phil. For him to give you a book is a very warm compliment.

January 23

Phil can't help being a coach. It's in his DNA. So even though he is as excited as the rest of us about our visit to the White House Monday to be honored by President Obama for winning last season's NBA championship, Phil also sees the visit as a distraction.

He realizes the impact the event can have on his players, so Phil will tolerate the ceremony, but he doesn't want the players to forget this is a business trip. So he's holding a practice prior to taking his team to Pennsylvania Avenue.

The Lakers play Sunday evening in Toronto, so they won't get into Washington until around midnight. I'm going to fly to the capital from L.A., landing much earlier in the day.

We are going to give the president a Lakers jersey and a ball. A White House official asked if there was anything else I wanted to give President Obama. I'll tell Phil to pick out a book for him.

I hope Michelle and their daughters are going to be there because I'd love the opportunity to meet them.

When we were honored by President Ronald Reagan, I don't recall Nancy being at the ceremony. And when President George W. Bush hosted us, I don't think Laura was there.

With all the things President Obama has to worry about right now, it is wonderful that he's taking the time to meet with us.

Phil will ask the players to reflect on the occasion, what it means to them as individuals, and what it means to them as a team.

January 25

Back in 1985, we went to the White House after beating the Celtics for the championship in Boston. We got on a plane after a short celebration. Our audience with President Reagan was in the Rose Garden because it was a warm day in June. We were riding a wave of euphoria in a moment of triumph.

Today's trip to the White House, though just as meaningful, was different. It was good timing to go in January in the first half of an eight-game road trip. It offered the players an opportunity to remember the long-term goal of this season, to flash back on what it was like to be crowned champions. It's possible to lose sight of that during the dog days of January.

Everybody was really jazzed to be here. The enthusiasm was high for the players because this president has been inspirational to so many of them.

I took my girlfriend Stacy Kennedy with me, and we arrived in Washington well before the Lakers' game in Toronto. It turned out to be frustrating because we couldn't find a place to watch it.

Not as frustrating as it was for Phil and the players, who lost 106–105.

Pau was called for fouling Hedo Turkoglu with 1.2 seconds to play. Turkoglu made both free throws to put the Raptors ahead by one. Then Kobe missed a long, difficult three-point attempt at the buzzer.

So Phil wasn't in a very good mood when he reached the hotel after midnight.

Every member of the team was permitted to bring one person with him for the trip to the White House. We didn't stick strictly to that rule, but we were able to keep the group at a reasonable size. There were wives, kids, other family members, and Lakers staff.

Phil's daughter Elizabeth, who lives in Washington, came with her husband Gregg. Phil also brought his son Charley, who flew in from San Francisco.

Pau brought his mother, as did Andrew Bynum.

Everybody had to submit his or her name, birth date, city of birth, and social security number a week in advance.

Today, the day of the ceremony, turned out to be absolutely beautiful. It was warm and sunny. We were pinching ourselves about how lucky we were. It had snowed so much over the holidays, but there was no white stuff on the ground today.

I took a lot of pictures because everywhere you look in Washington, a great photo opportunity beckons.

Since Phil stuck to his decision to have practice this morning, the families and friends accompanying the players for the White House visit went there about an hour before the team.

The players practiced from 10:30 to 11:30 AM, then met with kids from the community. The players arrived back at the hotel at 12:30, just as we were leaving.

The formal ceremony was at 2:00 PM. A tour of the White House had been arranged for us. Our guides could not have been more gracious, charming, helpful, or patient, happily answering all our questions.

We were each allowed to bring a camera, which surprised me. And, of course, most of us have camera capability on our cell phones. I was even able to tweet about the whole experience.

We saw the portraits of all the presidents and a lot of the first ladies. There was so much history to soak in.

I got this great picture of Charley with a portrait of JFK. Charley reminds me of that great leader.

In one room was an impressive portrait of Bill Clinton with a pretty red couch below it. When Lamar's wife, Khloe Kardashian, sat down on it, looking beautiful in an evening gown, I took her picture and posted it on my Twitter account. Media outlet TMZ decided to pick up all my tweets because Khloe's name popped up. So not only did my 23,000 followers see my photos that day, but anyone who went on TMZ also got a viewing.

The anticipation about meeting the president was growing minute by minute.

We were walking down a hallway from the White House Library to the Green Room when I spotted Bo Obama, the First Family's pet. A Portuguese Water Dog, he is just the perfect size. He's cute, weighs maybe 30 pounds, and is black and white with a beautiful shiny coat. He was coming my way with his dog walker.

I clutched my camera, but just as Bo got to within 10 feet of me, he was turned and taken outside. So I didn't get to pet Bo. I didn't even get a picture of him, but I was excited to see a dog living in the White House.

Once we were in the Green Room, all of us who were going on stage for the ceremony were briefed about exactly what was going to happen.

We had brought an autographed ball and a jersey with President Obama's name on it. I wasn't involved in assigning a number to the jersey, so I wondered what it would be. Sometimes they put No. 1 on a presidential jersey, but then I thought maybe they would give him No. 44 because he's the 44th president. He got No. 1.

We had designed a replica of the championship ring as a paperweight for our season-ticket holders. It turned out kind of blingy but pretty, with crystals instead of diamonds. It's what you might imagine Shaq's championship ring would look like.

Hopefully not being presumptuous, I thought the president, a huge basketball fan, might like one on his desk. So I stuck one in my bag, but almost didn't make it through security at LAX because when it came up on the screen, a TSA official stopped me and asked, "Ma'am, what is this?"

"See this Lakers championship ring?" I said, pointing to the one on my finger. "Well, this is an exact replica, but it's a paperweight. It's for the president."

The screener said, "You're going to see the president?"

"Yes, I am," I answered, with a big smile on my face.

He let me go.

When our players arrived, they were taken to the Blue Room. When I saw Kobe in a sharp suit sitting in a chair near the fireplace, he looked elegant. As I snapped a picture of him, he was all smiles. It was great to see Kobe so happy.

I took a picture of Derek Fisher and tweeted that this could be our future president. Okay, I know he is only the head of the players' union and captain of our team right now, but Derek has such an aura of leadership about him that there's no way to predict how far he might go in whatever direction he chooses.

I took off my championship ring and placed it on one of the chairs in the Blue Room. I wanted to see what the Lakers ring looked like in the White House.

Magic flew in from New York for the ceremony, but he nearly missed it because his flight was delayed. If he had been five minutes later, he wouldn't have been able to join us.

They lined us up by height, so although Phil wanted to be next to me, we were separated. I wound up on the end, which was fine with me. The only one who wouldn't abide by the height rule was Mitch Kupchak. I think he felt the coaches and players should be in the spotlight and he should be in the background.

We rehearsed walking out on the stage before the president came in.

Then we lined up again, and this time, the president walked in.

He could not have been sweeter or more charming. Before we got on the stage, he introduced himself to everyone, saying something to connect with each of us.

When President Obama got to me, I introduced myself, simply saying, "Hi, I'm Jeanie Buss."

He replied, "I know who you are."

I thought I was going to die.

Had an aide run my picture by him? Whether he really did know me or not, it felt like he did.

That's when I pulled out the paperweight, which I had removed from the box, and gave it to him.

I said, "I thought this might be something you'd want for your desk."

President Obama's face lit up. He took it and gave it to one of his aides. He at least acted as if he liked it, so that made me feel wonderful.

When the president reached Phil, he told him, "I have been watching you for a long time. I'm a Bulls fan. I was there for many of those games you coached."

It seemed there was mutual admiration at work. Under different circumstances, I can imagine a friendship developing between them. They could connect on so many levels, from basketball to Chicago to principles of leadership to social concerns.

When President Obama was elected, Phil predicted he would find common ground on which to govern. "It's like I always tell players," Phil said at the time, "you cannot only go to your left. Sometimes, you have to go to your right."

The president began his speech by praising my father, the Buss family, and the Lakers organization for how the team has been run the last three decades. I was nearly bursting with pride.

The president also mentioned that Phil hands out books to his players and added that he wished Phil could give Congress a book on how to get along and work together.

It was hilarious when the president got around to Magic. The president teased him about that unforgettable drive by Michael Jordan, when he switched hands as he elevated to the basket in the 1991 NBA Finals between the Lakers and the Bulls.

Magic kind of bit his tongue. It was funny because he wouldn't normally do that. But he wasn't about to trash talk with the president of the United States.

I got the feeling this was a nice break for President Obama, that he was just as happy that the Lakers were there as the Lakers were to be there.

Derek and Kobe made the team presentation of the jersey and ball.

When the 17-minute ceremony was over and the president turned around to thank us for coming, I said, "I've got two seats on the floor for you anytime you are in L.A. I really want you to come to a game."

He said, "I'd like that very much. I will come to a game."

I told the president, "I'm going to hold you to that. I'm going to keep bugging you."

So whether or not it's while he's still in office, I am confident President Obama will indeed come to see the Lakers.

He has sat courtside for a Wizards game, and we can make it work in our place as well.

I know we can because we already have. President Bill Clinton came out to see the Lakers when STAPLES Center first opened in 1999.

When they were building our arena, they were already committed to hosting the Democratic National Convention there in 2000. So security areas for that event were installed at the time of construction which have served us well in the years since, and will do so again whenever President Obama arrives.

My dad doesn't come to ceremonies like this because he feels they are too political. But I called him immediately afterward to tell him what President Obama had said, anxious to let my dad know he was acknowledged by the president for his amazing management of our franchise.

The president has invited Kobe, his wife Vanessa, and daughters Natalia Diamante and Gianna Maria-Onore to have breakfast with him at the White House tomorrow. What an extraordinary experience that will be for all of them.

I can't adequately describe a day like today to someone who is not fortunate enough to have experienced it.

It was such an honor and should make everybody appreciate what we have.

To the winners go the spoils.

PICKING STRINGS
TO LEARN THE ROPES

I PROBABLY SHOULD HAVE BEEN STUNNED AND NERVOUS, FEELING insecure and unqualified.

But I was none of the above.

I was 19 years old, had finished one year of college, and had never worked in my dad's sports empire, but he wanted me to start out as the boss, the general manager of the L.A. Strings of World Team Tennis.

Not only that, but my first duty would be to conduct the team's upcoming draft.

"I want you to know what it feels like to do this job," my dad said. "I want you to see if you like it."

I was too young to have doubts. I didn't know what I didn't know. My dad thought I could do it, so therefore, I could do it. He trusted me. What else did I need?

I just figured that this was my life. This was what I'd always wanted to do. And this was what I was going to do.

Besides, I felt I had been preparing for that moment for much of my young life.

The Strings were the first team my dad had owned seven years earlier. When WTT meetings were held in L.A., I was the gopher starting at age 14. I would go for the coffee and doughnuts.

But after delivering the refreshments, instead of leaving I would stay, sit in the corner, and just listen. I was fascinated with the whole operation.

Then, three years after the league folded, it was back. Before, the season had stretched over five months. This time, it would be just one month, to be played in July of 1981.

"What a perfect thing for you," my dad told me, "because it's in the summer and won't interfere with your schooling."

"But now that I have a job," I said, "I'm going to quit school. Why do I need to go to college?"

"You can't have the job," my dad said firmly, "unless you finish school."

I didn't understand why it was necessary, but what choice did I have?

As draft day approached, I went to my dad for help.

"The reason I gave this to you," he said, "is so that you can get used to making your own decisions. I have complete confidence you'll do great. Don't worry about it.

"I want you to have the responsibility. If things go well, you get the credit. If things don't go well, you'll find out what that feels like as well. I want you to experience what it's like to be in my shoes. That way, I'll have someone to relate to."

We had the No. 1 pick. Yes, I finally got a little nervous as draft day approached, but I don't think I did too poorly. I chose Martina Navratilova.

I knew all the players before the draft because I was a big tennis fan. What I wasn't sure of was who would work well together as a doubles team because, remember, the WTT format consisted of men's and women's singles and doubles, plus mixed doubles.

Once I had Martina, it was just a matter of picking players who could complement her. I selected Terry Holladay as her doubles partner. My first male singles player was Vijay Amritraj, who had also been with the Strings in the 1970s.

The draft was conducted on the phone with my dad nowhere in sight. Afterward, he called and said, "Okay, what did you do?" When he heard, he was pleased.

So was I after we won the championship in that abbreviated season.

I know there were some whispers behind my back about my only being in that position because I was the boss' daughter. I still get that.

What really helped me that first season was having the support of Billie Jean King. She was playing that year for the Oakland Breakers, but her ties to the league went much deeper. It was she and her then-husband, Larry King, who founded the WTT and came up with the unique format that created the first coed professional teams.

Billie Jean coached and played for the Philadelphia Freedoms in 1974. That made her the first female coach of a team that included male athletes, another in her many groundbreaking accomplishments (Elton

John's 1975 No. 1 hit, "Philadelphia Freedom," was a tribute to their friendship).

The fact that the playing field was equal for the sexes in the WTT was what Billie Jean loved most about it.

The players really enjoyed the team format because they normally travel, play, and win or lose on their own in a tournament situation. To be part of a team, enjoying the camaraderie and sharing their highs and lows, was a new experience for them. I know Martina found that very appealing.

Another person I can thank for making me feel comfortable in the tennis world was Dianne Fromholtz, who broke me in when I was 15 by taking me to New York to watch her play in the U.S. Open.

Dianne, just 19 at the time, was a member of the Strings in those days and dating my brother Johnny.

That didn't save her, however, from being traded when my dad had an opportunity to get Chris Evert. He sent Dianne to the Indiana Loves.

Since she was responsible for me while we were in New York, Dianne worried about me sitting in the stands alone. She got so distracted keeping an eye on me that it affected her game. So she asked the head linesperson if I could sit on the court.

It was the most remarkable thing. They put a chair out there and I actually sat on center court for the semifinals of the 1976 U.S. Open.

Unfortunately, Dianne lost to her fellow Aussie, Evonne Goolagong.

After that, nothing about tennis was going to intimidate me.

Johnny and Dianne were engaged, but never married. I don't think the trade had anything to do with their breakup. She was from Australia and just wanted to go home.

I met so many inspiring people in my first years in sports and learned so much from them.

The first season my dad owned the Lakers, he invited Jane Fonda to come to a game and I was introduced to her.

She reached out to shake my hand, and when I responded with a floppy wrist, she said in a firm but friendly manner, "When you shake somebody's hand, mean it. Grab their hand so they remember you."

I follow that advice to this day. And I give everyone a hearty handshake.

Tommy Lasorda was another person with good advice for a young person seeking credibility and acceptance.

"Don't tell people your problems," he said, "because 50 percent of them don't care, and the other 50 percent are happy you have them."

MY FATHER WASN'T THE ONLY ONE who used the WTT as a launching pad to soar to the next level of sports ownership. The Boston Lobsters—still one of the best team names ever—were once owned by Bob Kraft. You might have heard of the team he eventually took over, the New England Patriots.

I also moved on from the WTT, but stayed in the sport as we began staging a series of one-night exhibitions at the Forum.

When you are the promoter of a tournament, the question you get asked all the time is, who is going to be in the finals? Two weeks before the tournament even starts, people call and say, "Who is going to play on Sunday?"

They know, of course, that it depends on what happens on the court. But they want your opinion because, if it's not going to be two big names, if there was no guarantee it would be a John McEnroe against a Jimmy Connors back in those days, many fans aren't interested in handing their money over.

So putting on one-night exhibitions, where we could dictate the opponents, proved to be very lucrative for us.

My cohort in this venture was Linda Rambis. When I started working for my dad, she was still Linda Zafrani, working in ticket sales and marketing for the Forum. She sold Lakers and Kings tickets and everything else.

My dad saw she was very capable, intelligent, a strong female, and a real go-getter. He thought she and I would work well together, so he assigned her to marketing duties for the Strings.

She's seven years older than me, but still young enough to make me feel like we were peers, almost like sisters.

It was another smart move on my dad's part because Linda turned out to be a good role model for me. Yes, she had more experience than I did, but she wasn't preachy with me.

We not only became fast friends, but also worked well together because our business styles complemented each other. I was still in school, so Linda ran the day-to-day operation, enabling me to continue my education.

She and I developed a year-round tennis calendar. We put on tournaments like World Championship Tennis, originally started by Lamar Hunt, as well as the Avon Championships, formerly Virginia Slims, that began when Billie Jean and eight other female players asserted their independence from their male counterparts.

But Linda and I weren't satisfied with just tennis. Soon, we were promoting volleyball and gymnastics as well.

We were these two girls that people might not have taken seriously at first, but pretty soon we were meeting with key tennis figures like Hunt and Donald Dell, as well as people in the sports marketing world. I'm sure they got a kick out of us because we wouldn't take no for an answer. We were relentless, but we were fun. We could hang out.

In 1983, we were trying to convince Martina to play in an exhibition against her archrival Chris Evert.

But she and Chrissie didn't like to play each other except at the U.S. Open or at Wimbledon. They didn't want to be in a situation that might give the other one the edge the next time they met in a Grand Slam event. That was their mentality.

Martina had gotten really interested in basketball through her friendship with female superstar Nancy Lieberman.

That gave Martina an idea. "I'll play in a tennis exhibition if I can also play in a basketball exhibition," she told me.

We agreed, but, as it turned out, the date we settled on—February 28, 1983—was also the night of the final episode of *M*A*S*H*, the celebrated television series about a medical unit during the Korean War. In those days, fans had viewing parties for momentous shows like that and the "Who shot J.R.?" episode of *Dallas*.

People had suffered along with the *M*A*S*H* characters on a show that lasted longer than the Korean War itself, so they wanted to be there to bid the characters farewell.

And that's exactly what they did. With nearly 106 million viewers, the show was the most watched program in television history until the 2010 Super Bowl between the Saints and the Colts drew 106.5 million.

And at the Forum? We had 1,000 people to watch Martina play hoops. She was great, but the sparse crowd made it a disappointing evening.

We could have had Martina play again, but we preferred to have her focus on tennis. That meant more business.

We also wanted to put on a McEnroe-Connors exhibition, but at that time, because their rivalry was so hot, they were very selective about choosing a venue. The only time it was guaranteed they would play was when they drew each other in a tournament.

Linda had a better relationship with John, and I was closer with Jimmy. Believe me, there was a lot of begging and pleading. It was important to them that neither got more consideration than the other.

We promised them limos while they were in L.A. and whatever else they would need. We also committed to an ambitious advertising campaign, treating them like the top stars in Hollywood.

John's father pushed him to do it. Also, John liked going to Lakers games, so we got him seats on the floor. He was spending more time in L.A. because he was dating his future wife, Tatum O'Neal.

John will say to this day that he is, first and foremost, a Knicks fan. But the Knicks were constantly struggling, so he decided to root for the Lakers unless they were playing the Knicks.

We offered John and Jimmy $100,000 each. We even bought an insurance policy from Lloyd's of London in case one of them got hurt. With so much money at risk, we had to protect ourselves.

Even with all that, it took us a few years to convince them to do it. Finally, John and Jimmy agreed, and in April of 1984, our years of persistence paid off.

We got our money back and more. We sold 16,000 tickets and broke the all-time gross gate receipt record at the Forum with just under $600,000 in ticket sales.

That was mind blowing, and not just to me. No one could believe that two girls could pull off something like that.

We grossed more than any Lakers or Kings game. The old record had been set in the early 1970s when Muhammad Ali fought Ken Norton at the Forum.

Box seats were $100. It was like a rock concert having those two guys play each other. It didn't matter that there wasn't a tournament title on the line. What mattered to John and Jimmy was making sure they didn't lose to their No. 1 adversary.

The record for Forum ticket sales was broken at the end of that year when Kenny Rogers and Dolly Parton played a New Year's Eve concert, but we still held the mark for a sporting event.

Jimmy wound up playing for the L.A. Strings, and when he made a memorable run to the semis of the 1991 U.S. Open, he credited our team for helping to make that possible.

He enjoyed the team camaraderie and he asked his teammates to come to every one of his matches. That, he said, would inspire him.

We were all there, watching Jimmy come back to win after being down two sets to Patrick McEnroe, and come back to triumph again on his 39th birthday after being down to Aaron Krickstein. Jimmy's valiant performance finally came to an end in the semifinals when he lost to Jim Courier.

In 1984, John won the U.S. Open several months after he and Jimmy got a guaranteed $100,000 for a Forum exhibition. In contrast, John made $160,000 for his two-week run at the Open.

For players at that level, competing in the Grand Slams and on the rest of the tour was the way to get their rankings up. The higher their ranking, the greater their guaranteed appearance fee, so playing in the exhibitions was where they made their money.

After I finished college, Linda and I developed the Michelin Challenge. We would bring in four players and stage a semifinals and finals. But it was spread out over roughly a year, so there was a great match every couple of months. We would have McEnroe versus Connors, and then Connors versus Yannick Noah or Stefan Edberg or Ivan Lendl. It was a minitournament, a format that had never been employed before.

In 1993, the last year of Forum exhibitions, we matched up McEnroe and Pete Sampras. Pete was paid $125,000 for the night. For winning the U.S. Open that year, he received $535,000.

The tournament people had finally gotten smart and realized exhibitions were diminishing their events because fans wanted to cut to the chase if possible and just see the big names face each other. So tournament officials put us out of business by jacking their purses up above what we would pay.

The winner of the 2010 U.S. Open will pocket $1.7 million. Astonishing.

ONE OF THE THINGS I HAD TO LEARN in those early days was how to deal with the media.

As I matured, I realized media people have a job to do just as I do. The situation reminded me of a cartoon I saw about a wolf and a sheepdog. All day long, the dog would prevent the wolf from attacking the sheep. At the end of their respective shifts, however, each clocked out and then they had a beer together. The wolf had been doing his job, trying to steal the sheep; the dog had been doing his job, protecting the flock.

In real life, just because I am in a potentially adversarial situation with people professionally doesn't mean I can't respect them and, at the end of the day, be friends with them.

I just needed to realize that I can't control the media. Everybody is entitled to his or her opinion. I can't dictate to them what to write or broadcast, so I don't let it get to me if they express a view I don't agree with.

Back when I first entered the public eye, however, I hadn't developed that attitude, and I let one article hit me hard.

We had a World Championship Tennis event at the Forum featuring three of the top eight players in the world, all good on clay courts.

But two of them—Jose Luis Clerc and Guillermo Vilas—lost in the first round. It was a fast court, not the clay they excelled on. Patrons complained about the upsets.

A *Los Angeles Times* sportswriter ripped me and ripped the tournament. Ivan Lendl, ranked No. 2 in the world at the time, ended up winning the title, so we had a top player as champion. But that didn't alleviate my bruised feelings about the story.

Breaking out in tears, I told my dad, "I'm really sorry. I hope this doesn't embarrass the family. I did the best I could."

"What do you expect?" said my dad, referring to the writer. "He is probably an intern barely making $10,000 a year."

When I heard that, I started crying even harder.

"Now what's wrong?" he asked.

"That's how much you pay me!" I said.

I immediately got a raise. The worst article ever written about me ended up making me money.

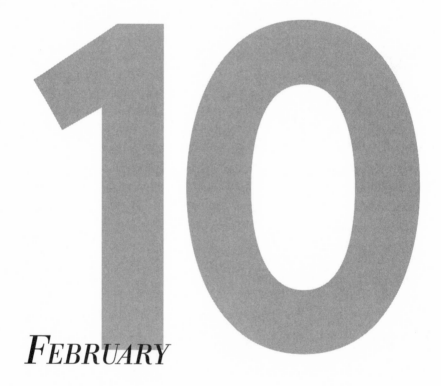

FEBRUARY

February 1

The timing was superb. Nearly halfway through this seemingly unending road trip, team personnel were reunited with family and friends for the White House visit. Without that break, the trip would have felt interminably long.

Thank goodness, the Lakers are flying home after tonight's game, two days short of two weeks since they left.

I've been on my share of Lakers trips and have enough pleasant memories to last me a lifetime, but there is one memory I could do without.

I don't take the team bus because I feel that's a private sanctuary for the coaches and players. But on one occasion, the separate transportation usually arranged to get me to the team hotel was nowhere in sight when we landed.

Since we take charter flights that usually land in isolated areas of the airport away from the general public, I couldn't just walk out and find a cab.

That left me no option other than the team bus. I stood right in front of the door as everybody was filing on, hoping someone would tell me where to sit. I know everybody gravitates toward their comfort zone—the players in one section and the coaches in another, with trainers, executives, PR people, and broadcasters settling into their familiar spots as well.

Del Harris was the coach then, but neither he nor anybody else seemed to be concerned about where I sat.

So I finally boarded the bus and discovered the only empty seat was in front of guard Nick Van Exel.

My rear end hadn't even touched the cushion when he said, "You can't sit there."

He said it loud. *Really* loud.

I wanted to disappear. I was aware I was in the team's sanctum, but I didn't know what to do, so I just sat there and put my head down. It was awful.

I'll never forget that feeling. Nobody wants to be treated like the uninvited guest. I will never, ever go on a team bus again. Ever. Even with Phil as the coach.

February 3
LAKERS 99, BOBCATS 97

When I first started dating Phil, I kept hearing Chicago this, Chicago that, Chicago, Chicago, Chicago. I told Phil that my goal was to see him more closely associated with the Lakers than with the Bulls.

Including this season, he has coached the Lakers longer than he coached the Bulls. Even so, I never thought he would replace Pat Riley as the winningest coach in Lakers history. I didn't think Pat's total of 533 victories would ever be broken.

With tonight's win, however, Phil surpassed him.

I still think Pat is more associated with the Lakers than Phil is, even though Pat also won a championship with another team. That's because we all witnessed the birth of Pat Riley, the coach. This was the nest he came from. We watched him become who he was, so the image of him crouched on the sideline in front of our bench will be forever ingrained in the minds of Lakers fans. Phil, on the other hand, will be thought of in terms of coming here in the second half of his coaching career.

Phil and Pat are friendly rivals with mutual respect for each other. They even trade notes on occasion.

There is no bitterness there even though their teams had many fierce battles when Phil was coaching the Bulls and Pat was leading the Knicks.

"I always appreciated Pat's gamesmanship," Phil told me. "He always brought out the best in me. People in L.A. don't know that."

In the years since my dad bought the Lakers, we have certainly had our ups and downs with coaches.

When my dad first took over, he wanted Jerry West to continue as head coach. When West turned him down, my dad made a brilliant selection in hiring Jack McKinney, a former college coach and a protégé of Trail

Blazers coach Jack Ramsay. My dad plucked McKinney away from Portland where he was an assistant under Ramsay.

In the short time he ran the Lakers, McKinney designed the system that would define the fast-breaking Showtime Lakers.

But in an unimaginable tragedy, McKinney suffered a serious head injury just 14 games into his first season when he tumbled headfirst over the handlebars of his bike while pedaling downhill on a Palos Verdes street.

He was on his way to play tennis with his assistant coach and longtime friend, Paul Westhead.

After the accident, Westhead took over the coaching reins, calling himself a "substitute teacher." But when the Lakers won the championship that season, my father's first as owner, Westhead was still the coach because McKinney had not fully recovered.

No organization would want to go through what the Lakers did with McKinney. There was so much heartbreak on one side and such success on the other.

As Paul's wife Cassie said at the time of the McKinneys, a family they had been so close to, "They can't share our joys, and we can't share their sorrows."

The Westheads had their own sorrows a year and a half later when the Lakers let Paul go.

The move came after Magic Johnson spoke out and said he wasn't having any fun and wanted to be traded.

My father, learning that the players were in revolt over an offense most of them felt was too stifling, had already decided to relieve Paul of his duties. Unfortunately, Magic went public before that happened and received heavy criticism because of the inaccurate belief that he had gotten the coach fired.

Fortunately, the perfect replacement was available: a former player/Chick Hearn sidekick/Lakers assistant coach named Pat Riley.

When Phil left the Lakers in 2004, I was all for Pat replacing him. I thought that would have been a good hire.

However, given Pat's situation in Miami—where he was not only the coach at the time but team president as well—it didn't seem to make a lot of sense.

But Pat was definitely intrigued by the idea.

February 9

I went on a tour today of an area that is groundbreaking for an arena.

And they didn't even have to break any ground to construct it. They just knocked down some walls.

It's Hyde Lounge at STAPLES Center, located on the third suite level, a club modeled after the one on Sunset Boulevard.

What makes this one unique is its location. The owner, Sam Nazarian, bought eight suites, then removed the barriers and created a club that features food from high-end restaurants, luxury décor furniture, a spectacular DJ, and, oh yeah, as an added attraction, the Lakers, Kings, Clippers, boxing, or whatever else is going on down on the floor.

The seating area faces outward when an event is going on, providing a perfect view from a great vantage point.

When the event is over, everyone turns around, the curtains are drawn, the music kicks in, the dance floor appears, and patrons are in their own private world, the most exclusive of all the exclusive clubs.

No other arena has ever done anything like this. It's revolutionary thinking. You need something like this here in L.A. where you are competing with so many venues that offer VIP treatment.

It's a hot spot, open until 2:00 AM every night, whether there is an event going on or not. It kind of reminds me of the Foundation Room at Las Vegas' Mandalay Bay.

Now, just because you are already in STAPLES Center doesn't mean you can get into Hyde, which holds around 250 people. Entry is by invitation only.

Sam, who owns hotels and clubs all over the world, told me he got the inspiration for this lounge from seeing pictures of Wilt Chamberlain's old house, which had accordion-type seating and was heavy on the leather.

To me, it's reminiscent of the old Forum Club. Nothing could ever be that good—I admit I'm a little biased—but Hyde is an impressive attempt. I know that if my dad walked in, he would feel right at home.

What my dad did 30 years ago, creating the Forum Club, was crazy in the opinion of some people. It was hard to fathom a nightclub existing inside a sports arena.

Crazy? It quickly became the place to be. People clamored to get in there with the same zeal they demonstrated in trying to get seats to the game itself.

My dad understood from the beginning that the key to making the Lakers appealing was equal parts sports and entertainment. Every arena now tries to copy that formula.

One word best describes my dad's philosophy: Showtime.

He certainly didn't invent the term. As a matter of fact, he borrowed it from a nightclub he used to visit regularly, a place on Wilshire Boulevard down by the ocean called The Horn.

It wasn't a big place, holding perhaps 150 customers seated at tables or in booths.

The evening would begin with the dimming of the lights. Then a singer, who had been seated inconspicuously at a table, would stand up and begin to sing, "It's Showtime." A second singer would join in from another table. Then a third.

When my dad bought the Lakers, he thought of The Horn, thought of the Showtime theme, and decided to incorporate it into his basketball operation.

How?

Well, to start with the Lakers had just drafted Magic Johnson, perhaps the most entertaining basketball player of all time. With Magic at the controls, my dad envisioned a razzle-dazzle, fast-break offense that would be as entertaining as it was efficient.

But what's entertainment without music? There had been an organist at the Forum, but my dad livened things up by bringing in a 10-piece band from—where else?—USC.

Athletes. A band. There was only one thing missing if my dad was going to emulate the atmosphere he enjoyed so much at USC football games: cheerleaders.

So next came the Laker Girls.

My dad planned to take advantage of the fact he was in the entertainment capital of the world by luring as many big-name celebrities as possible to sit in the courtside seats.

He figured that if he could make the Forum the place the *stars* wanted to be, it would become the place *everybody* wanted to be.

But if those stars, accustomed to interacting with the best entertainers in Hollywood, were going to be face-to-face with the Laker Girls just a few feet from their courtside seats, the girls had better be talented and sexy dancers with spectacular outfits.

And so they are and have been down through the years as a result of a vigorous recruiting and training program.

The first Laker Girls were song leaders from USC and UCLA. It's really amazing how far they have gone from there, literally as well as figuratively. Not only have the Laker Girls represented the NBA everywhere from Europe to Asia to Australia, but they have also entertained our troops in Korea, Japan, Israel, Italy, Bosnia, and Sarajevo.

Locally, of course, the Laker Girls perform at our games and at various charitable functions all over town.

My dad may have been out there on his own when he created the Laker Girls, but he wasn't alone for long. Soon other teams got in step with their own versions of our female squad.

The last to kick up their heels were the Celtics. The Boston Celtics Dancers made their debut during the 2006–07 season and this past year had their first dance camp.

If Red Auerbach were still around, he would be completely annoyed.

So when I look around Hyde Lounge, I have to smile. What began in the darkened atmosphere of The Horn and blossomed into Showtime has taken yet another entertaining twist. After 31 years, the party is still going on.

February 15

It was supposed to be an important weekend for me in Dallas, scene of the NBA All-Star Game at $1.2 billion Cowboys Stadium. I am a member of the league's labor relations committee that was convening there to discuss the prospects for a new collective bargaining agreement.

Instead, I wound up sitting at home watching the game on TV with Phil thanks to a fierce Texas snowstorm.

I had been scheduled to fly to Dallas last Thursday on a 1:00 PM flight out of LAX. Then I was transferred to a 3:00 flight with the hope that the storm would abate.

No such luck. I was moved to a 4:30 flight and finally, all flights to Dallas were canceled.

The meeting was Friday. When I contacted a league official, I was told, "We have so many people stranded in L.A. that we are trying to put together a charter for tomorrow morning."

"That's great," I said. "Just give me the information and I'll be there."

They had a flight leaving at 8:00 AM from the same area of LAX where the Lakers' charter plane normally departs. For once, Phil was going to take me there and wave good-bye.

I got up at 4:30 AM because I had to make arrangements for my dog. At 6:00, I received a call to inform me there would be yet another delay, this one of at least three hours because of the continuing weather problems. Our charter was supposed to be coming out of Dallas to pick us up, but conditions prohibited it from taking off.

That meant that even if I was airborne by 9:00 AM, I was going to miss the meeting. I hadn't planned on going to the game, so now there was no point in heading to Dallas.

I felt awful about not being there because I made a commitment to be involved in the creation of a new collective bargaining agreement, and it's a responsibility I take seriously.

Even though this was an off weekend for the Lakers, I couldn't relax because all I could think about was what they were doing at the meeting and how I wasn't there to be part of it.

I kept looking at my clock and saying, "They're still in the meeting. They're still in the meeting."

I was uptight.

"I should be there," I told Phil. "I want to be there."

"How do you think I feel?" he snapped.

Phil's admission that missing the All-Star Game bothered him caught me off guard.

Even though he said "I need the weekend off" over and over, there's still a part of him that feels he should be coaching that squad because his team is No. 1 in the conference. But All-Star Game coaches are not permitted to hold the position two years in a row and Phil had that honor last season. Still, that rule hasn't quenched Phil's fire.

The revelation that our feelings were identical resulted in a bonding moment that we both laughed about.

As it turned out, NBA commissioner David Stern described the committee meeting as a lot of theatrics.

Upon hearing that, my dad told me, "I'm kind of glad you didn't have to go through that."

This will be an ongoing process, but the important thing is to keep the ball moving.

Phil and I watched the All-Star Game and were both struck by how beautiful the setup was in that huge stadium.

Defense is not a cornerstone of that game, but it sure is fun to watch. We flipped back and forth between that and the Olympics.

Kobe didn't play because of a sprained ankle. He knows what is best for him, and I'm glad he made that decision. It couldn't have been easy for him, the ultimate competitor, to sit out a game played in front of 108,713 fans.

It was frustrating for league officials as well. One of the worst things that can happen when promoting an event is to have your star unavailable. And even amongst this group of players, Kobe is the star.

I've never had 108,000 people show up for an event I've promoted, but back when I was running the tennis program at the Forum, I occasionally had 16,000 fans fill the seats expecting to see a big name only to have that player drop out for some reason.

Two examples stand out in my mind. Ivan Lendl didn't play on one occasion because he said he had to have his teeth fixed (they didn't look fixed to me), and Tracy Austin couldn't play after having hot coffee accidentally spilled on her at a Marie Callender's restaurant.

No matter how understandable the reason, it's always disappointing.

Watching the weekend events, I came up with two ideas that might appeal to fans.

One would be to change the slam dunk contest. They should take the full All-Star squads—all those guys wind up attending the competition on Saturday night anyway—and make it a shootout like in hockey. It would be East versus West. The two sides would take turns attempting dunks, and the tension would grow as the competition neared its climax.

For the All-Star Game itself, I would like to see the players selected totally by the fans. Whoever they want to see, that's who they should see.

Then I would have the two coaches select their teams draft style, regardless of conference, alternating picks the way it is done in a pickup game on the playground or schoolyard.

I'll take him.

Then I'll take him.

And so on.

Do it on Saturday so a game jersey can be produced for Sunday.

It would put the coaches in a unique position. The fans could argue about who was picked first or second and who was picked last. No one would want to be that guy.

I know the All-Stars would never go for that format. It might be embarrassing to the players selected for the final few slots.

My inspiration for this idea is all those wacky reality shows I watch that Phil makes me turn off when he's home.

ALONG WITH AEG (Anschutz Entertainment Group), we have commissioned renowned sculptors/artists Julie Rotblatt Amrany and Omri Amrany to create a Chick Hearn statue. It hasn't been publicly announced, but the statue is almost done and Chick's widow Marge knows about it. It will be unveiled during the playoffs.

My dream is to commission another statue for the next All-Star Game because it is going to be here at STAPLES Center next season.

We dedicated the Magic Johnson statue in 2004 as part of the festivities the last time the All-Star Game was here.

Who is the next Laker deserving of the honor? Some would say Jerry West.

Others would favor Kareem.

It's a tough choice.

February 16
LAKERS 104, WARRIORS 94

While I am content with the Lakers' win tonight, the best part of the evening was the drive to STAPLES Center because it included a cell phone conversation with the surgeon who removed cataracts from both eyes of my dog Princess Cujo earlier today.

The surgeon told me she could say with certainty that the operation, which also involved the implanting of two lenses, was a complete success. My dog's vision, the surgeon said, will be about 95 percent of what it was before the cataracts formed.

What a gigantic relief. I went from being a nervous wreck to being thrilled beyond belief.

Princess Cujo was still coming out of the anesthesia, which is always risky because she is diabetic. But that didn't detract from the good news.

They may even let me take her home tomorrow, but not until they have made sure that her blood sugar is back to normal.

Performing this procedure on dogs is not new and can be very successful, but sometimes it can be hard to find lenses that fit because they are not made specifically for dogs. If they can't find a fit, a dog may get back only two-thirds of its vision following cataract surgery, but at least light comes in and the animal can make out shadows.

It's been distressing for me because Princess Cujo had deteriorated into nearly total blindness over the past two weeks. At first she had limited vision, then she could see only shadows. Finally, it got to the point where she was walking into walls. Her eyes had become gray and cloudy.

It was so upsetting because I knew she was getting depressed. She could no longer assert herself in her normal dominant manner. She couldn't even go up and down stairs because she had no depth perception.

I could tell she was trying to adjust, trying so hard to be her former self.

She was scared and couldn't understand what was happening. I couldn't explain to her that I was going to find someone to fix her eyes.

When dogs that run in a pack start to go through the dying process, they will hide because they instinctively know the rest of the pack will push out any weak links. And they don't want to be perceived as weak.

I've been told that 75 percent of dogs who are diabetic get cataracts. When they start to form, the dog's vision can go really quickly. There are dogs that go blind in a day or two.

Knowing that, I have been going through an agonizing few weeks. First, Princess Cujo had to undergo a procedure to make sure she really had cataracts and that her condition was worsening.

Then doctors had to run a test to make sure she could withstand the surgery because of the diabetes. It was a two-week process before she finally had the surgery.

It was performed by an eye doctor for animals in Culver City.

I've been warned that the postoperative stage won't be easy, either. Princess Cujo has stitches in her eyes and will have to wear one of those cone gadgets around her neck to prevent her from rubbing her eyes with her paws. Doing that could damage her chances for a full recovery.

She will have to wear the cone for two weeks, she'll need to have eye drops administered to her, and she'll be on pain medication.

I will have to have somebody with her at all times.

But at least she will be home. For me, that will bring new meaning to the old saying, "a sight for sore eyes."

February 17

I'm being pulled in three directions.

I picked Princess Cujo up today at the hospital, but even though she is home and doing better, she still needs a lot of attention.

That worries me, but just seeing her improvement makes it all worthwhile. Before the surgery, she pointed her head in my direction after hearing my voice or smelling me, but she couldn't make eye contact.

Now when I come into a room, she looks right at me and follows me around.

I went to tonight's premiere in Westwood of the HBO documentary, *Magic & Bird: A Courtship of Rivals*. It was tremendous and brought back a lot of memories of the Magic Johnson/Larry Bird era.

Phil went to dinner with some friends and wanted me to skip the premiere and go with them.

I graciously declined, feeling my place was at the premiere supporting Magic and representing the Lakers organization. Magic is part of the family and no one else in my family was attending.

Phil pouts a little bit when I don't choose him first, but it's important for me to do the right thing in terms of my position with the Lakers. I can't compromise by giving up who I am and what I've built over the years just to do what Phil wants me to do.

Time and time again, I think I've proved that my job is my priority.

I still laugh when I think about the day I first met Magic. It was in the summer of 1979. My dad had just bought the Lakers and I was staying with him at his house in Bel Air.

Magic, the top pick in the draft that year, was brought over to the house by Bill Sharman, then our general manager, to meet my dad.

When the bell rang, my father told me, "I'm still getting ready. Sit them down in the living room and ask if they want something to drink."

I opened the door and there was this big guy with a huge smile, a smile that just dazzled you. But I felt instantly comfortable with him because we were of the same generation. He was 19 and I was 17.

So in they came, Magic, Bill Sharman, and Dr. Charles Tucker, Magic's business advisor.

I sat them down, got them a drink—Magic asked for "a soda pop"— and with a big smile of my own told him, "I'm so excited you are going to be on the Lakers."

He replied, "I'm only going to be here for three years because I'm from Michigan and I want to play for Detroit."

I was stunned. I didn't know what to say.

I excused myself, ran to my dad, and told him in alarm, "Magic says he's only going to be here a couple of years. Then he's going to go play for Detroit because that's where he's from. What's going to happen?"

My dad, calm as ever, smiled and replied, "The first time he plays at the Forum, he is never going to want to leave."

I said, "Oh, okay."

My dad was right. Magic still hasn't left.

February 25

The Lakers won by just a point in Memphis on Tuesday night, leaving Phil unhappy with the way they were playing. Then we lost the next night in Dallas 101–96, and Phil was miserable.

So what else is new?

It's been that way lately. It doesn't matter if I'm feeding the dog or if I just walked in the door or if I've got my hands full of groceries. He's got to vent to me right then and there when he gets like that. He'll call the house phone and he'll call the cell phone and he'll keep calling until he reaches me.

Sometimes he'll be sitting on the team bus or the plane surrounded by people so he really can't say anything, but he's still mad. It's almost like we have to listen to each other breathe.

Am I supposed to change the subject and talk about something else? I have to play a guessing game. Are you upset because we didn't shoot well? Are you angry at the officials?

Warmer? Am I getting warmer? Hello?

Often, I get one-word answers.

TONIGHT WAS AN OFF NIGHT for the Lakers, and we co-hosted, along with the Los Angeles Sports and Entertainment Commission (LASEC), an event at STAPLES Center called Basketball 101.

There are only so many community events the Lakers can participate in, and we already have a casino night and a golf tournament. I thought we needed to focus some of our time and resources on promoting the game of basketball.

You don't have to play the sport to enjoy it as a fan. But by understanding the nuances of the game, some of the thought processes behind an offense, or why a particular matchup is good or bad, you can deepen your connection to it.

I learned from attending this event a few years ago how the point guard starts the play from the point of penetration and the attributes Phil looks for in a point guard.

I would like fans to have the opportunity to learn these things as well and ask any questions that come to mind. That's the idea behind Basketball 101, which began five years ago.

It started because of a good friend, probably the best friend I made in college, Kathy Schloessman, now the president of LASEC.

Kathy created an event in L.A. seven years ago called NFL 101 in conjunction with that league. It's smart for the NFL to keep a profile in the Los Angeles market even though there hasn't been a team here in nearly 16 years.

I was talking to her about that event, and Basketball 101 evolved from that conversation.

Over the years, we've had some great male speakers like Kareem and Michael Cooper, but we've also had women like Ann Meyers Drysdale, Lisa Leslie, and Penny Marshall describe what they love about the game. Nearly half of our fans are female.

Tonight was really special to me because Jerry West appeared for the first time. Jerry and Phil were on a panel discussion that lasted about 40 minutes.

I don't know where or how it started, but there's this notion out there that Phil and Jerry don't get along.

Not even close to being true.

The subject tonight was building a championship team, and who knows more about that than those two guys?

They even played against each other in the 1972 NBA Finals—where Jerry's Lakers beat Phil's Knicks in five games—and in the '73 Finals, where Phil's Knicks returned the favor.

Their discussion tonight was lively, just what you would expect from two highly competitive men.

The setup for Basketball 101 is unique because we divide the STAPLES Center floor in half. One side features tables and a buffet and the other side is set up exactly the way it is for a game so people can shoot baskets. In addition, we give tours of the Lakers locker room, the only time the public can visit the team sanctuary.

We also brought down four of the championship trophies—all those that have been won since we moved to STAPLES Center—so people could take pictures with them. We treat those trophies with great care. There are special handlers who move them, and security is a top priority.

I don't think any of our other interactive events are comparable to Basketball 101 because it is on the Lakers' floor, but the night is expensive at $500 per ticket.

Still, many people come back every year. A lot of companies buy tables and entertain clients, and there are always plenty of kids in attendance.

All net proceeds from the event are split between the Lakers Youth Foundation and the nonprofit LASEC.

I AM CONSTANTLY LOOKING for ways to reach out to new fans, especially female fans. One idea I tried a few years ago was well received but poorly executed.

It was an alternative broadcast with all women behind the microphone. My inspiration was an old TV show called *Mystery Science Theater 3000*.

They would show an old "B" movie and in the foreground would be the silhouettes of people watching it and commenting on it.

That's what I was trying to copy by showing a game with female-only commentary. Executives at our broadcast partner, Fox Sports West, liked the idea, and they could pull it off because they have two regional sports channels in this market.

So on the regular channel that night you got the usual Lakers announcers. On the second channel, you got "Lakers' Living Room." It was an opportunity to watch a game with myself, Linda Rambis, Shaunie O'Neal (Shaq's then wife), Marge Hearn, and Lisa Leslie, all of us wired for sound.

Unfortunately, I couldn't seem to explain my vision to the producer. Instead of showing the game with us in the background, or just having us off camera completely, the cameras were trained on us and the game was in the background.

It didn't work.

But as technology creates additional delivery platforms, people are going to want to hear variety in the voices coming from those platforms.

Whether it's your traditional broadcast or female-only broadcasts or comedians or the cast of *Hoosiers* reunited to reflect on their experiences while watching an Indiana high school basketball game, there are going to be all sorts of formats available.

The live content of the game itself will still be the main attraction. That won't change. Everybody will want to watch the Super Bowl, but they'll want to do so via the telecast they are most comfortable with and the broadcasters they relate to.

COLD DAYS IN MOSCOW, HOT NIGHTS AT THE FORUM

MY DAD TRUSTED A 19-YEAR-OLD KID TO RUN THE L.A. STRINGS of World Team Tennis, and I succeeded against all odds.

But that was a one-month season.

Then he entrusted me again to expand the tennis program, and Linda Rambis and I created the Forum Tennis Challenge Series.

But the Forum, like every other arena, had a voracious appetite. There are 365 nights in the year and any night an arena is dark is a wasted opportunity.

So my dad came to me and said, "Add more events."

My title expanded to director of Forum Sports and Entertainment under Claire Rothman, the president and general manager of the building. Claire, now retired, was one of the most respected executives in our business. Not just one of the most respected women. Her gender didn't matter.

She ran the Spectrum in Philadelphia in the late 1960s and then was hired by Jack Kent Cooke to run the Forum in the mid-1970s.

When my dad assumed command, he was very comfortable keeping Claire in control.

Concerts are the bread and butter of an operation like the Forum. So you really have to have a good relationship with the music industry, and nobody was better connected than Claire.

It showed in our lineup of talent. Everybody from the Bee Gees to Neil Diamond performed there, with several live albums by singers such as Barbra Streisand recorded in our arena. Playing at the Forum was a must for an artist; it was the Madison Square Garden of the West. Claire built a fantastic reputation for the Forum that I was fortunate to inherit in 1995 when she left.

She was and still is a mentor to me, always supportive. If I call her about an issue I'm wrestling with, she will talk me through it, analyzing the pros and cons.

Now 81, she's still amazing. She's exactly who I want to be when I'm her age. She looks fantastic, travels, and is a very well-rounded person with time for the arts and her family. She has always understood what is important in life.

But I didn't automatically have her respect. That wouldn't be Claire. I had to earn it, and that only came with time.

Rather than taking advantage of my family ties, I plunged into my job because I had a passion for it. While I certainly didn't want to disappoint my dad, I did it for no one but myself. I think that was what ultimately earned me Claire's seal of approval.

Don't get me wrong. Claire can be tough. She never babied me. Too often, peers and superiors in business will humor a member of the owner's family because they are afraid of losing their jobs. Claire was never afraid to be frank with me. She wasn't busting my chops. She treated me no differently from any other employee. And that was really important in my growth because she provided me valuable feedback. So when she did praise me, it meant a lot.

Claire's tough love also helped me gain the respect of other people I worked with.

She really took notice in 1984 when Linda and I broke the record for the highest-grossing gate with the McEnroe vs. Connors tennis match.

Concert days at the Forum were always a trip. If it was a country concert, there were 16,000 cowboy hats in the arena. If it was the Rhythm Nation tour, then everyone dressed like Janet Jackson. I joined in whenever I had the chance.

When Neil Diamond took up residence at the Forum for his record-breaking 10 consecutive sold-out shows in 1989, we got a memo warning us that we were not to address or even look at him if we ran into him during rehearsal. If he addressed us, we were to always call him "Mr. Diamond."

My reaction? I definitely wasn't going to sneak in for the sound check.

When the Grateful Dead performed at the Forum, you could go into the parking lot and buy a variety of different items including tie-dyed T-shirts and brownies.

Fans of some bands formed mosh pits. Those are the nights where you walk the building in advance, checking for any potential trouble, because a hard-core heavy metal crowd can turn on you in an instant.

One band set up gigantic pillars on either side of the stage supporting huge artificial eyeballs. They were positioned to stare at the crowd. It was the creepiest prop I had ever seen.

Sitting in the audience with those eyeballs glaring at them elicited uneasiness in some fans and hostility in others.

I was thinking we were going to lose control of that crowd. The band was manipulating the fans in order to get them to respond. There was an edge in the air and you could feel it. Mass hysteria can lead to a disastrous outcome.

Thankfully we didn't have an incident that night, but it was a reminder that a lot of things that happen at a concert are initiated by the act itself because the performers want to create a certain atmosphere for their show.

When The Artist Formerly Known as Prince decided to make one of his comebacks and chose our venue, it was a big, big deal because he hadn't done a show for quite a while.

It was the hot topic on all the local music stations and when the tickets went on sale, they sold out immediately.

The question was whether or not he was really going to show up.

Less than half an hour before the doors opened, with a huge crowd already gathering in the parking lot, The Artist Formerly Known As Prince, having not yet arrived, called the promoter and said, "I just can't do it. I'm not ready."

He wasn't inspired. And that was it for him.

But what about us? This was the kind of situation that can cause fans to storm the box office. You never want to cancel an event once people are on the premises. You don't know what might happen.

At least we hadn't opened the doors yet, because once you do that it's much tougher to get people out.

So we had to go out and inform the fans that the show was off. I decided to be part of the group announcing the bad news. When you are a manager, you don't send your people out to do something you wouldn't do yourself.

Buck Martin, a member of our staff, made the announcement through a bullhorn that the concert was being canceled.

There was no rioting, not even any yelling. The fans totally understood.

The attitude was, "Oh, he's not feeling it? Okay, that's cool. If he's not in the right place, then he shouldn't be performing. Just let us know when he's going to be here and we'll come back."

Fans of Prince truly love and understand him. If it had been some rock and roll bands, there would have been a riot.

For one of our shows, a ticket broker put aside about 100 seats in a good location, but somehow forgot to resell them.

That meant when the artist came out, he was going to see a huge block of empty seats in the middle of a supposedly sold-out arena. That would have made no sense.

The promoter was panicking. "What am I going to do?" he asked.

I quickly approved a plan that didn't sit well with me—moving people from the cheaper seats to the better seats at no additional cost. But what else could I do at that point?

People upstairs were brought down to fill in the glaringly empty section that would have been staring the artist right in the face.

There was one promoter who convinced his artist to price every ticket in the building the same. The first row was $20, and the last row was $20. All that did was create a greater incentive for scalpers because the price for the best seats was artificially low. So low that scalpers could get at least 10 times the face value.

I don't know if the artist was part of a kickback scheme or if he just didn't get it.

Live Nation, one of the country's largest concert promoters, has merged with Ticketmaster, one of the leading service companies of its kind, to become Live Nation Entertainment.

Ticketmaster also has a consumer-to-consumer resale company called TicketExchange. So, in essence, they are competing with ticket brokers for the secondary market business.

It's the artists who should be making that money. If someone is going to spend $1,000 to see Miley Cyrus and wants to sit in the first row, and the ticket has a face value of $50, who deserves that additional $950?

Miley.

OUR REALISTIC GOAL AT THE FORUM was to be booked 250 nights a year. Basketball and hockey filled 125 to 130 of those evenings. We also had tennis exhibitions, volleyball games, and the Los Angeles Lazers indoor soccer team. In 1993, we added roller hockey. If we had a good year with concerts, we would host 25 to 30. In a bad year, maybe 10. We also always had special family shows like the Ice Capades, Harlem Globetrotters, and Sesame Street.

To fill the remaining gaps, we booked gymnastics, indoor rodeos, and any other attraction that could draw a crowd of at least 10,000.

One sport we had to pass on was arena football because our scoreboard at the Forum was too low to accommodate the arc of the ball on passes and kicks.

My dad, always the innovator, thought we should look beyond our shores for potential events. He looked way beyond, all the way to the Soviet Union.

This was in the mid-1980s, before the fall of the Berlin Wall, the dismantling of the Soviet empire, and the end of the Cold War.

My dad sent me, along with Claire, Linda Rambis, and attorney Jerry Fine to Moscow. The idea was to bring attractions like the Moscow Circus and the Leningrad Ice Ballet to Inglewood. The first step was to open up the lines of communication with the Soviet cultural ministry.

I went there filled with optimism, too young and inexperienced to understand how difficult a task this was going to be. It wasn't, I would soon learn, like dealing with Rod Stewart.

For our first meeting, we were ushered into a conference room along with our translator.

In most of the meetings I attend, everybody just takes a seat wherever he or she feels comfortable. That's what we did, spreading out around the table.

When the Russians walked in, we were told, "No, no, no. You can't sit like that." They made us move so that we were on one side with their contingent directly across from us. Since we had five people, they made sure they had five people.

They served us Pepsi, very proud of the fact that they had an American drink.

The Russians directed most of their conversation to our lawyer because he was a man. We had previously exchanged letters, so we came prepared with questions about the production and operation of the shows and the costs they had presented us in their proposal.

After they answered our questions, we asked if we could have 15 minutes alone in the room to talk among ourselves.

When the Russians left, we started going over the details of what we had heard. For example, we were told they would supply the bears for the circus. One of us mentioned we would need appropriate cages for the animals.

When we invited them back into the room, the first subject the Russians addressed was cages for the bears.

How did they know we were concerned about that?

Hmm. Could the room have been bugged? Had they listened to everything we said?

Yes, I was very young and naïve. What made me think we were going to have privacy over there?

That incident was typical of that trip. The conditions were awful. We went in the dead of winter and were frozen the whole time. There were no locks on the doors of our hotel rooms. And the food was terrible.

Linda was nauseated because she was pregnant, even though she didn't know it at the time. I was throwing up because even though I was warned not to drink the water, I rinsed my mouth when I brushed my teeth.

The worst part was that the trip proved to be a waste of time. Trying to get through all the Soviet red tape was like hacking your way through a jungle.

Their proposed deal was one-sided and would have required a lot of money from us up front.

What if they didn't show up in Inglewood? What recourse would we have? With too much cost and too much risk, we turned the deal down.

And after all that, we didn't even get to see the circus.

At that point, we just wanted to get out of there, so Linda and I took off early and went to Finland.

Our other trips over the years in search of talent for the Forum were much more enjoyable. For instance, we went to Wimbledon and the U.S. Open tennis tournament every year, hoping to sign players.

Anytime a new sport came along, my dad, always looking for new business for our arena, would throw it on my plate. Which was fine with me because I learned a lot that way.

One day in the early 1990s, he told me my next venture would be roller hockey.

"What's that?" I asked.

"Hockey on roller skates," my dad said.

My immediate response was, "Oh my gosh, this is embarrassing. I'm promoting roller derby. There goes my career."

Where would we get our players? We were going to use in-line skates, very popular at that time, rather than the quad skates used at the 1992 Olympics in Barcelona where roller hockey was a demonstration sport. Should we go to Venice Beach, a hub for inline skaters, put a stick in their hands, and see if they could handle a puck?

Instead, we found a lot of hockey players use in-line skates to train and stay in shape during the off-season, so we recruited some of them.

The players were all minor league ice hockey players, largely from the East Coast Hockey League.

In ice hockey, players can stop so sharply that the ice comes flying up from their skates. Our guys got adept enough to make that same jarring turn and stop on roller blades, thus punctuating the action of the sport.

We played on the subterranean cement floor of the Forum. It was a bad surface, strewn with metal pipes designed to keep the ice frozen. And there were divots for tethering the high wire for the circus aerial show. Our players were basically skating on potholes.

But it was a cheap event to operate, so we gave it a try for one night to see if anybody showed up.

A few thousand did, and I absolutely fell in love with the sport.

With that game as a launching pad, a 12-team league—Roller Hockey International—was formed to begin play in 1993.

We, of course, had the L.A. team. What were we going to call it? You want to make sure you don't pick something the headline writers can rhyme with "loser."

It was important to me to come up with a name that would describe the sport. If we were the L.A. Pilgrims or the L.A. Tidal Wave, how would anyone know what sport we were promoting?

I decided to go to Mattel, makers of various toys including the famous Hot Wheels cars. I wanted to name the team the L.A. Hot Wheels. "You pay me $25,000," I proposed to the Mattel executives, "and I'll put your logo on our jerseys. It would be a great promotion for you."

They said it was a really good idea and that they'd get back to me.

They contacted me three days later to say they liked my idea so much that they were only going to charge *us* $25,000 to license their logo.

I said, "No, no, you have to pay me because I'm promoting your product."

Their reply? "No, no, we don't let people use our logo unless they pay us."

So much for the L.A. Hot Wheels. It would have been different, that's for sure.

I decided to go with Thunder Blades, but it got shortened to Blades. That identified hockey in two ways: the blade of the skate and the blade of the stick.

Next came the team's colors. From a merchandising standpoint, I wanted colors that would look good with blue jeans. I chose neutrals—black, silver, and white—to serve as the core, but then I added a pop-out color called Quebec blue, so named because it was the color worn by the NHL's Quebec Nordiques (now the Phoenix Coyotes).

For the logo, I hired the graphic artist who designed the Mighty Ducks of Anaheim's logo, Nick Newton. For the Blades, we wanted a logo that would be considered cool and could hopefully generate the merchandise sales we badly needed.

The league owned the patent on the puck, which was made of rubber and specially designed for our sport. The patent was going to be our cash cow. The sales of the puck and licensed equipment would subsidize the league until it could be a stand-alone business.

There were roller rinks springing up everywhere, and kids were even taking over tennis and basketball courts and setting up goals. The sudden explosion in popularity was the promise of a bright future.

And we would have the exclusive right to manufacture the puck. Can you imagine if the NBA owned the patent on a basketball or if the NFL had the patent on a football and those leagues earned a royalty for every ball sold around the world?

Unfortunately, the person filling out the paperwork for the puck patent designated himself, rather than the league, as the patent holder, reaping hundreds of thousands of dollars while also beginning the eventual downfall of the league.

But I didn't foresee a bad ending for the sport in those days. Just the opposite, in fact.

In-line roller hockey was invented in America. If we could make that version an Olympic sport, the U.S. would be favored to win the gold medal. And if there is anything that will propel a sport in this country, it's when the U.S. is good at it. Here was something we could own and build on.

I thought this was going to be my life and I was going to wind up in the roller hockey Hall of Fame.

I hired Bobby Hull Jr., the Hall of Fame hockey player's son, as my coach. I wanted him to build a team with as many American-born players as possible.

Our first game was against the Oakland Skates in the Oakland-Alameda County Coliseum Arena. When the Blades were introduced and skated out, I was so full of pride because here they were, wearing the colors I had picked, the logo I had designed, and the name I had chosen. They were like my children. I actually felt a lump in my throat.

It turned out to be a wild, high-scoring sport, which made it that much better than ice hockey. A typical game in our league would end 10–9 or 12–10.

In that first game, one of the Oakland players scored a hat trick. Some fans responded by throwing their hats onto the playing surface.

The ushers reacted by trying to throw those fans out of the arena. They didn't realize that was the traditional hockey salute for a hat trick. That's why they call it a *hat* trick.

By the second season, we found that playing on a plastic tile surface called Sport Court was perfect for our game. There were innovations in skate design. The manufacturing companies were flooded with orders.

It was crazy. Everything was coming together.

The players were paid by the game: $250 if they won, $100 if they lost. There were no contracts and the pay never changed over the years.

Within a year, the number of teams in the league doubled to 24. We had a 24-game schedule spread over July, August, and September. We played 12-minute quarters with a halftime, and the game lasted less than two hours.

Hockey Hall of Famer Mark Messier bought the team in Tampa Bay. The very first team to play at the Arrowhead Pond of Anaheim wasn't the Ducks, but the Anaheim Bullfrogs roller hockey club. Because that arena was brand new then and the Bullfrogs were always good, they would draw 10,000 people. The most we had at the Forum was 7,000.

Even with the low salaries, adding up our expenses for uniforms, travel, lodging, and all sorts of other items, roller hockey was a money loser for us, but to me it was a 10-year project. If we could bite the bullet and wait until the seven-, eight-, and nine-year-old kids playing the game became young adults, things would turn around and we would have our core audience. We just wanted to stem the bleeding until then and stay in business.

At that point, the only people coming to our games were die-hard ice hockey fans who were bored in the summertime. It's hard to market a sport very few adults have actually played.

We felt our best option was to nurture the grass roots rather than spend a lot of money on marketing. That meant sending our players out to make appearances at the many roller rinks that were popping up and holding clinics. As soon as our games were over, we had tables and chairs set up on the court where fans could wait in line, meet the players, and ask for autographs. We wouldn't even let the players shower first.

It made for a popular finale to our games. Whether we won or lost, fans would stand in line for up to an hour and a half to get a player's signature.

It wasn't popular, however, with one of our players. Chris Nelson, a tall, talented defenseman who grew up in L.A., complained about the autograph session. He preferred to shower and go up to the Forum Club, bitching and bitching about this added obligation.

I finally said to him, "Okay, you're right. If you don't want to do it, I don't blame you. But here's what I'm going to have to do. I will take your name off the back of your jersey and out of the media guide. That way, nobody will care if they get your autograph because they won't know who you are."

He decided to join his teammates and accommodate the fans.

Things improved gradually for our team. Our attendance steadily increased. The players got better and better.

Interest spread internationally. There were teams in Canada, Germany, and Japan. The sport was gaining ground.

Every ingredient was working the way we had hoped. The league got a big boost by signing a contract with ESPN. We had dates on national TV. We signed a deal with Fox Sports Network to show some of our games locally.

But in the last of our five years in the league, I was confronted with a harsh reality that severely damaged my faith in the integrity of Roller Hockey International.

The information came from my head coach, Mark Hardy, who has been a player and assistant coach with the L.A. Kings.

"All I want to do is beat the Bullfrogs this year," he told me. "I don't even care if we win a championship. I think the Bullfrogs win because they are paying players under the table. I can get a couple of really good guys to come in, but I have to know how much I can spend."

"I am not going to cheat," I said. "That would kill us, not to mention the fact that the economics would not support it. I am not going to ruin the league."

"I don't think I can ever win in this league if I can't do that," he said.

"Okay," I told him, "how much would it cost to win a championship?"

"What do you mean?" he asked.

"How much do you need?" I repeated. "You tell me. A hundred thousand? A million?"

"I don't know...like a hundred thousand," he said.

"Okay, I'll give you the hundred thousand," I said, "but if you don't win a championship, I want the money back."

No surprise. He wouldn't take the offer.

Ultimately, the league was sunk due to bad management by league executives, beginning with the stealing of our patent on the puck, a patent that would have underwritten all of the league's expenses. As long as the people running Roller Hockey International were there, the league was never going to pay for itself.

In 1997, knowing we would soon be leaving the Forum and paying rent upon the completion of STAPLES Center, my dad asked me, "Do you see our roller hockey team sustaining itself?"

"To be honest with you, no," I said. "Management has repeatedly done things to sabotage our success, even though it has all these great things going for it. It grew to 24 teams too fast. Owners are cheating by paying players under the table. Then the cheating owners decided not to pay the players at all, which could result in a lawsuit."

So we folded the team.

It was a shame, and a total heartbreak for me. The league lasted two more seasons and then it folded, too.

At the end, I was so angry that I wasn't even speaking to half of the league's executives. When I told them we were done, they didn't try to change my mind because they probably figured that at least they got rid of someone who was questioning their motives.

There went my chance to get into the roller hockey Hall of Fame.

MARCH

12

March 1

I have lost my Lakers championship ring twice in my life. The first time, years ago, left me utterly terrified.

The second time, at yesterday's Lakers-Nuggets game, left me smiling in the end, my faith in humanity validated.

I was taking part in a book signing at STAPLES Center for a book chronicling the Lakers' half century in Los Angeles. Bill Sharman was there as well, adding his name to mine on each copy.

Also sitting with us was the book's editor, Narda Zacchino.

After asking people at signings what name they would like on the book and who their favorite Laker is, I often offer them the opportunity to try on my ring.

When I hand it to them, they sometimes shake because they are so excited. They put it on their finger and usually take a picture. The experience of putting on a championship ring is one most people will never have, so I like to share the opportunity whenever I can.

And it gives them something to do instead of just staring at me signing a book.

When I hand them the signed copy, they hand me back the ring.

Many fans ask me to take a picture with them, a request I never turn down, so it's easy to get distracted.

Yesterday, as I went back to signing books, something felt different. Then it hit me all of a sudden. My ring was gone!

Narda was distraught.

"Oh my gosh, where is it?" she asked. "I've got to call security."

I tried to calm her down.

"Don't worry," I told her, "we'll find it."

She ran over to security while I just kept signing books, because there were many people still in line and the game was starting. I didn't want to be responsible for people missing the second half of the biggest game of the month because they were waiting for me.

Narda came back with our head of security.

"I'm fine," I told him. "This is not a crime."

Narda, seeing that I had continued to handle the customers in her absence, told me, "I can't believe you are staying so calm."

"I promise you," I said, "a Lakers fan would not steal my ring. I know it. I'm sure somebody walked away with it simply because they were so in awe over the experience of wearing it. They just became absentminded."

The ring was replaceable, and I was not about to order a lockdown of STAPLES Center until the ring was produced.

Maybe I could re-create a scene from my school days when an item would disappear from the classroom. The teacher would say, "I'm going to turn my back and that (fill in the blank) had better be back on my desk before I turn around again or there will be repercussions."

Soon enough, my instincts were proven correct. Within a few minutes, an older couple walked up and handed me the precious metal.

"I'm so sorry," one of them said, "that we walked away with your ring."

When they left, Narda shook her head and said, "I cannot believe that. You are so trusting."

I reiterated my belief in the goodness of our fans.

"A person who would wait in line and have Bill Sharman and me sign their 50th anniversary book isn't here to steal my ring. It doesn't happen that way," I said.

That doesn't mean I'm naïve. I know there are people out there who wouldn't hesitate to steal a championship ring.

I speak from experience because I came face to face with one of them in one of the most frightening experiences of my life. That was the first time I lost my ring.

It was in the late 1980s when the Lakers and our offices were still at the Forum. I pulled into the parking lot around 10:00 in the morning, my usual arrival time.

It was a quiet day with no game that night, so there was no one around as I got out of my car.

To enter the Forum offices, you had to walk down a few stairs to reach the glass doors that led inside.

As I moved in that direction, I saw a guy head quickly down those stairs.

I assumed he was going into the building, but then I saw him standing at the bottom of the stairs just waiting. That seemed odd. What could he be waiting for?

My intuition told me something was fishy, but instead of trusting my feelings, I told myself I wasn't going to be afraid. *Don't be a chicken*, I thought.

As I reached the stairs, he pulled a gun out and said, "Give me all your jewelry."

I had plenty to give. I was wearing an engagement ring from Steve Timmons, a volleyball player I would later marry.

I was also wearing a diamond tennis bracelet, a charm bracelet, a diamond Presidential Rolex watch, diamond earrings, and my Lakers championship ring, engraved with my last name.

It was horrifying. With no one around to stop him, I didn't resist.

I put my purse down so I could take my jewelry off. He grabbed it all in his hands and said, "Okay, go in the building and don't call the police, because I know who you are, I know where you work, and I will come back and kill you. I am going to watch you walk into the building."

As I picked up my purse to go through the glass doors, he realized he hadn't taken my money. He screamed at me, "Come back!"

By then, I had turned my back on him, a person holding a gun on me. Who does that? I didn't know what else to do.

When I didn't turn back around, he started yelling, "Hey, hey, hey!"

I was five feet from the door, so I took two panicked steps, grabbed the door handle, and ran into the building, all the while hoping I wouldn't hear the heart-stopping sound of a gun going off.

Instead, it was suddenly completely quiet, the mysterious figure having disappeared up the stairs.

I called the police right away, but they never found him or any of my jewelry.

To this day, I am convinced he didn't just happen to be there when I arrived. He obviously knew me and knew my routine.

The police asked me to help them create a sketch of the armed robber, but I couldn't oblige. I hadn't looked at his face. I had just looked at the gun. I do remember he had a hat on and a white T-shirt with baggy pants.

The police also brought me in to look at a lineup. I couldn't positively identify any of the people they had assembled. But when one guy stepped forward, my palms started sweating and my body had a violent reaction. My guess is that was probably him, but I couldn't be sure.

I told the police I didn't want to go through that again. It was too emotional, too hard on me. It was like reliving the incident.

When I told my dad what had happened, he was horrified. It's a terrible thing to experience.

For months after that, I was scared every time I pulled up at the Forum. I had nightmares about the robbery for a long time.

I learned a great lesson that day: always trust your instincts.

March 7

MAGIC 96, LAKERS 94

Tonight was the Lakers' third straight defeat, the team's longest losing streak since Pau Gasol joined the team just over two years ago.

For this organization, losing three in a row is catastrophic. When I think about teams that lose 10, 12, 15 in a row, I imagine that's got to be really exhausting and demoralizing.

While on Twitter last night, I saw Ron Artest had tweeted a photo of his new hairstyle. His hair has been dyed blond and the word "defense" is etched into it in three languages: Hebrew, Japanese, and Hindu.

I knew Phil was out to dinner in Orlando, but he had his iPhone with him, so I cut and pasted the photo of Ron's hair and emailed it to Phil.

"Be prepared for this tomorrow," I wrote in the email. "Here's Ron's new hairdo."

I wasn't just passing along juicy gossip. I felt this was information Phil needed to know so that when he walked into practice today, he had already gone through the process of calculating what is on Ron's mind.

I'm sure his decision to go blond will, once again, elicit comparisons to Dennis Rodman, but as Phil says, they are nothing alike. They are both great basketball players, but the similarity ends there.

I think Phil just wants to know what is going on with Ron. Is he bored?

I think his barber is from Orlando, so my guess is Ron figured, Hey, I got a day off, so what else am I going to do? Since I'm playing on national TV, I'll do something for the fans.

Phil has rules, but he also knows he has to adjust because he can't treat everybody the same. He goes with his intuition.

Athletes train their bodies constantly, but they also have to train their minds in order to get the best performance out of their bodies. Phil understands that.

Over the years he has learned what players need, both physically and emotionally, to get through the long season. Maybe he doesn't always do the right thing, but I don't think any coach has ever done a better job of figuring his players out than Phil.

He'll figure Ron out.

March 8

A month ago, I was sitting home agonizing because bad weather had caused me to miss a league committee meeting in Dallas during All-Star weekend.

I made up for it today. I didn't miss a thing, bouncing from meeting to meeting at the league office in New York.

I flew in Sunday and today attended a meeting of the labor relations committee concerning negotiations for a new collective bargaining agreement; a planning committee meeting to discuss revenue-sharing ideas; and an interview with Michael Jordan, who is seeking league approval after reaching an agreement to purchase the Charlotte Bobcats.

Every prospective owner has to go through this process.

Obviously, Michael was no stranger to anybody in the room. We know his basketball credentials and we know he's got the branding smarts. The Jordan Brand, a division of Nike, is still one of the biggest-selling brands even though Michael hasn't been on an NBA court in seven years.

The only question about him is, how focused would he be as an owner? Does he really want to take on a potential headache?

Michael impressed me in the meeting. We all know MJ from his playing days and his memorable commercials, but this was Michael Jordan, the serious businessman. He looked dashing in his suit and tie, once again bringing style with him. I think he's really into being a successful owner. That's good news for the NBA and the fans in Charlotte.

Michael was already a part-owner of the Bobcats when the majority owner, Bob Johnson, got an offer from a group headed by George Postolos, former president and CEO of the Rockets. Written into Michael's agreement was the stipulation that he had 30 days to match any purchase offer.

It's one thing to have an option to buy, but quite another to exercise it. Especially on short notice.

Michael is expected to bring in other investors, but during the 30-day window the onus was on him. He stepped up in typical Michael fashion, just beating the clock before his option expired.

I had the good fortune to sit next to Dallas owner Mark Cuban at the meetings. He and I have a friendship based on mutual respect for each other.

I also have a lot of fun teasing him, whether it's about tweaking Phil or his appearance on *Dancing with the Stars*.

Mark asked me what it was like before he came in for his initial interview, seeking approval to purchase the Mavericks. He wanted to know what was discussed.

I was honest with him. I told him he was carefully scrutinized by the owners. They wanted to know what he could bring to the league.

They saw a young guy who had made a lot of money overnight, a member of the newly minted dot-com billionaires. That made the owners cautious because he didn't come with an established track record that could offer some clues as to how he would operate in the NBA. He was an unknown entity.

As it turned out, Mark has brought a lot of fresh ideas to the league. That's not surprising. He has a brilliant mind geared toward creative thinking and awareness of new technologies.

Before arriving at these meetings, he spoke at MIT. Mark is a hero to the people we refer to as the "geek squad."

Using statistics as the guiding light for the analysis of personnel is a trend in sports, personified by Oakland A's general manager Billy Beane and popularized in the book *Moneyball*. Mark is the leader of that trend in our league. He has even extended his use of statistical analysis to include the referees' tendencies and calls.

I look forward to seeing Mark at these meetings because he has a unique way of thinking. A lot of what he says has merit.

But only to a point, as far as the rest of the owners are concerned. You can't run every team in the NBA the same way. That's what makes the league so inimitable. What goes on in Boston is different from what goes on in L.A. You can't just come up with a formula and apply it to 30 different markets.

I'm all for taking emotion out of the mix when you are judging talent, but we can't forget the players are flesh and blood, not just names in a fantasy league. Simply assigning a number to someone is not enough. Elements like character and leadership have to be factored in.

Mark is also adept at marketing, understanding his product and his audience, but sometimes he seems to be speaking his own language. But trust me, I will always listen to what he has to say.

While talking to Mark made me optimistic about the long-term future of the league, I was pessimistic about how we were going to resolve some of the nagging questions that plague every professional sports league, such as labor peace and revenue disparity between large and small markets.

Overall, it was a lot to digest in one day.

March 9

Lakers 109, Raptors 107

Phil is concerned about the team. The Lakers' loss on Sunday to Orlando was their 18th of the season. Last season, the team lost a total of 17 games, and we've still got a month to go in the regular season.

It's disappointing to Phil. He expects better. He wants his players to show who they really are. They are being questioned.

I don't think comparisons to a year ago are fair because this isn't the same team. That's nothing new for Phil. In his 10 years here, he has had an ever-changing roster with Kobe being the only constant. Even Derek, a key component of Phil's Lakers teams, was gone for three seasons.

Change doesn't bother Phil. He accepts it as part of life. Both of his parents were ministers. His father believed that once he had delivered his message over the span of a few years, it was time to move on and find new listeners.

I think a big difference this season is the absence of Kurt Rambis. Phil misses him, especially on the road.

PHIL IS CRACKING THE WHIP to try to shake his players out of their malaise.

He made them sit and meditate for 20 minutes today at practice.

The idea is to get the players to clear their minds. For some of these guys, the way they clear their mind is to be physical. Now he's asking them *not* to be physical. They have to contemplate what's going on. They can't avoid it.

Phil sees meditation as a way to get his players connected, to channel their energy and their focus onto each other. It can be a very powerful tool.

There were players on Phil's teams in the past who would make funny noises while they were supposedly meditating.

Even in those instances of disruption, even if players insist "Oh, I'm not into it," Phil still requires them to go through the motions. He believes just getting the players to quiet down can be a form of meditation even if they don't realize it.

Phil has also tried to get me into meditation. The way he practices it requires the use of a kneeling board. You get on your knees with your legs bent and your butt sitting on the board. That gives you support and keeps the brunt of your weight off your heels.

I found it very uncomfortable. I couldn't really stay in the moment because all I could think about was how much I wanted to unfold my legs.

To Phil, it is really important to stay in the proper form. He thinks an athlete should be able to will his or her mind to override any resulting physical discomfort. I can see where that would be important in the teaching he does.

But I don't agree with that as it pertains to those who aren't in athletics. It shouldn't matter whether or not you are in the proper position. If, for example, you are unable to get out of bed because of an ailment or a disability, does that mean you can't meditate? That doesn't make sense to me.

I think there are different forms of meditation. I found that walking my dog works for me because it's a quiet time. I don't have my BlackBerry with me, giving me the chance to get in tune with the world around me.

I think meditation is different for each individual.

ONE ISSUE WAS RESOLVED before tonight's game. After shaving his head, Ron Artest is no longer a blond.

Even then, there was some residual purple dye on his scalp. Phil laughed about that.

Somebody in the trainer's room found a way before the tipoff to remove the dye, giving Ron a clean look.

And hopefully with tonight's victory the Lakers are off to a clean start to the final month of the regular season, leaving their struggles behind.

March 17

It may only be the middle of March with hopefully a lot of time remaining in this season, but we have already run out of time for setting ticket prices for next season.

At a luncheon meeting with my dad today, the decision was made to raise our prices slightly. We have the largest payroll in the league and must pay a substantial luxury tax. The team has justified that cost so far, but we must generate the revenue to continue to meet our financial obligations.

Hopefully we'll be able to offer our fans the opportunity to again watch the defending champions next season. The problem is we have to decide on our ticket prices before we know how we do in the playoffs.

It's a long process. We are required to submit our price list to the league for approval. Then we have to start billing for season tickets for next season, with the notices going out during the playoffs. There will be a deadline of sometime in July when people have to pay or lose their seats. That's why we have to make these decisions sooner rather than later.

The suggested price list originated with Tim Harris and Veronica Lawler, head of our season-ticket operation.

Along with their suggestions, I brought my dad an aggregate list of what other teams are doing pricewise. He doesn't look at all 30 teams, only those that are competitive with us, what they offer and what we offer. He was already aware of most if not all of that information. He keeps up on all aspects of finance around the league.

The state of the economy was also factored into our price increase. We've got to be very careful because there is sensitivity about prices these days. Everything's got its limits. My dad has a good feel for that, intuitively knowing when to push and when not to push.

Thankfully, we have kept the right balance, since our renewal rate last year was the highest in the league at 96 or 97 percent.

And beyond that, we are fortunate enough to have a waiting list. Although a fully refundable $100 deposit is required to get on the list, it has grown nearly as big as our list of season-ticket holders.

There are about 11,500 of them. In addition, there are approximately 4,000 to 5,000 premier and suite seats.

The remaining 3,000 tickets can't be sold as season seats because if we get to the Western Conference Finals or NBA Finals, those seats are turned over to the league for media and some of the NBA's partners. You can't ask somebody to buy a season ticket and then not be able to offer it to them for all the playoff rounds.

That's why on a game-by-game basis, we always have seats we can release for over-the-counter sales.

That is also why we don't specify to those on the waiting list which seats we may be available. We may never have anything to offer them.

My dad learned that lesson when he first bought the team. He wanted to free up 10 of the 100 courtside seats for the lawyers and accountants who had been involved in his complex purchase of the team.

Those seats on the floor were—if you can believe it—$15 each in 1979 when my dad took over.

He knew how difficult it was to buy those seats, since he had been trying to find an available pair for himself for a decade.

So my dad doubled the price to $30 each.

No cancellations.

He went to $60.

Still, no one budged.

My dad kept raising the price, and today those seats are $2,700 each for the regular season and start at $3,000 apiece for the playoffs. And it's still almost impossible to find an empty seat.

My dad found a unique way to explain the price hikes to his courtside-seat holders.

Having invited them to a meeting at the Forum, he decided on his approach as he walked through the parking lot.

He told his audience he had noticed a fleet of Rolls-Royces and BMWs parked outside. Quoting the prices of the day, he told them that while the average car costs $12,000, they were willing to spend up to $120,000—or 10 times the average price—for a luxury car.

So, my dad said, I think you should be willing to pay 10 times the average price for a courtside seat.

Like I said, there were no cancellations.

My dad, of course, comes from a real estate background where no two pieces of property are priced the same. When he bought the Lakers, there were two or three price levels for seats and that was it. Upstairs and downstairs. He told me that was not how real estate works. People will pay more for the better location. It's always about location, location, location.

It was my dad who created the Senate Seat program at the Forum. Those were basically suites without walls that included waitress service and parking. It was my dad's way of selling year-round seats in a building that didn't have suites. Once my dad was successful, other arenas copied the idea.

This is a good place to clear up a common misperception about Jack Nicholson not paying for his seats.

He's bought them every year since 1972. He likes that arrangement because as a paying customer, he's not obligated to do any sort of promotion for the organization or serve as a celebrity spokesman.

That's fine with us. Just Jack sitting there is statement enough.

And it is no coincidence that he is sitting next to the visiting team. That is called home-court advantage.

The one time he asked to be involved was when Chick Hearn passed away. Jack was happy to do interviews about the legendary broadcaster.

I LEARNED LESSONS ABOUT MARKETING and finances prior to my dad's third season as the Lakers' owner when he announced he was signing Magic Johnson to a 25-year, $25 million contract, then the richest in sports history.

That stunned fans and the media alike, but my dad told reporters, "In a few years, you will come back to me and tell me this is a bargain."

Based on Magic's crowd-pleasing charisma and championship-producing skills, it didn't even take a few years. Especially considering the way other salaries soared in the ensuing years.

My dad saw the publicity value of the contract. A million dollars per year was intriguing, sexy, and headline generating.

Of course, that was before salary caps. Back then you could do something like that, but nobody had ever thought of it before.

Even without the benefits he envisioned reaping from the contract, my dad could justify it for one simple reason. Ultimately, aside from lost interest payments, it didn't cost him anything.

It was a period of high interest rates. My dad explained to me that if you put $5 million into an account with an interest rate of 7.5 percent compounded yearly and didn't touch it for 25 years, you would have earned enough to pay Magic his salary plus get your principal back. So he secured the best player in the NBA and had his principal investment returned.

Now *that's* a bargain.

Magic was still operating under the terms of that contract when he had to retire after testing positive for HIV.

My dad told him, "I want to honor that contract. My plan is to give you a piece of the team. You've given me and the Lakers so much value." My father got a great deal of pleasure out of doing that for Magic. My dad has always treated people fairly, never going back on his word.

In the early years of my dad's ownership of the Kings, Marcel Dionne, Dave Taylor, and Charlie Simmer skated together on what was known as the Triple Crown Line.

When Charlie went into a contract year, my dad was determined to keep that line together. He and Charlie's representatives negotiated for several months, finally coming to a verbal agreement.

But before the contract was signed, Charlie shattered his right leg in a game against Toronto.

My dad could have said, "What contract? I don't remember agreeing to anything."

Instead, he signed the contract even though it took Charlie over a year to get back to full strength.

My dad is classy that way.

That doesn't mean he's a soft touch for tough agents. My dad is an effective negotiator and a good communicator, always explaining his position.

His grasp of finances is amazing. When the economy started to go down, he accurately predicted how much the league would lose in ticket revenue. He anticipates where the market is going and he can read trends. He stays true to the numbers and doesn't get overly emotional.

But his economic sense is based on more than just numbers. It's also a matter of understanding people's psyches. Are they going to be spenders or savers? How will they be affected by the job market?

Reading people and reading numbers is a combination that makes for a great entrepreneur and a world-class poker player.

March 18

Having played three times in the World Series of Poker and in various other tournaments over the years, my dad knows when to go all in and when to get out.

He also knows it is always better to know everybody else's hand before you have to play your own.

With that in mind, my dad is not about to make a decision on a coach for next season until he sees how this one turns out. If we don't win the championship, the inclination will be to make a change. The easiest thing to change would be the coach because most of the other key components are under contract.

What concerns me is that there are a lot of intriguing coaching jobs out there that may be gone by the time Phil knows his fate with the Lakers. If he does not come back to our organization and there is no other appealing direction to turn, he would have to sit out a year. If a new collective bargaining agreement is not signed, there could be a work stoppage, which would mean Phil would have to sit out another season after that. If he was gone for two years, my guess would be that he would never come back.

At this point, if Phil is not their choice I think the Lakers might offer the job to Byron Scott, and he'd take it, no matter what the terms, because this is his dream job.

Am I supposed to believe that Byron being in my dad's suite had nothing to do with a possible job in the future? I don't know.

My dad is going to do what he thinks is best for the team, which I certainly understand.

It will be so much easier if we win a championship, but there is nothing easy about repeating in this league.

WITH THE TIMBERWOLVES IN TOWN for tomorrow's game against the Lakers, Phil and I had dinner with Linda and Kurt Rambis last night. The conversation was spirited and lively, but it was bittersweet because we all miss Kurt. However, when Phil and Kurt started talking Xs and Os, Linda and I gave them some space. Old habits are hard to break.

March 21

LAKERS 99, WIZARDS 92

We held our first-ever Lakers Fan Jam this weekend at the Los Angeles Convention Center next to STAPLES Center.

We created a Lakers theme park with interactive activities for the whole family. Our goal was to connect with fans who never see the Lakers live because they can't get a ticket, and to make them feel part of the experience.

We partnered with the NBA, owners of the Pop-A-Shot (the league's version of an arcade game), the bungee run, and the seven-, eight-, and nine-foot-tall hoops, all of which are on display annually at the All-Star Game in the NBA All-Star Jam Session.

All of the Lakers made an appearance over the two days. People had to wait hours for an autograph Saturday, sometimes failing to get the one they wanted because we only had each player for one hour. They had practice Saturday and a shootaround and a game today.

For my autograph session, I teamed with Marge Hearn. We took Saturday morning when the players were at practice. I absolutely adored the experience because it was a chance to interact with so many fans.

Marge said her "Fran" would have stayed all day.

We included an attraction Chick in particular would have appreciated: an area where people could pretend to do play-by-play of a Lakers game.

After Marge and I were done, Kareem signed autographs for an hour, which was terrific because people went wild when he came out on the stage.

He is one of the most intelligent, thoughtful athletes who ever made a living playing this game. Unfortunately, because he is naturally introverted the public has often missed out on hearing from an intriguing observer of humanity unless they have taken the time to read some of the interesting books he has written.

Our fans couldn't get enough of him this weekend. They let him know how much they appreciate him.

Even though that still makes Kareem a bit uncomfortable, I think he's learned to embrace public adulation more in recent years.

On Saturday evening, Lamar Odom and Shannon Brown took a shot at the Guinness World Records mark for consecutive free throws by alternating shooters in 60 seconds. The previous record was 10. They made 25.

We had trouble fitting everybody into the Fan Jam Saturday because we were so overwhelmed by the demand.

That demonstrated how much this team means to this city. We can only fit 19,000 people into STAPLES Center for any given game, but Lakers fans go way beyond that number. Without them, this organization doesn't exist.

This weekend was a learning process. Now that we have given birth to Fan Jam, it will continue to evolve and improve.

The enthusiasm is certainly there. In two days, charging $15 per adult and $10 for children 12 and under, we sold more than 25,000 tickets.

March 24

LAKERS 92, SPURS 83

Jillian Samueli, daughter of the owners of the Anaheim Ducks, reached out to me for career advice, so I met her for lunch today.

I am often approached by students who want me to mentor them, but I never feel comfortable in that role because when they say they want to follow in my career path, I have to tell them that's not possible. My career path was based on my dad buying a team and giving me a job. How do you tell people to groom themselves to be in a position like mine? If this wasn't our family business, I don't know if I'd be where I am.

When Jillian, who is 24, contacted me, I figured this was somebody I could finally relate to. Maybe she can benefit from some of the experiences I've had and avoid some of the pitfalls I've seen.

I could see she's serious about wanting to be involved in the team that her family purchased five years ago.

For the last two years, she's been working in every department of her organization, something I can identify with. She also spent six months interning for the Toronto Maple Leafs. I'm sure it was difficult for her to leave her family and work for another organization, but it was a smart choice to experience sports management from someone else's point of view.

I gave Jillian advice that would have served me well at her age. I told her, "You've got to live your life in a conscientious manner because you will be scrutinized. It isn't merely a matter of what you can get away with. It's about doing the right thing, because that is the only way you are going to have integrity in this business. And that will cause people to believe what you say. If you take a public role with your team, integrity will be your most valuable asset. In this day and age, any mistakes you make, no matter how far in your past, will find their way back to you."

I enjoyed the afternoon. I gave Jillian my thoughts about growing up, what I wanted to accomplish, and how I went about reaching my goals. I got as much out of it as she did because it enabled me to look back at where I was when I was Jillian's age and reflect on the road I took to get where I am now.

She's different from me in that neither of her siblings—she has two sisters—are interested in the sports business. So if it stays in the family, she will be the heir apparent.

Her mom Susan is very active as the co-owner, a rarity in sports. The Samuelis remind me of the McCourts, owners of the Dodgers before they split up.

It's good for Jillian to have a powerful role model in her mother, giving her something to strive for. Jillian has made me a fan and I will be cheering for her as she continues on her path.

ALTHOUGH I WAS CAREFUL not to get involved in all the gossip surrounding the McCourts' divorce, I did discuss them with Jillian because I think their situation offers her a valuable lesson.

The McCourts' misstep, I told her, was taking their personal problems and putting them in the public eye. You don't ever want to do that, no matter who you are.

Enjoying a cigar with Phil after the 2000 NBA Finals. Yes, I took a couple of puffs. Just one of those things you do after winning (even if it doesn't taste that good).

Flying on the Lakers' team charter in 2002. I don't ever sit with Phil, so he comes back to visit me in the tourist section. I think he was quizzing me on the New York Times crossword puzzle.

This is a self-portrait of us on beautiful Flathead Lake in Montana in 2009. One of the many benefits of Phil's extraordinarily long arms is he can hold the camera far away enough to fit us both in the picture.

I was giddy over meeting Jay-Z. His jacket felt like heaven and he smelled really good! I hope he attends some NBA meetings soon since he is part owner of the New Jersey Nets.

If you ever have the pleasure of meeting Dodgers legend Tommy Lasorda, keep your ears open because you will learn something. I admire him as a professional and marvel at his energy.

Mark Cuban is smart and funny. I voted for him during his run on Dancing with the Stars. My favorite performance of his was the I Dream of Jeannie TV show tribute. He made a very good Major Nelson.

Tobey Maguire is a devoted Lakers fan, and when he found out how much I loved horses he invited me to be an extra in his 2003 film, Seabiscuit. I loved getting into costume and spending the day at Santa Anita Park reliving the 1930s era. The red lipstick was fantastic!

The Dog Whisperer himself, Cesar Milan, joined me at a Lakers game to help raise funds for the Morris Animal Foundation. He creates as much stir as any movie star when he's sitting on the floor. People want the best behavior out of their dogs and Cesar knows the formula.

Jim Carrey attended an L.A. Kings hockey game with his daughter Jane in 1997. As a gift I presented her one of Shaq's shoes. She got a kick out of it, as so many people do. One of my friends once put her baby in Shaq's shoe for a photo. His feet are impossibly big.

*Celebrity Lakers fans Penny Marshall and Ice Cube join legend Kareem Abdul-Jabbar and me in the exclusive Chairman's Room to celebrate the 20*th *anniversary of the Lakers' 1985 championship. That team is very close, probably because it was the first Lakers team to defeat the Boston Celtics in the Finals.*

My best buddy, Linda Rambis. We have shared so many experiences we are like a modern-day Lucy and Ethel. Or maybe Paris and Nicole. Or maybe just Linda and Jeanie.

The Lakers scorekeeper for 48 years, John Radcliffe passed away in 2009. We wanted to honor his wife Carolyn and their daughter Suzanne with a Lakers championship ring. I was humbled by Carolyn's graciousness. The scorer's table was renamed in John's memory.

One of the perks of my job is I get to play Vanna White and hand out the NBA championship rings. In 2009 we had each current Lakers player paired with a Lakers legend. It was Lakers fan nirvana! With so much talent on one court, I was surprised they didn't start a pickup game.

I think this is as close to a wedding photo as Phil and I will ever get. I'll take a championship ring any day. I cannot help but smile when I see his face. This was an intimate moment in front of 18,997 people!

This was taken in the Gold Room of the White House in 2010. In the past some players have complained about taking this trip, but that wasn't the case this time as all the Lakers were excited to meet President Obama. Derek Fisher looks presidential and ready to run in 2016.

Danielle Robb, Stacy Kennedy, Linda Rambis, and me in my "Kobelieve" T-shirt about to embark on the 2010 championship parade. During the parade fans were trying to throw a bottle of Hennessy to Ron Artest as a gift and it missed my head by inches. Good times.

Lakers win! I hoped this would be the ending to our 2010 season when I started writing this book. I stay away from the stage after a win, so Phil had to fight the crowd to find me for a hug. I felt so proud of him and all the players. I wish that feeling could last forever.

I first met Jamie McCourt when Phil and I went to a Dodgers game right after she and her husband bought the team. She had her PR person, assistant, and bodyguard all with her.

I don't understand the need for a posse. How do you get to know someone when he or she is surrounded by three other people? How do you engage in a one-on-one conversation? I never had an opportunity to get to know Jamie as a person, although we interact with the Dodgers organization all the time.

I would say the Dodger I interact with the most is Tommy Lasorda. I'll do anything for Tommy.

Jamie's style may have worked for her when she was with the team, but it wouldn't be comfortable for me.

I can't operate that way. I don't have someone else booking my calendar. I don't have layers of people you have to go through to get to me. I think it's important to be accessible rather than insulated from reality.

You have to interact with fans. You have to know what people are saying. Sometimes the Lakers are criticized or Phil is criticized or I am criticized. I don't let those things damage me, but I take everything in. I listen, because if you hear it again and again, maybe there is something to the feedback. But if you have people blocking the message, you've got no idea what is going on.

If your only gauge of public sentiment was reading the columns of T.J. Simers, Mark Heisler, and Bill Plaschke in the *Los Angeles Times*, entertaining as they are, I can see where you could become even more cut off.

In isolation, your inclination would be to deliver one message in response to criticism and tell everyone to take it or leave it, rather than having a two-way conversation with both the media and the fans.

I have always chosen to interact and take the criticism head on, no matter the consequences.

13

PASSIONS AND PRIORITIES: WIFE, PLAYMATE, AND NBA GOVERNOR

EVEN THOUGH IT'S BEEN MORE THAN 20 YEARS SINCE THAT DAY I stared down the barrel of a gun outside the Forum, I can still remember the resentment that briefly overcame my fear when the robber asked me to take off my engagement ring.

I was thinking, *This isn't mine to give you. This is from the man I'm going to marry. It's his.*

That man was Steve Timmons, an Olympian whom I had met in 1986 when I was promoting volleyball at the Forum.

We dated for nearly three years before we got engaged, and my passion for my job almost got in the way of his proposal.

Steve was scheduled to play in a beach volleyball tournament in Chicago and he asked me to go with him.

I turned him down.

"I need to stay here because I've got a tennis event at the Forum," I said. "This is my job and I've got to keep my priorities straight."

We got into a big fight about it.

"I don't understand what your big hang-up is about my not going to Chicago," I said. "You are going to be playing in a tournament anyway."

Then he dropped the bomb, right in the middle of our fight.

"Because I was going to ask you to marry me," he said.

"What?" I said after doing a double take. "Did you just ask me to marry you?"

"Yeah," he said, "I guess I did."

He had made arrangements for us to go to the top of Chicago's Sears Tower where he had planned to propose.

Not a good move on my part to turn down his travel plans, but how could I know what he had in mind?

Instead, he just gave me the ring and I said yes.

For a long time, I wanted to be Mary Tyler Moore, the career girl. Watching her show about an independent woman as I was growing up, the message was planted in my mind that you didn't really need a husband. You had your friends at work, your social girlfriends, and your dates. That seemed like a really cool life. I think that show was a big influence on a whole generation of women like me.

I was crazy about Steve because he was really bright, creative, and talented. I got to share the Olympics with him, both in 1988 in Seoul and in 1992 in Barcelona. I was proud of him for making those U.S. teams, and grateful for the fond memories I have of those experiences.

He had 80 percent of what I wanted in a mate. I was 28, three years younger than he was. I thought, *I'm already ancient. Who am I to think that if I keep looking I'm going to find somebody who is 100 percent of what I want? Nobody is perfect, especially me. I shouldn't look past somebody who has a lot of good qualities.*

I should have realized that the way the botched proposal weekend went was a sign the marriage was not going to go well, either.

I didn't go to Chicago even after I agreed to marry him, and that was one of his constant issues with me: that I made work too much of a priority over him.

After a yearlong engagement, we eloped and got married in Carmel on Valentine's Day, 1990.

That's the day I picked because I figured that way he'd never forget our anniversary.

When I told him the day, he said, "When is Valentine's Day, February 15th?"

I thought, *Oh, this is trouble.*

One of Steve's best friends, fellow volleyball player Karch Kiraly, and his wife Janna came along and served as our best man and matron of honor.

We had a big reception a few months later. My dad came with two dates. My mother was there, along with my brothers, my sister, Steve's family, and his volleyball teammates. It was fun.

But not for long. Soon after we got married, Steve signed a two-year deal to play volleyball in Italy for Il Messaggero Ravenna. Karch had previously signed with the team, which was based in the town of Ravenna on the Adriatic Coast south of Venice.

The club was run first class all the way, and we were treated wonderfully. But it was hard for me to go there and not be a businesswomen in my new surroundings. In that town, I was merely Steve's wife. That was uncomfortable for me because I was accustomed to my independence. I never changed my last name to his.

I would go to Italy for a month and come home for a month because I was still working full-time back in Los Angeles. And then, it was back to Italy for a month. That was also difficult.

It was fortunate that I was working on tennis events because most of the big tennis agents had offices in Europe. So that made it a little easier.

Still, my workload was hard on our marriage. It seemed to Steve that whenever we tried to carve out some time together, something would happen that would require me to get back to my business and my family. That frustrated him.

I didn't make my marriage my top priority, and I know that was not right. Even when we were back in Manhattan Beach, I would plan on being home from work by 6:00 PM, but things would come up at the office and I wouldn't get home until 7:30. So we ate dinner late. Phil has the same issues with me now.

But there were bigger issues between Steve and me. I have more of an "A" type personality and he was more of a chill-and-be-with-his-guys kind of person. That was tough for me to navigate, trying to operate in two different worlds.

While we were in Italy, Karch and Janna had their first child, Kristian. I grew close to this adorable baby as I watched him take his first steps. When Steve and I divorced, I lost contact with Karch and his family because they were Steve's friends. I also missed some of the other volleyball people I had spent time with, but that's what happens in a divorce.

The beginning of the end for Steve and me came when I gave him an ultimatum. That really surprised him. But looking back, I think we were on our way to breaking apart.

We were remodeling a house on The Strand, one of the most pedestrian-heavy streets in Manhattan Beach. I would come home and he would say, "What do you think?"

And I would ask, "What are you talking about?"

Steve had rearranged all the furniture and hung paintings and I wouldn't even notice. I'm not a creative person, while he had a real artistic eye.

I didn't fully appreciate that in him and I'm sure that was disappointing to him.

I thought Steve should understand how important my work was to me. Again, different priorities.

During the remodeling, we moved into my mom's condo in Manhattan Beach. She was living in San Diego at the time.

Steve had told me the remodel would take a couple of months, but it was going on a year and there was no end in sight. He was so creative that every time they knocked out a wall, he had another idea. It was an out-of-control project, a money pit. It was extremely stressful.

I was not thrilled about being 30 years old and living with my mom.

It all came to a head the day Steve told me he was about to leave on a weekend fishing trip with his buddies. I asked him not to go, telling him I really thought we needed the time alone to work out some issues in our marriage.

He said, "No, I've got to go. They are picking me up in half an hour."

That's when I dug my heels in.

"If you walk out that door," I said, "I am not going to be here when you get back."

He wouldn't budge.

"I'm going to go," he said.

He did.

And I went, too, making good on my threat to move out.

It was immaturity on my part, but once I drew the line, I didn't know how to erase it.

It wasn't just about the fishing trip. Steve and I had several challenging issues separating us. He traveled a lot. We didn't see eye to eye on money matters. And we didn't have a friendship to fall back on. I'm still friends with most of the men I've dated. But with Steve, when the marriage was over, the relationship was over.

I was angry and felt abandoned, something I've always had a fear of, so I wanted out of the marriage.

I got married thinking I would never go through a divorce. That was, by far, the most humbling experience of my life. It really makes you question your judgment. Although it was the right thing for both of us, it was devastating.

I moved in with my dad, Steve moved out of my mom's condo, and that was it. We have had maybe two more conversations since. I saw him once at a party, but didn't speak to him. I didn't know what to say.

My mom and dad were very supportive of me, but they wanted to make sure I wasn't being too rash. In retrospect, I probably was overreacting. But looking back, I believe it worked out for the best because Steve is now happily married, and I had the opportunity to be free to focus on the things that were really important to me without having to settle. I could do what I wanted without someone saying I couldn't.

SIX MONTHS BEFORE MY DIVORCE, John McEnroe and Tatum O'Neal had split up. John and I, friends for more than 10 years and both on the rebound, dated for a few weeks.

It started when he played in an event at the Forum, just one of those things that began with a "Hey, let's hang out."

But it wasn't meant to be. We soon realized there was a reason why we had always been just friends and no more than that. Our brief involvement was more about comfort and friendship.

He soon met and started dating Patty Smyth, the beautiful and super-cool rock and roll woman he is married to now, and John and I reverted back to our old platonic relationship.

I WAS 32 WHEN I GOT DIVORCED. I thought to myself, *Now what?*

I thought about all the things I still wanted to achieve, and one of them was to be part of the *Playboy* family. It wasn't like I said, "Gosh, I'd really like to be naked in a magazine. Let me see who I can call."

When I was growing up in the 1970s, my dad owned the Playboy Club in Phoenix and my Aunt Susan, his sister, was a bunny. So *Playboy* is something I have always felt comfortable with.

I contacted Marilyn Grabowski, the magazine's West Coast photo editor, and asked her about applying to pose for the magazine.

I did not mention my application to my mom or dad beforehand. After all, I *was* 32 years old.

"We start with a test photo shoot," Marilyn said. "So why don't we do that? Then we'll send the photos to Chicago and that's where they will approve or disapprove you for the magazine."

The test photos were shot at a house in the Hollywood Hills.

I didn't go into the shoot planning to make any demands. I wasn't about to say, "This is who I am and this is what I want to look like in the magazine." I wasn't going to try to pretend to be anything I wasn't.

We took the pictures and I was pleased with them, but I had to wait months to hear if I was going to make it or not.

Finally, they approved me. It didn't come with any requirements on their part like, "Oh, you need to get a breast enlargement and fix this and fix that." They wanted me just the way I was.

That was very flattering.

They wanted to do my actual shoot for the magazine at the Forum. The idea was to show what went on behind the scenes and in the locker room.

It was fitting that most of my pictures were taken there because that arena was such a big part of my life. To have that as the setting made it much more special to me.

But when the time came to actually disrobe, I was nervous. It's a moment of truth. Anytime you venture in front of a camera, there's anxiety. It's always intimidating. It doesn't matter if you have your clothes on or not.

I quickly realized, however, that it was only a big deal to me. The six or seven other people on the set—the makeup person, hairstylist, lighting technician, photographer, and assistants—were only concerned with doing their jobs.

Any hang-up you might have about your body is your hang-up, no one else's. You've got to be comfortable in your own skin.

It's all business on the set. It's not like they play music and make you feel like you're in a strip club. They want to get their shots and they want them to be lovely.

It was hard work. I know that sounds silly because I was lying down for half of the shots. But it's physically challenging because you have to turn this way and that to get in the desired poses and then stay perfectly still.

My body was exhausted when we were done, but my brain hadn't been challenged all day. That's when I knew I couldn't be a professional model; I need more intellectual stimulation.

I'm not saying modeling isn't challenging, because it is. It just that it's not for me. I cannot quiet my brain for that long.

The people on the set were professional and supportive. We shot over several days, six or seven hours per session, because once they spent two hours getting the makeup on and my hair done, they wanted to get as much accomplished as they could before they broke the set down and had to start all over again the next day.

The shoot was totally out of my hands. They are the experts. I wasn't worried that they weren't going to make me look attractive. They are artists, so good at creating beauty, and giving you a look that enhances you. I had complete faith in them.

I have to admit, it was flattering to be the center of attention, to be the star for a day.

I have known Hugh Hefner for 30 years, but once I started the process I didn't talk to him until the photo shoot had been completed. I wanted to be in the magazine based on my own merits, not because of my dad's relationship with Hef.

I didn't tell my dad I was posing until the release date for that month's magazine had been set. He said he had no idea that was something I had aspired to do.

His best line was the quote he gave to the media: "It will be the first issue of *Playboy* magazine that I will never see."

That was perfect. He was saying, "I approve of the magazine, but it is still my daughter."

It was humbling when I first saw the layout, but I was really happy with the way the photos portrayed me. Hef was very complimentary when he saw them.

Playboy subsequently asked me if I would agree to tape messages for a 900 number where people could call and hear me talking. They would be instructed to press #1 if they wanted to listen to my thoughts on sports business and so on. I politely declined.

When I was asked by the media what my next step was, I told them there were no additional steps, and that I had no plans to continue modeling.

It was simply something I wanted to do, and if I hadn't pursued it, no matter how it turned out, I would have regretted it because I would have made a decision based on other people's expectations of what I should or shouldn't be. I can't imagine missing that experience just because I was worried about what other people would say about me.

I have learned there are going to be people who don't like me, no matter what I do. It isn't about me. It's about them.

I'm thrilled with the choice I made.

I understand posing for *Playboy* magazine is not for everybody. My point is that if there is something you have always dreamed of doing, don't be intimidated or held back by the opinions of others. You will never know if you can reach your goal unless you try.

Could I do it now at 48? There is no way I would consider that. But 1995 was the right time for me.

In my opinion, no one who has posed for the magazine should have any regrets. All the women who are part of the *Playboy* family benefit from the manner in which the brand empowers them and presents them with various opportunities. That was especially true back in the 1970s. It was a chance for so many women to earn money, go to college, and gain their independence to do whatever they wanted to do. I have always been very supportive of all of them.

I get asked to sign my *Playboy* photos all the time, both in person and by mail. That will never go away. When I least expect it, someone hands me a copy of the magazine to autograph.

I had been warned by Patti McGuire, Jimmy Connors' wife and 1977 Playmate of the Year, to expect that. People would come up to her at a tennis event while Jimmy was playing and ask her to sign her *Playboy* photos.

Phil has seen the magazine. It has nothing to do with why he loves me or doesn't love me. He doesn't judge me like that, but he does tease me about the photo spread all the time.

I had a few people come down on me. Even some women in the sports industry voiced negative opinions of me in media publications. It just confirmed again that there are people who don't know me who are going to judge me. If I had listened to their idea of what my career should be or what my choices in life should be, I'd be living their lives, not mine.

MY FIRST BOARD OF GOVERNORS MEETING was in April of 1995. It was the same month my photos came out in *Playboy*. Talk about timing.

Each team is allowed one governor and up to three alternates. The governor is expected to be at every meeting. But with the schedules of these very successful people, they can't be available for every meeting, every vote, and every conference call. That's why there are alternate governors, like myself, who are allowed to attend the meetings.

My dad hadn't missed a board meeting until last year. As a matter of fact, he was the head of the board for many years, a prestigious title reflective of the respect the NBA family has for him.

The meetings are held twice a year: in October before the start of the season and in April before the start of the playoffs.

It is important to NBA commissioner David Stern that we have an active board that can provide him with feedback.

I was excited to finally be part of the NBA decision-making process after years of dealing with second-tier sports like World Team Tennis, indoor soccer, volleyball, and roller hockey. At those meetings, there was a lot of stress because most of the teams in those leagues weren't making money. Around the table at those gatherings, the questions always revolved around which teams were going under and who was struggling the most.

Again and again, I heard those owners say, "In order to stop losing money, let's add more games to the season."

I never understood that theory. Selling seats is like selling fish: if you exceed the customers' demand, a portion of your product will just sit there and rot. Until you sell all your seats, there is no point in adding games. Overextending is the kiss of death in any league.

I figured I would hear none of that at my first NBA meeting. It was the mid-1990s, the heyday of Michael Jordan. The league was growing, its games were a big event on NBC, the *Seinfeld* and *Friends* network, and the Dream Team had participated in the previous Olympics. We had arrived. We were at our peak.

I thought that when I got to the board meeting, everybody would be jolly because business was so good. People would be patting each other on the back, smoking cigars or putting their hands behind their heads with their feet propped up on the table.

Unfortunately that wasn't the case. Instead, it was like every other meeting I had gone to in every other league. Remember the movie *12 Angry Men*? This could have been called *12 Angry Owners*, except there were more than twice that many.

The meeting was held in a Manhattan hotel ballroom. Wearing a business suit, I walked in with my dad feeling fully prepared, having studied all the issues on the table.

Representatives of the same team sit together. At that time, John Jackson, who had run the boxing program at the Forum, was the other Lakers governor, a position now held by my brother Joey.

I didn't want to draw attention to myself, so the fact that my *Playboy* pictorial was hitting the stands that same month was not ideal.

It wasn't long before the attention came my way. "Let's welcome our newest addition," the commissioner said, pointing in my direction. The owners gave me a round of applause. I was embarrassed and blushed. I simply said hello and gave them all a little wave. Then I buried my head in the notes I was dutifully taking.

I received some particularly unwelcome attention when we broke for lunch. In the buffet line, the owner standing behind me reached out and squeezed my rear end.

Maybe he felt that since I was in *Playboy*, that's what I was looking for. Any woman of my generation would know that is not the case.

I whipped around and gave him a dirty look. He avoided my gaze and pretended like it never happened.

I never told my dad what had occurred.

The unfortunate gesture shouldn't be seen as any sort of indictment of NBA owners. Women have had to deal with stuff like that in every business. I am not the first. It was no big deal. It didn't diminish me as a person.

When the meeting resumed, someone from another team came over to my dad and said, "Jerry, there is a vote coming up this afternoon and I would like you to vote our way. It's really of crucial importance to me and vital to our organization. If you do this, you can count on me to vote with you on something that is important to your team."

These guys are the most competitive people in the world. That's why they own sports teams. They don't want to see another owner get an advantage. What this owner was asking for would have benefited his team perhaps at a cost to some of the other clubs. My dad saw right through that.

Although that owner didn't get my dad's vote, he did get my father's attention. You have to be a politician and work on building a consensus when you are face to face with your peers at these meetings.

I thought that because the owners were flourishing, they would be anxious to see their fellow owners enjoy success. I assumed they would feel that the better everyone does, the better the league will do. But it's not like that. It was an eye-opening experience for me.

I have to admit, I was a little jealous of anyone at that meeting who had a relatively new arena because we were still in the Forum, which was becoming archaic by that time. All the talk was of suites, VIP service, and high-tech video boards, all the things the Lakers didn't have despite all the success they had enjoyed. There were no plans at that time to build STAPLES Center.

David Stern runs the board meetings. I know some of his critics think he's too dominant, but I strongly disagree. I think he is a dynamic speaker and leader who is often able to get people to put aside their own best interests to achieve harmony. His mission is to make people understand that the bigger the pie, the bigger their slice.

David expresses that logic to not only the owners but also to the players' union, our sponsors, and our broadcast partners.

He has praised my father for being one of those who always votes for the well-being of the league, even if certain issues don't necessarily favor the Lakers.

I think David has been one of the most progressive commissioners in all of sports in terms of including women and minorities in various positions. The NBA has been recognized by the Institute for Diversity and Ethics in Sport for leading the way in diversity of gender and race.

There were several high-profile women at that board meeting, including Susan O'Malley, president of the then–Washington Bullets; Val Ackerman, special assistant to the commissioner and later president of the WNBA; and Heidi Ueberroth, director of the NBA's International Media Programs and now president of NBA International.

When I looked around the room during my first board meeting, I realized I was never going to be able to relate to a Bill Davidson, owner of the Detroit Pistons, or an Abe Pollin, who ran the Baltimore/Washington Bullets, now the Washington Wizards. Owners for 20 or 30 years even back then, there was no way they were ever going to listen to a new person like me. What was I going to be able to contribute?

So I decided I would do my best to absorb, to learn how the process works, but to keep my mouth shut and not interfere.

I realized that while I might never be a peer of the existing group, I was going to have something to offer future owners when they joined the league. I would be the veteran who could clue them in and answer their questions.

Since then, people like Mark Cuban, the Maloofs, Dan Gilbert, and Robert Sarver have joined the NBA's exclusive club. These owners are closer to me in age. Of course, they are self-made, powerful men, successful and rich beyond my wildest dreams, so I can't completely relate to them. But I've made the effort and I have been rewarded by being included on committees in recent years.

It takes time. I attended league meetings for more than 10 years without missing one before I was brought into the inner circle.

But my dad is still the legend. Everybody wants his opinion, especially David Stern. I will never replace Jerry Buss, but hopefully I add value by being who I am.

APRIL

April 1

Phil came home really down after the Lakers' 2–3 road trip. Considering how difficult their journey was and because they had no game today, I thought he would give the players the day off. He didn't.

There is a lot of sniping and grumpiness evident among both players and coaches, all of whom seem disgruntled by the trip.

This is what can happen when a team goes on the road and its weaknesses get exposed.

Phil will never make excuses, but we have key injuries to Andrew Bynum and Luke Walton. Luke, out because of a pinched nerve in his lower back, will hopefully return Sunday, and Bynum, hobbled by a strained Achilles tendon, will be back sooner rather than later.

I know these are the dog days of a long season, but there is a lot of hysteria out there about our chances in the playoffs, and I'm dismayed that people are being so critical. What is going on?

HEARING QUESTIONS ECHOING AROUND Southern California, my dad decided to personally calm the fans' nerves by showing up at today's practice at our El Segundo headquarters to connect with the players and demonstrate his support for them.

As soon as my dad walked onto the court, Derek Fisher, Ron Artest, Sasha Vujacic, and a couple of other players rushed over to welcome him. My dad has been producing champions since before many of these players were born, and his physical presence still brings energy to the room.

Nice timing by Dr. Buss, the best owner in sports.

I BECAME INVOLVED TODAY as well when I got a call that reinforced my feeling that fans are overreacting to our slump. It was from David Singer, producer of *Mason & Ireland*, the afternoon sports talk show on our flagship station, 710 ESPN.

"Will you please be our guest on the air?" David asked. "People are ready to jump off a building because the Lakers had a 2–3 road trip."

"What am I going to say?" I asked.

"Just hearing you address the issue," he replied, "will go a long way."

So I went on the air and told listeners that when we looked at the schedule last summer—one that was loaded with home games at the start of the season—we knew that some early success might lull fans into a false sense of how good the team was.

Some were even talking early in the season about the Lakers equaling or surpassing the Bulls' regular-season record of 72 wins. That will never happen because there is a new factor that didn't exist when Chicago set the mark in the 1995–96 season: TNT NBA Thursday.

Eight years ago, when the NBA agreed to an exclusive national broadcast for Thursday night games on TNT—the league's answer to *Monday Night Football*—it largely took one day out of the week for scheduling games because there are only three on Thursdays.

As a result, there are a lot more back-to-back situations, especially for the Lakers and Celtics, both of whom are very popular with TNT. When the Lakers play on a Thursday night at home, they have to play Friday night on the road because back-to-back home games are not scheduled.

Making it even more difficult, the TNT game in the western half of the country usually starts late to accommodate the earlier game in the East, and it runs long because of commercial breaks. That means a late departure for the airport, a late arrival in the predawn hours on the road, less sleep, less energy, and thus less chance of victory.

We are going to be facing that next week when the Lakers play Thursday night in Denver, then get on a plane, lose an hour, and play Friday night in Minneapolis.

When I told Phil that was a potential disaster waiting to happen, he said, "Just remember, in the playoffs, there are no back-to-back games."

TNT NBA Thursday has become a pop-culture phenomenon thanks to the studio broadcast team of Ernie Johnson, Kenny "the Jet" Smith, and

Charles Barkley. "Sir Charles," as he is fondly called, is so popular that he hosted *Saturday Night Live*, a role usually reserved for Hollywood stars and current high-profile athletes.

I could watch Charles, Kenny, and Ernie talk about anything. When they are on, it is must-see viewing and the ultimate reality show because you never know what Charles is going to say next.

The partnership between the NBA and TNT is a valuable asset for both entities. So TNT NBA Thursday is here to stay, which means, I believe, so is the Bulls' claim to the best regular-season record in NBA history.

April 2

Lakers 106, Jazz 92

This was a really good day even before the Lakers got a much-needed victory against Utah because we announced the signing of the greatest player in the NBA today, Kobe Bryant, to a three-year contract extension.

Hopefully, we'll have a chance to win some more titles with him. Back-to-back-to-back-to-back wouldn't be too bad.

I'm sure this agreement makes Kobe feel secure because he knows where he's going to be for a long time. He doesn't have to think about that anymore. He can maintain his focus on winning more championships, maybe more than Magic, Kareem, or Michael ever did.

What was noteworthy about this negotiation was that it was kept out of the media.

Since I am not involved in basketball decisions I was not part of the discussions, but it was with great relief that I heard the news last night.

Phil wasn't part of the conversations either, and it is probably better that way because he can stay in the moment and focus on winning now rather than worrying about the future.

It was certainly something that was on the minds of my dad, Mitch Kupchak, and my brother Jimmy. After winning a championship last season, they made a big commitment to Andrew Bynum and Pau Gasol, and if we didn't get this commitment from Kobe, it would have been disconcerting. The nucleus of this team is pretty special.

Just survey the rest of the league. It seems every team in the NBA is building its roster with the idea of trying to beat a Lakers squad that has so much power and depth.

This negotiation with Kobe was a lot different from two other instances when there was a question about his future with the team: once when he was a free agent in 2004, and the other when he asked to be traded in 2007 because he wasn't happy with the team's roster. This time, there wasn't any agony or much uncertainty, either for the team or for the fans.

THERE WERE PLENTY OF BOTH in the spring of 2004 after we lost to the Detroit Pistons in the NBA Finals. The futures of Kobe, Shaq, and Phil were all up in the air.

It was a lot like the tension before we got Shaq following the 1996 season. We had traded our center, Vlade Divac, with the hope we could get Shaq, who had played out his contract with Orlando and was a free agent. It was a huge risk because we couldn't talk to Shaq until the free-agent window of opportunity opened.

My dad was anxious about trading Vlade, who was both talented and popular, in order to free up cap space for Shaq and to get a shot at acquiring Kobe. My dad told me, "We are preparing for something that may not work out. If it does, it will be a huge home run. If it doesn't, then at least we tried and we'll figure out something else."

The move stressed me out. It may have been beyond my control, but I still lost a lot of sleep over it.

There is a tradition of great big men in our organization, from George Mikan to Wilt Chamberlain to Kareem Abdul-Jabbar, so if we could sign Shaq, we would continue that tradition and cement the franchise for another six, seven, or eight years.

Fast-forward to the end of those eight seasons and it became hard to watch what was going on with Shaq.

The Lakers didn't want to lose him, but negotiations weren't going well. Because Shaq's contract was grandfathered in from the previous collective bargaining agreement, he could earn more than players operating under the then-current CBA.

Still, my dad and Shaq had different numbers in mind. My dad was willing to extend Shaq's contract at $22 million per year. That would have easily made him one of the five highest-paid players in the league. Shaq, however, had made it clear he wanted something closer to $30 million.

Shaq still had a year left on his contract, but if he went into that final season dissatisfied, could we tolerate a guy who was screaming at my dad in the preseason to pay him what he thought he was worth? What if he just walked away when his contract expired? Wouldn't it be better for the Lakers to get something for him while they still could?

I don't think that when Shaq drew a line and said he wouldn't go any further down the pay scale, he imagined the Lakers would seriously consider trading him. Who trades a player like Shaquille O'Neal at that point in his career?

My dad, that's who.

I find it interesting that Shaq ended up signing a five-year deal with Miami for $100 million one year after we traded him there. He could have stayed with the Lakers and made more.

Trading Shaq had nothing to do with Kobe. It was totally a money issue.

Besides, their relationship wasn't as bad as the media made it seem. Phil never had a problem getting them to play together. There might have been personality conflicts off the court, but never on it.

For Kobe, the issue was the depth of Shaq's commitment to staying in shape. How do you motivate him other than calling him out publicly like Kobe did?

That's quite different from the media's claim that the situation had deteriorated so badly that Kobe demanded, "It's me or Shaq." If that had been the case—in light of the fact that my dad had made it clear he didn't want to lose Kobe—why would the Lakers have made Shaq a contract offer?

Nothing was certain.

At a home game during that period, an injured Kobe sat on the Lakers bench wearing Clippers colors: red, white, and blue. I thought to myself, *Wow, that's a message.*

The Lakers could have traded Shaq and lost Kobe in free agency at the same time. That was a realistic possibility.

Everyone was on pins and needles as the day of decision neared. Vacationing in Italy, my dad called Kobe and made an impassioned plea. It was my dad's strategy to be the last person to talk to Kobe before he made his decision.

Because Kobe was our free agent, we could offer him substantially more than any other team could. The rules give an advantage to the club attempting to keep its players when they become free agents.

I honestly think Kobe didn't know what he was going to do until the end. He really liked the idea of having different possibilities because he is somebody who is motivated by challenges. And going to a new team, no matter which team, would be a challenge.

So yeah, there were a lot of anxious moments.

When Kobe agreed to stay with the Lakers, my dad called from Italy to tell me, but I wasn't totally relieved until I saw it on ESPN. That made it official.

While Lakers fans were excited to have Kobe back, the loss of Shaq was tough, especially when it came to dealing with season-ticket holders, because we had gone through the renewal process before sending him to Miami. As rumors of Shaq's imminent departure spread, we received plenty of emails from our season-ticket holders who had already purchased their seats.

I know there were people who thought, *Oh, you did this on purpose. You waited to get the money from me before you traded Shaq.*

That, of course, was not the case.

There were a few people who wanted refunds after the trade. I think we got 12 cancellations. We looked back to see when those customers had bought their tickets and it turned out they had been purchased in 1996, after Shaq joined the Lakers. So I think those were people who were bigger fans of Shaq than of the Lakers.

Some season-ticket holders were actually happy Shaq was gone.

April 3

Before the season started, Sasha promised Phil that even if he disagreed with what Phil or any of the assistant coaches were telling him, he wouldn't talk back.

And if he broke that promise, Sasha said, "I'll buy the whole coaching staff dinner."

Sure enough, in Oklahoma City last week, Sasha reacted poorly when Jim Cleamons gave him instructions. When Brian Shaw interceded, he and Sasha had words.

It happened in a public setting, on the bench during a game for all to see.

Sasha is frustrated because of a lack of playing time, but that doesn't excuse his behavior. It was inappropriate.

"You need to listen to our feedback," Sasha was told by the coaches, "and live up to your obligations."

Phil's twin sons, Ben and Charley, are in town for the Easter holiday. The three of them went to dinner at a restaurant down the street from our house in Playa del Rey.

Guess who Phil ran into?

With all the dining choices in the area, Phil coincidentally picked the place where Sasha, his dad, and his girlfriend, tennis star Maria Sharapova, were eating.

Sasha picked up the tab for Phil and his sons, telling Phil, "Now I've taken care of my obligations."

"No," insisted Phil. "What about the other coaches?"

Sasha bought the rest of the coaching staff breakfast yesterday morning and was rewarded by Phil in last night's victory over Utah, getting into a game for the first time since his confrontation with the coaches.

I should talk to Sasha and tell him that when he was out with a shoulder injury a month ago, Phil told me a couple of times, "I really miss Sasha. I need him."

Every guy in the NBA has been a superstar on either his high school, college, or national team. Most of them soon learn they aren't going to be superstars in the NBA, but that role players are also very important.

Sasha hasn't learned that yet. I believe that he thinks because he's not a starter, because he doesn't play 30 minutes a game, that he's not part of the equation. He was signed not only for his offense but also for the defense he played in the playoffs last season. He is like a mosquito out there, annoying opponents and guarding them effectively. I wish Sasha would realize how valuable he is to the team.

April 5

I am absolutely thrilled by the news my father has been elected to the Naismith Memorial Basketball Hall of Fame. He deserves it not only because of the championships the Lakers have won under his ownership and the spirit my father has instilled in this city, but also because he has enriched the league, both philosophically and economically, in ways that will last forever.

A chemistry major in college, my father continued to mix different elements when he became owner of the Lakers, blending sports and entertainment in a unique formula that maximized the fan experience at Lakers games.

He has been copied by others, but will never be duplicated. His vision and his ability to execute that vision make my dad unique, and that's why he belongs in the Hall of Fame.

My father is a humble person. He normally doesn't enjoy having a big fuss made over him. He doesn't like attending ceremonies in his honor or having things named after him. Over the years, people have wanted to place his name on everything from racetracks to hospitals, but he was never really interested in such tributes, even though he sincerely appreciated the offers.

I once asked him if there was any honor he would enthusiastically embrace, and he said there were two that would mean a lot to him.

One was acceptance into the Hall of Fame, and the other was a star on the Hollywood Walk of Fame.

Now, my father has both.

His smile when he learned he had been voted into the Hall of Fame was different from any smile I've ever seen on his face. It wasn't the unbridled joy of winning an NBA title, but more a look of satisfaction about the recognition of his accomplishments.

The Hollywood star was meaningful because it represents the city my dad loves. He made Los Angeles his home so many years ago, coming here with little more than his optimism and his energy.

This city, he feels, nurtured him and provided him with an environment in which he could be successful. And to him, Hollywood epitomizes L.A.

The star was difficult to obtain because it isn't bestowed on entrepreneurs. To qualify, one must be a success in the entertainment or media business, which includes movies, music, television, and radio. The powers that be couldn't seem to get their minds around the idea that my father belonged there. He's not a media or entertainment star, we were told.

I campaigned for him by pointing out that my dad launched Prime Ticket, the first regional sports cable network. I said he should be included as a broadcast pioneer.

And that's the way he was accepted. Below his name on his Hollywood star is an icon of a television set.

And in August, my father's name will take its rightful place in Springfield, Massachusetts, in the hallowed halls of a sport he has served so well for so long.

WHILE PHIL WAS HAPPY ABOUT my father's selection, he was disappointed that his longtime assistant, Tex Winter, considered the father of the triangle offense, was again overlooked.

Even though Tex is in the Hall of Fame as a contributor, it would mean a lot to Phil to see Tex voted in as a coach.

Tex has been an inspiration to Phil. What began as two coaches working together evolved over the years into a father-son type of relationship. Phil's own father passed away when Phil was in his mid-thirties.

Phil was impressed by Tex's brilliant basketball mind even before they worked together. Phil had studied the triangle and understood its philosophy and value.

Tex understood Phil. When they were together with the Bulls and the Lakers, Tex was comfortable standing up to Phil when he didn't agree with him.

Phil appreciated and respected that because there are not a lot of people who would dare to do that.

Phil will continue to hope that he and Tex will be reunited someday in the Hall of Fame.

PHIL WAS IRRITATED BY yesterday's 19-point loss to the Spurs at STAPLES Center.

He knew he was going to pay for letting that frustration bubble over and criticizing one of the referees in his postgame press conference. Once you single out a referee by name, you've gone over the line by making it personal.

Sure enough, it was announced today that Phil was fined $35,000 by the league for his remarks.

I reprimanded him for his outburst when he got home. I pointed out that he is the national spokesperson for the Positive Coaching Alliance. How, I asked him, can you be Mr. Positive Coach when you are publicly questioning the motives of someone doing his job?

"I understand your disappointment in the outcome of the game," I said, "but when you go public with your feelings through the media, you're going to have to answer for that."

But that's Phil. He's emotional. He cares. I know a lot of people watch him sit courtside and think he doesn't have a pulse. That's just not true. When the game doesn't go well, his emotions churn inside of him and sometimes, when he goes in to face the media in an agitated frame of mind, his unhappiness comes out the way it did yesterday.

That was predictable. Phil gets edgy about having to talk to the press after a loss anyway. He was disappointed in his players yesterday and probably let them know that in the locker room. So he was coming out of an emotional situation and into a room full of cameras, microphones, and notebooks. That's not the best timing. If he could face the media two hours after a game, he would never say what he did. It's the heat of the moment that makes him react that way.

There are two sides to Phil's personality. He is a very fiery, competitive person who has worked hard at balancing that part of his nature with a desire to be calm, focused, and well balanced. He struggles with that like the rest of us do. He always wants to be on the better side, to tap into Buddhist values, but he's not always successful.

It's unfortunate because now airing his feelings is going to cost him a lot of money.

Believe me, Phil didn't devise a plan, making those remarks to get some subliminal message out. He would never employ a strategy that would prove to be so expensive. If he visualized himself writing the check, he might have kept his passion in check.

The Lakers cannot pay that fine. If we allowed a coach free rein—if we agreed to pay any fines he might incur—matters could get completely out of control. It's important that the league reminds Phil of its guidelines for public statements by hitting him in the wallet.

PHIL JOINED THE POSITIVE COACHING ALLIANCE nearly a decade ago when he heard that many kids drop out of organized sports because of a negative experience with their coaches. That, to Phil, is tragic. Kids shouldn't have to suffer through that type of experience. So Phil agreed to be a national spokesperson for the PCA.

He is not alone. Bill Bradley, Larry Brown, and Doc Rivers are just a few of the many sports figures who are members of the organization's national advisory board.

April 11
TRAIL BLAZERS 91, LAKERS 88

The Lakers continue to struggle and the negativity seems to be everywhere. Today, not even Phil was immune to it.

He is taking a lot of heat for drawing up a play for Pau Gasol to take a last-second three-pointer with the Lakers trailing the Trail Blazers by three at STAPLES Center.

When Pau missed, the questions began. Why would Phil do that? Did he forget he had Kobe on the floor? Is Phil falling asleep on the bench?

Portland's plan was to try to foul whoever had the ball, opting to give up two points, if necessary, rather than three. In searching for someone to get an open shot, Phil figured Pau would be the man least expected by the Trail Blazers to get that assignment.

It wasn't a desperation play, Phil said. Pau is a good long-range shooter. The plan worked perfectly as Pau, indeed, was left open, but the ball just didn't go in.

If it had, Phil would have been a genius. Because it didn't, Phil is supposedly losing his touch.

April 17

Here we are, on the eve of the playoffs, and Phil spent two hours tonight reading a cookbook and figuring out what he wanted to make for dinner.

For him, cooking is a stress reliever. Every coach has some refuge from the pressures of the game. Kurt Rambis, for example, likes to ease his mind by washing cars.

Phil's time in the kitchen was well spent. He made a fabulous dinner consisting of halibut, roasted sweet potatoes, and risotto with broccoli and onions. He really topped himself this time. This dish has become one of his best.

Even though there is trepidation among Lakers fans after watching their team lose six of its last nine games heading into the postseason, Phil remains a calming influence. He's been through this so many times before. He knows it's hard to keep a team playing at 100 percent efficiency all season long, but he's confident he will extract the maximum effort from everybody starting tomorrow.

Everybody, that is, whom he puts on the floor. Tonight, the number of reserves he can call on has shrunk by one. As Phil was making dinner, trainer Gary Vitti called to say he had the result of tests performed on DJ Mbenga, who was inadvertently hit in the left eye in practice earlier today. A hole was detected in DJ's retina and he immediately underwent laser surgery.

That sounds really serious. I figured he'd be out a long time based on the cataract surgery performed on Princess Cujo. Gary, however, said he was told DJ could possibly play in 72 hours.

That's amazing, I told Phil. After her surgery, Cujo had to wear a cone around her head for three weeks.

"Maybe," said Phil with a grin, "I should get DJ a cone."

Phil loves DJ because he's one of those players who sits on the bench and gets only a sparse amount of playing time, but when he gets in there, he plays like a starter.

Phil was already worried because Sasha will be out for the first round due to a sprained ankle, just when he was finally getting his groove back.

April 20
LAKERS 95, THUNDER 92
Another day, another $35,000.

For the second time in 10 days, Phil was fined that amount for remarks about the officiating. Last time, he zeroed in on one particular referee. This time, his target was less specific. Prior to the start of this playoff series against Oklahoma City, Phil wondered aloud about the fact that the

Thunder's Kevin Durant tied LeBron James for the league lead in free-throw attempts per game.

When I saw David Stern, I brought up Phil's twin fines. I wanted to beat David to the punch because I knew it was a subject he was planning to mention to me.

"I don't know why Phil says the things he says," I told David. "I can't control him. I can't make him stop. I know he is letting off steam, but to me, uttering those remarks almost makes the situation worse."

"I'm going to keep fining him," David said, "as long as he keeps talking about the officials."

I can understand that.

IT DRIZZLED BRIEFLY BEFORE tonight's game, but fortunately it didn't rain on Chick's parade.

This was the evening we unveiled the Chick Hearn statue in front of STAPLES Center at a ceremony attended by various members of the Lakers family, several of whom spoke. Also present was a large crowd of fans and, of course, Marge.

There are others in Lakers history who are also worthy of a statue, but being aware of how our fans feel about Chick, and knowing the street outside STAPLES Center is named Chick Hearn Court, we felt he was the logical choice.

The rainfall reminded me of the day in 1986 when Chick received his star on the Hollywood Walk of Fame. While tonight's moisture didn't amount to much, there was a torrential downpour that day on Hollywood Boulevard, so powerful that it was difficult to get to the ceremony.

At first, when those memories came flooding back to me, I feared it might be that way again today. But then the sun came out, and I couldn't be more pleased with how the event turned out.

Some people are honored with a bust. Others, like Magic, Wayne Gretzky, and Oscar De La Hoya—the three athletes on the STAPLES Center Walk of Fame—are given a full-body sculpture, standing as towering figures above the crowd.

For Chick, we had a different idea. We wanted him sitting, headphones on, clearly in the middle of a broadcast, an empty seat next to him where fans could pose with him, either putting their arms on his shoulder or pretending they are his color analyst.

It's perfect for Chick because he was so fan friendly. He would talk to everybody who approached him about their common love of the Lakers and the game of basketball. We wanted to capture his spirit and joy, and hopefully we did.

We didn't tell Marge about the dedication ceremony until it was scheduled. If the economy or some other factor had required us to put it on hold, she would have been terribly disappointed. When we did reveal the planned ceremony to her, she was thrilled.

When Marge went to sit next to the statue at the end of the ceremony, she put her hand on her lips and then on the lips of Chick's likeness. I felt, for that moment, she was closer to him than she had been in the eight years since he passed away. You could feel the bond they had shared, a marriage unsurpassed in terms of love and companionship.

I'm sure the ceremony was emotional for her. But to be able to give her this night, to let her see how beloved he still is, was wonderful.

The Lakers also owe a debt of gratitude to the people at AEG who own and manage STAPLES Center. They understand the value of creating areas at the venue where fans can gather. We are fortunate to have partners who value the fans and the community as we do.

April 22

THUNDER 101, LAKERS 96

Even though the Lakers won the first two games of the series, I knew Phil would be uneasy about heading to Oklahoma City. Sure enough, he texted me today that he managed to sleep only four hours last night, restless as he thought about what lay ahead.

He called me from the team bus while on the way to the arena but, because he is uncomfortable saying too much while surrounded by coaches and players, the connection was more emotional than verbal. The important thing is, he knows I'm there for him.

It was obvious watching Game 3 that the Lakers were stymied as they tried to force things rather than sticking with the game plan.

Phil doesn't feel the Thunder is better than his team. While he respects Oklahoma City's talent, he is confident the matchup favors the Lakers because of our big guys.

But the key could be Andrew Bynum's ability to regain the stamina and consistency he demonstrated before missing the final 13 games of the regular season due to a strained Achilles tendon. We really need him, because the Thunder doesn't have an answer for him.

WHEN PROMOTING PRESEASON games, I love to schedule the Lakers for the first event in a new arena because everyone wants to be a part of history while also checking out the venue. It's an easy way to sell tickets and expose the Lakers brand to an out-of-market audience.

We accomplished that goal at the Ford Center in Oklahoma City in the fall of 2002, back when the Thunder was still the Seattle SuperSonics. The Lakers and the Nuggets played in the first game on the Ford Center court. In those days, I didn't foresee an NBA team moving to Oklahoma City, but I knew after our preseason game that it could be a good market. We did really well in ticket sales.

The Oklahoma City fans showed their support again when the Hornets moved there from New Orleans for two seasons in the wake of the devastation caused by Hurricane Katrina in 2005. Although the Hornets relocated with only a month's notice, they were very successful as measured in terms of both attendance figures and corporate support.

Oklahoma City's fans are passionate about sports as they are again demonstrating with their fervor in their own team's first-ever home playoff games.

April 25

I talked to Phil after last night's loss in Oklahoma City that tied the series at 2–2, and he was very subdued. I tried to be upbeat and get his mind off the game.

He arrived home around 2:30 in the morning. I let him sleep in because he had given the team the day off, even though he later went to our El Segundo headquarters to meet for a couple of hours with his coaches to go over the game tape which, I'm sure, had to be painful to watch.

It was not a well-played game on our part. Pau missed the first two free throws in the first 10 seconds of the game and I thought, *Really? Is this how it's going to be?*

Well, that's exactly how it was.

I watched the game alone while doing my laundry. Anything to keep me busy so I didn't have to sit still.

Phil talks not only to his coaches and to me about the games, but to his kids as well. Having watched basketball their entire lives, they are good at giving him feedback and he trusts them.

His daughter Brooke is close to getting her PhD in psychology, so Phil finds it helpful to talk to her about the emotional state of the players.

We had dinner with Kurt and Linda Rambis last night and Phil talked to Kurt about the team as well. He was the architect of the Lakers' defense last season and has as much insight into the workings of this team as anybody. Kurt offers an additional set of eyes with the advantage of a little bit of distance.

I booked a massage for Phil to relax him. He also works out with a trainer, but even though we live by the beach, he will not take walks on the sand because he knows he'll be surrounded by well-meaning fans who won't give him the space he needs at times like this.

That's why his favorite escape is to get on his motorcycle. When Phil wears his helmet, nobody knows who he is.

I WENT TO THE *LOS ANGELES TIMES* FESTIVAL of Books at UCLA today to sign copies of the book celebrating the Lakers' 50 years in Los Angeles.

I dreaded facing the fans because I figured they were going to be upset and drill me with directives to pass on to Phil.

Instead, I was pleasantly surprised at how encouraging everybody was. They were actually cheering me up. When I hear that we are only as good as our last game, that's mostly the media talking. Our fans have been supporting us for decades.

One person told me that her 83-year-old mother keeps a stat book on the Lakers as a hobby. I can see her now, wearing a purple-and-gold outfit, diligently marking down every point, rebound, and assist.

Some people suggested off-season trades. I appreciate that they think we can send three or four of our bench players to Cleveland and get LeBron James. Everybody wants to be a general manager.

Or a coach.

April 27

LAKERS 111, THUNDER 87

When we were driving to STAPLES Center for tonight's game with the series tied 2–2, I told Phil, "Wow, this could be the last time we ever drive together to a Lakers game."

"Perish the thought," he said. "This is not the way it is going to end."

Having said that, Phil has nevertheless been lighting a lot of incense around the house. There's a burning smell in every room. It's a way for him to get into another mind-set or perhaps change the energy around him. He's been very meditative the last few days.

The best way for me to clear my mind is to distract myself by getting my nails done or walking my dog.

Phil has told the team, "You have to be focused. Stop the outside activities. This has to be your priority."

One of Phil's biggest concerns is that we are shorthanded because of injuries.

Oklahoma City has 15 players on its roster while the Lakers left a spot open. It's too late to change that now. Players can't be added during the playoffs. It would have been good fortune if we had filled that last slot with a utility player.

With somebody.

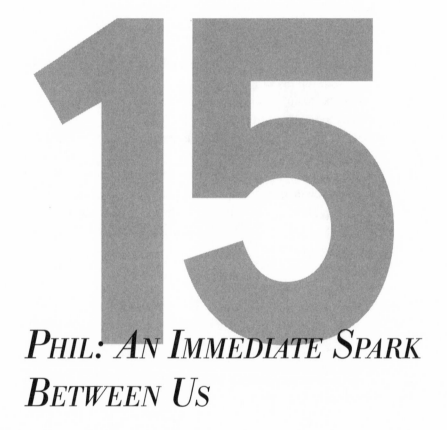

15

PHIL: AN IMMEDIATE SPARK BETWEEN US

AFTER THE LAKERS WERE SWEPT OUT OF THE PLAYOFFS IN 1999 by the Spurs, my father told me he wanted to hire Phil Jackson to coach the Lakers.

Bad idea, I told him.

Yes, I knew full well about the six titles Phil had won with the Bulls, but I also knew we had two of the biggest stars in the league in Shaquille O'Neal and Kobe Bryant, and the last thing we needed was another big ego to disturb the already delicate balance between the two. Better to let those guys be the stars, I figured, than some coach who might come in and try to be the center of attention.

What we needed, I said, was a lesser-known but still competent coach who could stay in the background.

I had just been named to the position I still hold—executive vice president of business operations for the Lakers—but I thought I knew what was best for the club.

But I didn't know Phil as a coach, and thankfully my dad doesn't always listen to my input.

As far as Phil the person goes, I also knew little. To me, he was a motorcycle-riding, Grateful Dead–loving hippie.

Didn't know if he was married. Didn't know if he had kids. Didn't care.

As a matter of fact, I avoided him at his introductory press conference. But when we finally did meet, I was impressed. I was struck by his personality, his imposing size and strength, and that voice. I was overpowered by his presence.

He was, all of sudden, a man in my eyes. A very attractive man.

And so, when word went around the office that he was in the process of getting a divorce, it caught my attention.

When my co-workers presented me with a cake on my birthday, I sent Phil a piece.

He stopped by my office to thank me and asked me out to dinner.

At first, I hesitated. It's not that it would be unusual to be friends with our coach. I had enjoyed a warm but always professional relationship with all our coaches during the years I had been working in the organization.

Mike Dunleavy came to my Forum tennis events. Del Harris would come to my office before every home game with three different ties and ask me to help him pick one to wear. I don't know if that was because he needed a female's opinion or if he was just superstitious.

But in Phil's case, I felt an immediate attraction. That made me feel awkward when I accepted his invitation, but deep down I hoped there was something there between us.

Having not found a house yet, Phil was staying in Century City, so I selected a conveniently located restaurant named Dominick's on Beverly Boulevard in West Hollywood. Another reason I picked it is that it's a really small place, so we would be less likely to run into people.

In this town, there are some restaurants—Mr Chow and The Ivy to name two—that seem to have paparazzi stationed outside night and day. Those are the places you go when you want to be seen with somebody. What I wanted was quiet conversation.

We had so many things to talk about in terms of the NBA in general and the Lakers in particular that the conversation could have gone on for hours.

We didn't, however, just talk about business. Even at that first dinner, we were very open about our feelings. I asked Phil up front, "Why am I here? Are you opening this line of communication for business or do you feel something? Because I have to tell you, I feel something."

I had just turned 38, I was single, and I approached my love life the same way I approached business matters: frankly and honestly.

It soon became obvious from the conversation that there was a mutual attraction, a spark between us. To me, he was extremely interesting and handsome, but I didn't know what his intentions were. I had no idea where he was in his life. So my guard was up, but that didn't stop me from feeling something special.

I certainly wasn't looking for a relationship with someone I worked with. While I was open to meeting somebody, I wouldn't have thought that was the match I was destined for.

I told Phil, "I don't want to have a secret affair with you. If we are going to see each other, important people in this organization are going to have to know about it, beginning with my boss...my father."

As I said, it wouldn't be unusual for me to be friendly with our coach, so being seen with Phil wouldn't raise any suspicions on its own. But I felt that trying to hide a real relationship could compromise both of us with my family, his family, and the organization.

I was determined to be honest with not only my dad but Jerry West and Mitch Kupchak as well. I wasn't sure how this was all going to work, but unless we agreed on full disclosure, I told Phil there was no need to continue. There wasn't going to be a clandestine relationship.

"Let's just see where things go," Phil said. "I don't want to define anything, but I understand your concerns. So if you feel that's important, then please tell the people you think need to know."

I know it was kind of premature on my part to bring it up so soon, but that's what you have to deal with as a couple when both of you are in the same company.

I'm not the first person to have met somebody at work.

It was extremely difficult to approach my father on a subject like this, but I felt it was the only way my relationship with Phil could work and not affect the organization.

The timing was bad because both Phil and I already had a lot on our respective plates. The Lakers were in training camp and he was running two-a-day workouts. On my end, we were in the process of moving from the Forum into STAPLES Center. Not only did that mean setting up new offices, but we were also preparing for opening night in the new arena.

Nevertheless, I wasn't going to be swayed from my determination to be transparent about my relationship with Phil.

I waited about two weeks and then told my father I needed to talk to him. A couple of days earlier, I had told my brother Jimmy about Phil and me, hoping he would tell my dad. I wanted that to happen so that when I did sit down with my father, he would have had a chance to process what Jimmy had told him, looking at it both logically and emotionally.

Jimmy's reaction had been, "Are you kidding?" He couldn't believe it.

I understand that because I didn't see it coming, either. I had never dated anybody in the Lakers organization and everybody knew I had not been real happy with Phil's hiring. Plus, Phil was very different from the men I had dated in the past.

When I finally sat down with my father at his house in Playa del Rey, his first comment was, "I'm glad you are dating someone older, someone who will appreciate you."

He handled it well. He didn't think of the organization first. He thought of his daughter. He wanted me to be happy.

But he also warned me about possible drawbacks. What if it didn't work out between Phil and the Lakers? After all, he was still a brand-new coach at that point. We weren't even in the regular season yet. It was October.

"I understand that," I told my father. "I don't know where this is going. I don't know how long it is going to last. But I'm not interested in doing anything undercover, living a secret life."

Once I had disclosed the relationship to my boss, there was no reason to be secretive. Phil and I weren't broadcasting our relationship to the world, but we weren't hiding it, either.

It took a while before people realized we were a couple.

Jerry West later told Phil he was surprised to hear about the blossoming romance. There are so many women in Los Angeles, Jerry told him. Couldn't you have found somebody without these complications?

All of a sudden, Phil was dating the owner's daughter. Was this part of some master plan?

Certainly not; it was just the opposite. Phil and I didn't have any clear plans for our future.

Even with my father's blessing, there were going to be difficulties. Phil still had to break the news to his family and figure out his situation.

His five children, including Brooke, who had moved with him to L.A., ranged in age from 20 to 31 at the time. Whenever children are involved, that's always an added complication in a new relationship.

And the kids were already experiencing emotional upheaval because of the divorce and Phil's acceptance of the Lakers job. He had been separated from June, his second wife and the mother of four of his children, for a while, but I think his departure for the West Coast was jarring for the children because they had spent most of their lives in either Chicago or Montana.

I was probably just one more thing the offspring didn't want to see coming over the horizon. I could relate to that stress having come from a family that had also experienced divorce.

Most people around me saw how content I was, so they were delighted for me. That certainly included my mom as well as my dad.

It was Phil who moved to Playa del Rey first. If he was going to be in L.A., he wanted to live on the beach.

I bought a house half a mile away. Then I bought another house a little bit closer to him. Finally, the house next door to Phil was put up for sale, so I bought it. In the course of seven years, I had moved closer and closer to him.

My friends make fun of me because I don't live in my houses very long. I've lived in nine different places since being on my own.

I handled the transactions myself without requiring anyone to look over my shoulder. I guess it was the real estate DNA passed on to me by my dad.

He went with me to the first place I purchased, but after having been taught by him about location, square footage, upkeep, and long-term considerations, I felt confident I could make the right decisions.

About three years ago, I was at it again. I sold the house next to Phil's and bought another one. But because my new home wasn't ready, I moved my belongings temporarily into Phil's house.

Once I moved in, I didn't want to leave and Phil didn't want me to go. That's how we ended up living together.

It took Phil to get me to finally put down roots.

THE 2003–04 SEASON HAD COME with high expectations for the Lakers because two high-profile free agents, Karl Malone and Gary Payton, had chosen to take less money and join the team in a quest to win their first championship.

We centered our marketing campaign around the slogan "Lakers Reloaded," playing off the hit movie *The Matrix Reloaded*. Having lost to San Antonio in the playoffs that year, the Lakers were gunning for another championship, and Payton and Malone seemed like the perfect ammunition.

Painfully for me and all Lakers fans, the team fell short, losing in five games to Detroit in the NBA Finals.

In the postgame news conference, there was a foreboding of the change to come.

"This summer," Shaq said, "is going to be a different summer for a lot of people…. Everyone is going to do what's best for them, including me."

Phil brought his five children to the podium for his comments, explaining that this was an important moment for the Jackson family.

It was all falling apart before my eyes.

Shaq was at a contract impasse with the organization, and we weren't sure if Kobe was staying either. Derek Fisher was about to opt out of his contract and Rick Fox was contemplating retirement.

There was a feeling that this was the end of an era, the end of the Lakers as we knew them.

When Phil returned from Detroit, he was ambivalent about staying on. He didn't want the team to break up, but if it did he knew he would be part of that breakup.

I think the feeling within the organization was the same. If the team wasn't coming back, then why bring Phil back?

My dad had already told me he didn't think he could keep the team together. If we did lose Shaq, and perhaps Kobe, and we had a team that wasn't a contender, would Phil even want to stay?

My dad wondered if Phil would lose interest. He didn't seem to my dad to be a coach who would want to go through a rebuilding process.

I just listened because I never get involved in those decisions.

Even if I had been tempted to say something, would I be saying it because I was advocating what was best for the organization or what was best for Jeanie?

I knew I couldn't be unbiased in that situation.

My dad had tried to sign Phil to a contract extension early that season, but that proposal had been taken off the table in January. So the writing was on the wall.

Phil wouldn't campaign for a new deal back then, so I knew when he went to meet with my dad after the season ended he wouldn't fight for his job. He went in completely open, like a leaf in the wind. In whatever direction Phil was pointed, he would go.

Had my dad said, "We really need you to stay," Phil might have stayed.

My greatest fear was that if Phil left, our relationship would be over as well. If he was no longer the coach of the Lakers, what did that mean for us? That's the part that scared me to death.

Phil wasn't interested in marriage, so there was nothing that bound us together other than coming to work at the same place every day.

When he went to meet with my father, I stayed home, waiting and waiting and waiting for Phil to come back.

Finally, he walked in the door and said, "That's it. I'm done."

I always knew that at some point, Phil and the Lakers would have to part ways. I had hoped that would occur as far in the future as possible. Certainly not this soon.

We already had plans that night to see *A Prairie Home Companion* at the Greek Theater with Phil's daughter Brooke and her husband Jack.

When the four of us got in the car, Phil had a bottle of champagne with him. He opened it up and we all drank a toast to the end of his career as Lakers coach.

Phil was very upbeat, but I was numb. I didn't know what to say. I couldn't imagine what would be next for him.

Phil wasn't worried at all. He started talking about all the things he wanted to do and all the trips he wanted to take and all the specific sights he wanted to see.

He planned a trip to the other side of the world in December and January to visit Luc Longley, one of his former players with the Bulls, in Australia. Phil would also stop in Sydney for the Australian Open and take a motorcycle tour of New Zealand.

Because the Lakers were in season, I couldn't join him on his two-month journey. That was hard on me and caused my old abandonment issues to resurface.

When I talked to my dad about Phil's departure, he said, "It was time for a change, but the Lakers are going to remain competitive."

That was the basketball side of my father's decision to not bring Phil back.

As for how it affected me from a personal standpoint, my dad told me, "He won't marry you. I don't understand why. You are going to have to figure out how you feel about him. But I can't understand why he won't commit to you when you make it so obvious you want that commitment."

I felt really vulnerable.

Phil came back from his trip, then took off for his summer home in Montana. There was no reason for us to break up because we got along really well, but I just couldn't envision what our life was going to be like.

WHO WAS THE NEW COACH going to be? What was going to happen? There was a lot of turmoil.

Nobody in the organization would talk to me about who Phil's successor might be. Everybody was either being secretive or felt it was too sensitive a matter for me to deal with.

My only involvement in the process was to supply the emails from our season-ticket holders regarding their thoughts about the coaching situation.

I was pleased when I learned the Lakers had asked permission to speak with the Miami Heat's president, Pat Riley. Like other Lakers fans, I had a strong desire for the familiar and the successful. Pat turned down the job, but he didn't turn down the opportunity to get Shaq in a blockbuster trade a few weeks later.

Ultimately, the front office decided to hire Rudy Tomjanovich, who had won back-to-back NBA championships with the Rockets in the mid-1990s. My dad likes to go after winners.

Phil thought the selection of Rudy was curious. It's not that he didn't think Rudy could do the job, but Phil felt Rudy didn't fit in with what he was told the Lakers were trying to build.

I found myself in an awkward situation because neither Rudy nor his wife Sophie ever reached out to me. Not that I was that important in terms of the basketball operation, but one would think that given my position as a Lakers executive vice president, they would want to connect with me at some level.

Maybe Rudy thought it was best not to befriend me because I missed Phil so much. He was being protective and didn't want to upset me, or perhaps there was something else going on. I don't know. Either way, I didn't understand it.

But he wasn't that way just with me.

Here was a guy who had the great fortune to be with one organization—the Rockets—his entire career, going all the way back to his playing days. So he didn't have to work at getting to know the security guy downstairs or the person who ran the ticket office in Houston. Rudy knew everybody connected with the Rockets because he had been there so long.

I'm sure Rudy knew it was going to be different here, but he never seemed to feel comfortable in his new surroundings. He didn't reach out to get to know anybody on the business side of the Lakers. It is impossible to be successful in this industry when you can't build a consensus within your own organization because you haven't created and nurtured relationships.

It didn't make sense to me that he didn't sit down with Kurt Rambis to talk about the possibility of Kurt staying on the coaching staff. I guess you could say Rudy wanted a fresh start, yet he hired Frank Hamblen, who had been on Phil's staff since he arrived in L.A. I thought that was odd. Kurt, at the very least, deserved the courtesy of a conversation whether Rudy hired him or not. Kurt was a big part of Lakers history.

Rudy's link to the Lakers, on the other hand, included one of the darkest days in team history. Rudy was the player who was famously and seriously injured by a punch to the face thrown by the Lakers' Kermit Washington, a blow that put an ugly exclamation mark on a Lakers-Rockets brawl in a 1977 game. Rudy was so badly injured that he had to undergo five operations. An agreement on a settlement of Rudy's lawsuit against the Lakers wasn't reached until after my dad bought the team.

Getting over the negative images from the past would be a challenge under the best of circumstances, but coming off so many major changes, especially the trading of a superstar like Shaq, made it that much more difficult.

Rudy brought in assistant coaches who were qualified but had no past connection with the Lakers, except for Hamblen. A move like that was bold, but it didn't reflect the loyalty our fans had grown to know and expect from the Lakers.

Rudy had a five-year contract and probably figured he had plenty of time to win over the fans.

WHEN PHIL AND I SAID OUR GOOD-BYES as he embarked on his Australia trip, I was sobbing, feeling that was the end of our relationship.

Phil told me, "You have to have confidence in our love."

The only confidence I had was drawn from the fact that we had spent so much time together. Still, it was with pure dread that I faced the future.

Then a wonderful thing happened. We missed each other. He would call me every day, and it seemed the farther we were apart, the closer we grew to each other. Our love wasn't about the convenience of time and space, but a connection of our hearts. I had never experienced such a complete bond with someone. I knew then that we were going to make it.

But there were still rough times ahead.

Prior to the 2003–04 season, Phil had committed to writing a book to chronicle what many had believed would surely be a championship season. He wrote it as a journal in real time, the entries unfolding as the season progressed.

The book was released at the start of the 2004–05 season. There were passages I knew would cause discomfort to some in the organization. It even caused friction between me and John Black, head of the team's public relations department. John wanted to refute the book by issuing a statement saying it contained "several inaccuracies," without elaborating on any of them.

I asked him to reconsider because that might make it difficult for Phil to ever rejoin the Lakers.

John was taken aback by the idea of Phil coming back. He assumed Phil would ride off into the Montana sunset. John remained adamant and issued the press release on October 14, 2004.

I was trying to rebuild a bridge that seemed like it had just been blown to smithereens.

BY JANUARY, THE LAKERS' OVERHAULED ROSTER was struggling to find a rhythm, teetering just above .500. Shaq, Rick Fox, and Gary Payton had been traded, Derek Fisher had left as a free agent, and Karl Malone had retired.

It was taking a while to get used to a new team that was more about fast breaks and less about defense.

Unfortunately, after 43 games (24–19) Rudy resigned, citing health problems. He had suffered from bladder cancer more than a year earlier and realized, he said, he wasn't ready to jump back into the rigors of NBA coaching.

Frank Hamblen was named to replace Rudy.

I HOPED PHIL WOULD CONSIDER coaching again. Although losing in the NBA Finals is tough to shake off, I got the feeling he still had more to give because he was watching NBA games and following all his former players.

Near the end of January, Knicks coach Lennie Wilkens, a Hall of Famer, resigned. That was the perfect job for Phil.

I couldn't wait to tell him about the opening, but he was somewhere in the Australian Outback with no cell phone reception.

I was going crazy waiting to talk to him because I felt so strongly that Phil's joining the Knicks was meant to be. It would ease the pain of his separation from the game he loved and bring him back full circle to the team that had drafted him. All the misery I had experienced was going to make sense.

Three days went by before I finally spoke to Phil. He was surprised to hear the news about the Knicks' coaching change, but he didn't indicate he was ready to apply.

After he arrived back in the States, the most astounding thing happened one night when we were home watching the Lakers on television.

It was a close game, coming down to the last play. The camera had zoomed in on Kobe in the huddle and Phil could read his lips.

Kobe called one of Phil's favorite plays: the "What the f**k" play (so named because Phil's mentor, Knicks coach Red Holzman, used it but was always saying, "What the f**k was the name of that play?").

That was when I saw a glimmer of hope. Kobe and Phil were still on the same basketball page. Maybe, just maybe, there would be a reconciliation someday.

The Knicks did eventually come calling for Phil, and he spent an afternoon in April with Isiah Thomas, then the team's president.

I certainly wasn't going to stand in Phil's way. I encouraged him to listen to everything the Knicks had to say, but I was also going to let everyone know that my fondest wish would be for Phil to rejoin the Lakers.

It might have been selfish because his return would be good for me, but I knew it would also be good for the organization.

The Lakers won just two of their last 21 games in the 2004–05 season, finishing with a record of 34–48 and failing to make the playoffs for only the second time in the Dr. Buss era. The only positive of the whole experience was we got the No. 10 pick in the next NBA Draft, with which we selected Andrew Bynum.

In the end, both sides took a leap of faith. My dad opened his checkbook wide, Phil accepted his offer, and on June 14, 2005, in front of a large media gathering at STAPLES Center, Phil told the basketball world, "This is something I never thought could possibly happen. It's a pleasure to come back."

MAY

May 1

After the Lakers eliminated the Thunder in six games with a 95–94 victory in Oklahoma City last night, Phil arrived home at 2:30 in the morning with a big smile on his face. He was proud of his players' performance on a hostile court.

It reminded me of the look he had after the Lakers eliminated the Orlando Magic in Game 5 of the NBA Finals last season, a look of total satisfaction.

But relief might better characterize the feeling after last night's game. It came down to the final second. Pau Gasol, poised under the basket, controlled a missed shot by Kobe and put the ball in the hoop for the series-clinching points with 0.5 showing on the clock.

It's said that luck occurs when preparation meets opportunity. Pau was prepared. He didn't stand around hoping Kobe's shot would go in. In case it didn't, Pau was ready to respond.

Phil likened last night's clincher to Game 7 in last season's Western Conference Semifinals against Houston, when the Lakers bonded as a team and fused into a championship club. Games like these can bring out the urgency and the focus needed for playoff basketball.

Phil was concerned after the last month of this year's regular season, but he never lost hope, never thought the team wouldn't be able to find its momentum.

Still, he had warned me before the playoffs started that the toughest series in any postseason is often the first round because that's where upsets occur if a team is not prepared.

Oklahoma City's lack of playoff experience showed. The Thunder learned the difference between the regular season and the postseason. This series should serve that team well as it continues to grow.

Phil's satisfaction was fleeting. By the time he got up today, he had already switched gears mentally and was formulating a game plan for the Lakers' next opponent, the Utah Jazz.

May 2
LAKERS 104, JAZZ 99

During the drive with Phil to today's game, I got a text from my dad. He wanted me to know he has invited Mike Dunleavy to watch the game from his suite. After resigning from his job as head coach of the Clippers this season, Mike was let go from his position as general manager as well.

I already knew, of course, that Byron Scott had been my dad's guest in his suite earlier this season and I have since learned Jeff Van Gundy also accepted an invitation.

My father told me he feels sorry for fired coaches, so he offers them a suite seat.

I wrote back, "That's cool. I like Dunleavy, too. I'll let Phil know in case anybody asks him, so he's not surprised."

Phil was behind the wheel when I got the text. He nodded his head. He doesn't let stuff like that distract him.

An interview I did with Ramona Shelburne for ESPNLosAngeles.com concerning Phil's future seems to have caused some controversy. All I said was that even if Phil doesn't come back to the Lakers, he is going to coach in the NBA next season because he is healthy enough to do so. Physical ailments will not be an issue.

I spoke out because I've heard people imply Phil won't go anywhere because I wouldn't allow him to do so. I want people to know I don't use emotional blackmail. I'm not going to threaten to break up with him. Our relationship is not like that. Phil is not a hostage.

If that's the perception, then I become a detriment to his career. While my job is here with the Lakers, I am not going to be the reason he doesn't go somewhere else.

I have very good role models in Linda and Kurt Rambis. They've made it work. So it's not unprecedented for the significant other of an NBA coach to live in a different city.

Linda and I would be NBA widows together in Los Angeles.

The negotiations for Phil's new contract are between him and Dr. Buss. I am staying out of it. The media has theorized that Phil has to take a pay cut in order to remain with the Lakers. While I don't know where that information is coming from, it's understandable since the next-highest-paid coach in the NBA makes about half as much as Phil does.

If my dad wants to spend less on a coach and that will make him happy, then that's what he should do. If Phil wants to go somewhere else to continue coaching and that will make him happy, then that's what he should do. So maybe for both of them to get what they want, there is going to have to be a change.

If the media reports about a pay cut are true, I see the logic. My dad is certainly not saying Phil hasn't done a good job. But the economy, in general, has been poor, and the NBA in particular is facing an uncertain future because the collective bargaining agreement with the players' union expires after next season. We have to be prepared for all possible scenarios by keeping expenses down.

Once my dad has crunched the numbers, he'll decide what he is willing to pay while still offering one of the top salaries in the league for a coach.

In effect, my dad is saying, "This is the amount of money the job pays, Phil. Would you like to apply?"

Last year, Phil floated the idea of skipping some of the road games and letting Kurt, then still with the team, take over in his absence. Phil knew that at some point Kurt would get offers to be a head coach somewhere else and would leave if he didn't see an opportunity with the Lakers. Phil felt he was standing in Kurt's way, but he could at least give him some road games to coach.

Nobody in the organization liked that idea, though it might have been a good solution: reduce Phil's salary in exchange for reducing his travel time and slowly training his successor.

May 4
LAKERS 111, JAZZ 103

It's May, playoff time, the time when every decision Phil makes is scrutinized, analyzed, and often criticized.

As the stakes on the court grow and the demand for courtside seats grows at the same proportion, we in the front office must make decisions on who sits in some of those seats, decisions that are also scrutinized, analyzed, and sometimes criticized by the ever-growing number of celebrities and pseudo-celebrities who want in on the fun.

We have our regulars, of course, like Jack Nicholson, Dyan Cannon, Penny Marshall, Dustin Hoffman, Leonardo DiCaprio, Denzel Washington, Tobey Maguire, Lou Adler, and David Beckham, to name a few.

We want the celebrities here, but we want the right mix, so we also try to connect with the younger generation by including stars like Zac Efron and Vanessa Hudgens.

While we are a celebrity-friendly venue, we don't give away the tickets. Celebrities and VIPs have to buy them, something they are willing to do, happy to be able to attend a Lakers game.

The requests come from everywhere. Donald Trump's assistant called our office today looking for seats. Most bona fide celebrities like Donald will have 10 different feelers out in search of the best seats, including calls to the NBA and whichever network is televising the game.

Sometimes, someone will call and say, "Don't you know who I am?" When we Google that person, it turns out they were on a sitcom in the '90s, but haven't done anything since.

Our definition of a celebrity is not limited to entertainment and sports. Take someone like Captain Chesley "Sully" Sullenberger, the pilot who saved so many lives by landing his disabled plane on the Hudson River. If he called, he would be someone I would consider an of-the-moment celebrity, a person our fans would be excited to see.

Most of the time, though, it's the movie stars who get first consideration, especially those who have movies soon to be released. By sitting in courtside seats, they become more visible, causing people to talk about the opening of their film. Going to a Lakers game, especially a playoff game, has become a reliable element in the marketing of a movie.

For our organization, it means more work for our public relations department because now magazines such as *People*, *Star*, and *Us Weekly* request photo credentials for every game.

A lot of the calls for tickets go to Linda Rambis, John Black, and Tim Harris.

Celebrities don't scream at me because they know they will never get me on the phone again. Of course, that doesn't stop their assistants from screaming at me.

On the flip side, there are stars who personally write a thank-you note for receiving tickets, like super-cute Chris Pine, or send a gift basket, like super-sweet Tobey Maguire, or a beautiful necklace, like super surfer Kelly Slater. Completely unnecessary, but I believe these people were brought up to be courteous, so I graciously accept their thoughtful expressions of gratitude.

When other NBA owners, like Mark Cuban, need tickets even though their teams aren't playing, we always try to accommodate them.

Along with the demand for seats comes a request to eat and drink in the Chairman's Room before and after games and at halftime. Because the room is small and private, passes are required.

One person desperately pursued Tim for a pass. The man insisted he was a celebrity. When that argument failed, he sent Tim pictures of himself *with* celebrities.

"Here are the people I hang out with," he said. "Therefore, I should have a pass to the Chairman's Room."

He didn't get it.

We must also decide who is shown on the video board.

Unless the celebrities are sitting on the floor, we will ask their permission before putting a camera on them. We figure if they are sitting in courtside seats, they know they are going to be seen. If they are sitting 10 rows up, maybe they prefer to be left alone. We don't ever want to make anyone feel uncomfortable.

At one game, Neil Diamond had a courtside seat but didn't want to be recognized, so he wore a fake mustache and a baseball cap.

The problem was the mustache was hanging halfway off his face. Since Jeremy Piven was sitting next to him, I texted Jeremy and said, "Tell Neil to fix the mustache."

The next day a friend emailed me a picture of that droopy piece of fake facial hair dropping off of Mr. Diamond's face.

IT'S NOT ALWAYS A LAUGHING MATTER. Back in the 1990s, after the O.J. Simpson trial, we anticipated that at some point Simpson might come to a Lakers game.

How would we deal with it if he did?

Sure enough, he showed up with a ticket—we were still at the Forum in those days—and things went smoothly until he decided to leave.

When O.J. reached the parking lot, he started going nuts because his car wasn't where he had left it. It turned out it had been towed because he had parked it illegally in a red zone right in front of the emergency entrance. He apparently didn't believe the rules applied to him.

The moral of that story is, you can get away with some things, but you could never park illegally at the Forum.

May 6

It's the middle of the playoffs and we've had two nights off at home.

Phil has been relaxed, spending both evenings in the kitchen cooking great meals. When I got home tonight, the house smelled wonderful. He had barbecued steaks and gotten really creative by making scalloped potatoes from his own recipe.

It's easier to be relaxed when your team is up 2–0 in the series, but Phil respects Jazz coach Jerry Sloan and knows it is not going to be easy to win in Utah. Jerry always has his teams well prepared.

Phil's relaxed mood fades when he watches playoff games on TV and he gets intense.

He doesn't root for teams, but he'll predict who is going to win a series and he's right 99 percent of the time.

Phil reacts when he thinks a coach has made a poor decision, whether it's a defensive assignment or a substitution.

In those situations, he's just like a fan. He'll get irritated the same way fans sometimes do about him.

Occasionally he'll ask me, "Do you know how that play got messed up?"

I'll say no.

"Well, let me show you," he'll say.

He'll hit the rewind button and run the play over, frame by frame, pointing out where everyone was and where they should have been.

It takes slow motion for me to see what he sees instantaneously.

May 10

LAKERS 111, JAZZ 96

The Lakers have swept the Jazz, resulting in joy and celebration from the Lakers' locker room in Utah to the sports bars of Los Angeles.

I stayed home and watched the game by myself as I usually do. Occasionally, I will communicate with the people who follow me on Twitter, but I like to be alone so I can focus on the game without distractions in a familiar chair in a comfortable setting.

Plus, I can hit the rewind button and see where an unsuccessful play broke down. Phil has influenced me in so many ways.

People ask, "Don't you get nervous during games?"

I don't because I know how hard the players work. You get nervous when you think you're not good enough or you're not prepared enough, causing you to feel exposed and vulnerable. I know the team has talent and will do its best.

I'm not superstitious. I don't feel I have to wear the same shirt as long as the team keeps winning, nor do I think the Lakers are going to lose because there was a black cat on my street.

Sometimes, I will tweet, "People, put on your purple and gold."

I don't say that because I think the Lakers' fortunes are riding on the number of people who are wearing the team's colors.

It is because I want everyone to feel like they're a part of the Lakers' success, because the fact is the fans are a big part of it.

I believe in channeling positive energy. If wearing a certain lucky shirt or wearing purple and gold makes fans feel positive, then I think that can make a difference.

Tweeting to Lakers fans to wear purple and gold is a perfect game-day diversion for me. It also creates a lot of cute photos. People send me pictures of their kids and even their dogs in Lakers gear.

May 17

LAKERS 128, SUNS 107

One of the reasons I love this time of year is that it's family time. Since I and all of my siblings have roles in the operation of the Lakers, the climax of the season brings us all together.

For much of the year, our paths rarely cross. I'm usually in the office every day. Jimmy, our vice president for player personnel, is out on the road scouting players. Johnny is also a vice president, researching new business opportunities. Janie oversees the Lakers Youth Foundation from her home, which is a two-hour drive from L.A. Joey is establishing the Lakers' player development system, including our D-League team. Jesse is busy studying and learning all aspects of the game.

We all text each other during and after games. Last year, when the Lakers won the championship, I watched the game with Jimmy and my dad at my father's house. Janie and my brother Joey were at the game in Orlando.

Everybody on the basketball side of the operation reports to Jimmy. I bring the business end into the equation. If the payroll is going up, we have to take that into consideration when looking at ticket prices and our advertising and broadcast revenue.

I will ask Jimmy, "How much are you planning on spending? How much money do I need to bring in?"

Sometimes, we are not on the same page. For example, if a decision is made from a basketball standpoint to trade a player, I might point out that this player is a fan favorite. His departure could impact season-ticket sales and our broadcast partners. It is my job to draw attention to these issues.

How do we resolve the matter? My dad makes the final decision.

It's fortunate we have my dad in the leadership role. There is no reason for him to ever retire because we can do the day-to-day tasks while Dr. Buss provides the vision.

I have to admit, sometimes it's an uncomfortable situation for me because of my relationship with Phil. I wouldn't recommend mixing business with pleasure to anyone. But surprisingly, with all its potential conflicts, it happens a lot in family businesses. I know because people reach out to me as a positive role model.

JANIE IS TWO YEARS YOUNGER than I am, but when we were young she was taller and stronger, so when we had the normal sisterly fights, she could pin me to the ground.

That was when we were kids, but as we grew up, I—as the big sister—played the role of mentor to her. I am so proud of my little sister.

We have remained close, but our lives are so different. She has a husband, my brother-in-law David Drexel, and two kids, 17-year-old Riley and 13-year-old Sierra.

I see my nephew and niece more now that they are older and join us at Lakers games. When they were younger, it was hard for me to make the two-hour drive to see them because of the demands of my job.

Even today, we don't see each other as much as I would like.

May 19

LAKERS 124, SUNS 112

When I look back at footage of the Lakers' home-court championship victories from the Showtime era, I realize how much things have changed.

When those games in the 1980s would end, the fans would flood onto the court in jubilation.

Not anymore. Security personnel now form a protective ring around the court during playoff games.

Perhaps the change in safety measures occurred because of the horrific stabbing of tennis player Monica Seles by a deranged spectator as she sat on the sideline during a rest break at a 1993 tournament in Hamburg, Germany.

Or perhaps it's just the age we live in, with the threat of terrorism always in our collective consciousness. You don't know what people are thinking now when they approach a player.

That's why it was so alarming when a spectator tried to walk onto the court to get access to the players after Game 1 of this series two nights ago.

And that's why I'm so grateful to actor David Arquette, who leaped from his courtside seat to help a security guard control the interloper.

When the guard was pinned to the ground by the spectator, David jumped in to help subdue him.

We have one of the few buildings that require fans to walk through a screening device to make certain no one comes in with guns or other weapons. Still, nobody knew for sure what this guy had on him or what his intentions were.

The man was stopped and because David is a celebrity, it became a headline story on TMZ. Fortunately, a story with a happy ending.

When I saw David tonight, I thanked him for being so brave and asserting himself in a potentially dangerous situation.

IT SEEMS LIKE KOBE IS FEELING better than he has in months and that is reflected in his performance in this series.

From Phil's demeanor, I can tell he smells a championship. This is the sweet spot of the long season for him. But he remains wary of the Suns despite the Lakers' 2–0 lead in this series.

Phil is particularly concerned about Steve Nash. Those worries are permeating Phil's dreams. I can no longer stop him from wrestling my pillow away from me in his sleep. He's obsessed with basketball right now.

May 23
SUNS 118, LAKERS 109

We were spoiled by the sweep in the previous round. It would have been nice to do it again, but against a team as talented as the Suns, a team bound to put up a good fight, it would have been unrealistic for anyone to expect that.

Still, the Lakers didn't follow the game plan Phil had designed. They are still up 2–1 in the series, but they have their work cut out for them.

The Suns' big men came through in Game 3. Amar'e Stoudemire scored 42 points and Robin Lopez hit eight of 10 shots.

Phoenix surprised the Lakers with a zone defense, and it seems everybody is telling Phil he can't run the triangle against a zone. Phil is not about to panic. He'll come up with some adjustments.

He would have preferred not to have his team shoot 32 three-pointers, especially since only nine were successful, but the Lakers couldn't get the ball inside.

Phil was disappointed by Lamar Odom's poor performance today, but felt like he shouldn't yell at him because Lamar already felt bad enough.

It didn't help that Phil could get only seven minutes out of Andrew Bynum. Andrew is trying to play through the pain of his knee injury, but he's not as mobile as he needs to be.

When I talked to Phil after the game, I told him to watch the play when Andrew went up to block a shot. The Suns' Goran Dragic leaned in on Andrew's body and Andrew wound up coming down on his bad leg.

I told Phil the look on Andrew's face made me cringe.

Phil couldn't see the play from where he was sitting, but when he watched it later on tape, he told me, "I don't know why Andrew didn't say anything to me."

"Because the kid does not complain," I said. "He'll do whatever you want him to do. It's so endearing."

Andrew has been very mature in the way he has handled the pressure and pain of having to play hurt.

May 24

Phil says he won't make a decision on whether he will coach next season until he gets a complete medical exam at the end of this season.

Some people have interpreted that to mean something is physically wrong with him. My dad called me to inquire about Phil's health.

I assured my father that Phil is actually feeling better than he has in several years. He just wants to know that if he makes a commitment to coach, he will be able to see it through.

It's hard to get Phil to make a commitment—as I know better than anyone—but once he does, he is determined to live up to it.

Phil's hips, both surgically replaced, don't bother him anymore. He hasn't had heart problems since he had a stent put in seven years ago. His energy level is really good. He has a kidney stone, but it continues to shrink and the pain has faded thanks to the medication he has been taking for the last couple of years.

He has high cholesterol and would probably be better off if he lost some weight. It goes up and down. During the season, he tends to put on pounds from eating on the road and eating late at night. In the summer, he'll lose the weight because he'll swim every day and be able to eat healthy food on a regular schedule.

Phil is much more proactive with his health than he used to be. He makes better dietary choices, takes supplements, and drinks a lot of water.

His only ailment is a sore knee.

He has come a long way since that nightmare episode seven years ago that still causes me to shudder.

WE WERE PLAYING THE SPURS in the 2003 Western Conference Semifinals. When I dropped Phil off at the airport for the flight to San Antonio for the opening two games, he was sweaty and clammy. He said he didn't feel well and was exhausted even though it was early in the day.

His words stuck in my brain. So when I knew Phil had arrived in San Antonio, I called our team internist, Dr. John Moe, and conferenced Phil in because I didn't trust Phil to call him on his own. The doctor told Phil that he needed to see him immediately.

Phil wasn't about to leave the team, but he promised he would go for a checkup when the Lakers returned after the two games in San Antonio.

He coached those games but clearly wasn't himself. I could see him hanging his head most of the time. It wasn't because the Lakers lost both games. I know the way Phil reacts to defeat and this was much more than that. This was a man who was too tired to raise his head. Even watching on TV, I could tell his complexion wasn't right. He looked pale.

I can't even look at a tape of those games all these years later because it's so alarming to see how bad he looks.

When the Lakers arrived home, I took Phil straight to the doctor.

While awaiting the completion of a series of tests, Phil coached Game 3 at STAPLES Center on a Friday night.

But when we got the test results Saturday morning, there was no way he was going to coach Game 4. One of his arteries was 90 percent blocked.

When the doctors, Moe and cardiologist Phillip Frankel, told me the name of the artery, I said I didn't know one from the other.

"We nicknamed that one 'the widow maker,'" they said, "because if it closes completely, the patient dies. It's the worst-case scenario to have that one blocked."

Listening to those words was like having an out-of-body experience.

The fact that Phil coached in that condition, especially in a pressure situation like a playoff game, is frightening. He could have had a heart attack during the game.

If the worst had happened, I suppose it would be better to have an attack at a game where you've got doctors next to you and an ambulance on the premises rather than having it happen at home at 2:00 in the morning with just me there.

Thank goodness we didn't have to worry about that. Phil underwent an angioplasty Saturday morning, the stent was inserted, the blood started flowing normally, and he looked and felt much better.

He spent the night in the hospital and I stayed there with him, sleeping by his side on a cot.

With the Lakers scheduled to play Game 4 on Sunday morning, Phil claimed he felt well enough to coach. The doctors didn't agree.

In addition to the need for more recovery time after the procedure, there was a complication caused by an antibiotic Phil had been given. His body had an allergic reaction to it and his face ballooned to what seemed like double the normal size. With fluid in the lower part of his face, he looked like a chipmunk.

Even if there had been no concern about jumping back into a stressful situation 24 hours after the angioplasty, Phil couldn't have coached because of his appearance. It would have been distracting to the team.

I think, in some ways, missing the game was more upsetting to Phil than his heart condition. His reward for a long regular season is the postseason. For him, it was like eating the outside of an artichoke only to be told you can't eat the heart, the best part.

Phil loves the chess match within the basketball game in a playoff series, matching moves with the opposing coach.

If it had been a preseason or regular-season game, it would have been easy for me to convince him to miss it. But to sit out a playoff game and maybe lose an opportunity to win a championship was maddening to him, especially with the Lakers down 2–1.

The fact that Phil wanted to coach the game was courageous, but when he threatened to do so, I said, "Are you crazy? You need to call Mitch Kupchak and tell him you are not going to be there."

We came home, turned on the TV, and I had to literally sit Phil down to watch the game because he was so restless.

He truly believed when he woke up that morning in the hospital that he was going to coach that game, and I think it still bugs him to this day that he didn't.

If I wasn't there with him, he would have gotten in his car and driven to STAPLES Center instead of letting assistant coach Jim Cleamons fill in for him.

There was one point where Phil stood up in front of the TV and yelled, "Timeout!"

I told him, "You are not at the game, honey."

When I looked back and realized I had missed the warning signs, I became an advocate for the prevention of heart disease. It's up to everyone to notice changes in those they love, especially when they are involved with a person who is as driven as Phil.

People like Phil are able to will themselves to ignore pain and discomfort because they are committed to what they are doing with such passion. That overrides any concern about their health.

The first warning sign in Phil's case was the clamminess I noticed from holding his hand. The sweat wasn't warm; rather, it felt like it came from a cold body. That was followed by the paleness and the exhaustion.

It was hard for me to nag Phil about getting medical attention. Since I was just the girlfriend and not his wife, and since we had only been seeing each other for a few years at that point and were not yet living together, I didn't feel like I could force him to see a doctor.

Now that I have become the person closest to Phil, I must assert myself when it comes to his health issues.

Fortunately, he hasn't had another health problem scary enough to cause a doctor to utter those two dreaded words: widow maker.

May 25

Suns 115, Lakers 106

After today's loss that tied the series at 2–2, I was taken aback by text messages I was getting from my friends. People were saying, "Hey, Phil's got to step it up. Phil's got to figure out this zone defense."

Wow, people sure jump off the bandwagon as soon as it gets a little shaky.

We lost two games to the Suns on their home floor, but were competitive in both. I'm frankly surprised to see how anxious our fans have become. The zone defense Phoenix threw at us not only threw us off our game, but seems to have thrown off our fans as well.

There is no question the Suns are a worthy foe. Steve Nash is spectacular and their bench put our bench to shame.

Still, it rattled me that people could have so much doubt. Hopefully, I have skin thick enough to take all the criticism coming our way, especially the hurtful comments about Phil.

He never falters in the faith he has in his team, especially when he knows if there is a Game 7 it will be on his home court. When the Lakers lose at home, that's when Phil has a reason to be alarmed.

He has been impressed with the job Phoenix coach Alvin Gentry has done. This is Alvin's fourth head coaching job, but as Phil pointed out the circumstances have to be right for a coach to achieve success.

In this case, the man and the circumstances are a perfect match.

May 27

LAKERS 103, SUNS 101

Everybody thinks Phil is so stoic and unemotional. But if you know him like I know him, you can read his emotions from the slightest movement of his eyes. And what I saw tonight, watching the game on TV, was not a happy face for Phil.

Not after Ron Artest missed a three-point attempt with the Lakers up by three and just over a minute to play, then tried another three-pointer two seconds after the 24-second clock had started anew and missed that one as well.

That let the air out of STAPLES Center.

If I were Ron, I wouldn't have gone back to the bench to face Phil after that second shot.

Everyone assumed Ron would be staying on the bench, pulled out of the game by Phil. Everyone was wrong. Phil left Ron in.

One of Phil's strengths is his willingness to stick with players who are struggling when he feels they have something to contribute. Some coaches in the league lose control on the sideline and throw towels and yank guys out and humiliate them in front of the fans, but Phil's not that way.

Oh, he lets you know with a look in his eye that you are in trouble. But he also gives you the opportunity to redeem yourself.

And so it was with Ron.

Following his two misses, the Suns, on their third three-point attempt in a row, tied the game when Jason Richardson banked in a shot with 3.5 seconds to play.

That's when the value of Phil's patience became evident.

Kobe missed a three-point attempt with 2.5 seconds remaining, but Ron beat Richardson to the rebound and banked in the game winner as time expired to give the Lakers a 3–2 lead in the series.

Ron showed the instinct to be in the right position at the right time, just as Pau did when he scored the game winner against the Thunder to clinch our first-round series.

The result was another special moment in Lakers history.

UNFORTUNATELY, I HAD TO WATCH the game from home because I was sick.

I felt ill last night after Phil grilled steaks on the barbecue for dinner. I thought it might be stress because the series had come down to three games, but I knew it was more than that when I woke up this morning still feeling sick.

Around lunch time, I felt worse.

When Phil came up to our offices to eat after practice, I told him I didn't think I was going to make it to the game.

It was important for him to know that as soon as possible because he has to leave a little earlier from our house if he's alone and can't use the carpool lane.

Before he left the house, he kissed me good-bye. I laid down, fell asleep, and didn't wake up until 5:30 PM, almost missing the game. As it was, I had to fight to stay awake once the telecast started.

The announcers were saying Alvin Gentry was sick, too. He was sitting on the bench with a trash can nearby in case he got sick again.

He was tougher than me. He made it to the game.

Although I was distressed that I couldn't be there to support Phil and the team, I knew I had made the right decision.

And while I would have loved to have experienced the thrilling victory in person, by staying home I saw something fascinating that I would have otherwise missed. It was a segment on the pregame show about Phil's lost year with the Knicks. He was out the entire 1969–70 season because of a bad back, a season in which the Knicks won the championship.

They clinched the title in the unforgettable Game 7 of the NBA Finals against the Lakers, a game that will forever be remembered as "the Willis Reed game" because of his dramatic appearance. Thought to be out because of a torn muscle in his right thigh, Willis limped onto the court and scored New York's first two baskets of the game, his inspired teammates taking it from there to soar to victory.

Knicks coach Red Holzman had asked Phil to work with the photographer for the Knicks and Madison Square Garden, George Kalinsky, to produce a photo journal of that season. That was Red's way of keeping Phil engaged.

A copy of the journal, containing some amazing photos, was shown on the telecast tonight.

Perhaps Phil's best photo in that collection is of Willis on the floor after his injury and the emotion of the people around him. Phil beautifully captures that instant when all seemed lost for the Knicks.

As good as Phil was as a photographer, Red saw even greater potential in him. If you are going to be traveling with us this season, Red told Phil, I'd like you to write notes after every game about things you observe. That prompted Phil to see the game in a different way, analyzing it from a coach's perspective.

I had tears in my eyes when Phil recalled in an interview how much it meant to him to be part of that team even though he wasn't able to contribute on the court. That, said Phil, was when he first started to think about coaching.

Marv Albert, the Knicks' play-by-play announcer, offered his insight about what he saw in the young Phil Jackson that season. Marv felt he was looking at a coach in the making, one with heart and soul.

It was a great history lesson for me, one I would have missed if I had been at the game.

I TWEETED THAT I WAS HOME SICK and got a tremendous response from some of my 28,000 followers.

You are never alone if you are on Twitter. I felt connected to my Lakers Twitter family, as we exchanged messages during the game just as I would have if I had been sitting with friends at STAPLES Center.

WHEN PHIL CAME HOME after the game, he gave me a kiss on the forehead and said, "Did you record the game? I need to watch the second half."

He wanted to see exactly how the Lakers blew an 18-point, third-quarter lead.

I went to sleep, definitely an NBA widow until the season ends.

May 30

We were all prepared for a Game 7. I made all the necessary preparations because we couldn't assume the Lakers would win on the Suns' home court. But they did, beating Phoenix yesterday 111–103 to win the series in six games.

I was particularly pleased Phil was able to show all the doubters that his team could operate effectively against a zone. The Lakers found a way to thread the needle. It was exciting to watch them score in the middle and again be the offensive team we've known and loved.

Kobe was not going to be denied. We are lucky to have him and Derek Fisher, because when things aren't going right on the road, they can both hit the big shots that rally their teammates and quiet the crowd.

No, Phil did not appreciate the flagrant foul by Sasha Vujacic on Goran Dragic in the fourth quarter that ignited a run by the Suns. But that incident didn't cause Phil to forget how much he missed Sasha on defense when Sasha was hurt.

He might have been the momentum killer, but as in the case of Ron Artest one game earlier, Phil let his player stay on the floor and make up for his questionable actions.

PHIL IS ALREADY PREPARING to meet the Boston Celtics in the NBA Finals. He gave the team the day off today, but he was up at 7:00 this morning doing laundry. When the washer and dryer are running, I know Phil's mind is also working, thinking of the next game and the next challenge.

Brooke, her husband, and their kids are coming over for some family time. Phil will be fun to be around today.

Tomorrow, it's all business as he charts a trail to the season's final peak.

17

A Gender Gap?
Don't You Believe It

DESPITE ALL THE YEARS I'VE BEEN IN THE BUSINESS WORLD, I still run into executives who butter me up, thinking I'm naïve. They act like they are taking me seriously, but then when it comes time to close a deal, they'll say, "Let me talk to Dr. Buss."

"You know," I'll reply, "I could go back to my dad and relay our discussion to him. But he is just going to turn around and say, 'Jeanie, you make the decision.' So you are going to waste about a week while I go through that process, and then I'm going to come back to you and we'll be right back where we are now. And I'll still make the decision. So which way would you prefer?"

That usually settles the matter.

For years, I heard "tell your dad this," "tell your dad that," or "get your dad to write a check." A co-worker told me that someone from a company we were negotiating with said, "Jeanie is sweet and everything, but I really need to meet with her father."

People assume I had those problems when I entered into the business as a teenager but have long since put them behind me. The reality is that it doesn't matter if I'm 19 or 48. In business, some people are going to try to dismiss me or put me in my place. That's the aggressive landscape in which I operate. If I let that affect me, then they win.

But that won't happen, because having long ago established myself in my career, I can keep things in perspective when I hear demeaning comments. I am realistic in assessing my own strengths and weaknesses.

When you are in a business negotiation, everybody is trying to gain a competitive edge, and people will use any tactic they think will give them the upper hand.

When some businessmen deal with women, they try to use gender as a means of advancing their agenda. They may claim they don't want to talk to a woman if she doesn't have a college degree, or if she didn't go to grad school, or if she doesn't have a law degree, or if she has a baby at home. They are going to try to put women down any way they can and make them seem like the weaker party.

I've been asked to fetch coffee at a meeting where I'm the only woman.

It's a means of jockeying for position, trying to one-up the woman they are dealing with so they can elevate themselves into a power role.

If a woman in business believes her gender is a negative, that it puts her at a disadvantage, then she *is* at a disadvantage.

I don't think being a woman is a drawback. Anyone who believes I'm vulnerable because I'm a woman has got it wrong. My advice to other women in business is to not regard yourself based on your gender, but rather on your intelligence, your experience, your conviction, and your passion.

I was once one of eight people in a roller hockey meeting, but the only woman in the room. The discussion got a little heated and one of the guys used some profanity.

He turned to me and said, "Oh, excuse the language."

It was like, oh, you frail little butterfly. We have to be so gentle around you.

"I don't really appreciate that language," I said. "But if you are going to apologize, then you should do so to everyone in this room. What you said was inappropriate, but not just because of me."

By singling me out, he was indicating I was inferior. I didn't feel inferior, so the strategy didn't work. He turned red when I called him out on his remark. Rather than moving his argument forward, he had been derailed.

At business meetings, I'm usually not the only woman in the room anymore. We are not the majority, but there are many more women involved in sports now than when I started 30 years ago.

That is very gratifying, but I don't think I personally have had anything to do with that. I'm not a pioneer.

To me, the ultimate trailblazer for women is my role model, Billie Jean King.

I will never forget coming into my dad's office six days before my 12th birthday, seeing him point to a TV, and hearing him say, "Come watch this. It could affect you in ways you can't even imagine."

There on the screen was Billie Jean playing Bobby Riggs in the tennis match that became known around the world as "The Battle of the Sexes."

It was a battle Billie Jean won, not only for herself, but for all of us who followed.

It was an important time for women, although I was too young to appreciate it. A year earlier, Title IX—a law requiring gender equality in all educational programs receiving federal funding—had been passed. That resulted in the opening of doors to female students in both academic and athletic activities in schools across the nation.

I have tried to take advantage of the opportunities this legislation provided my generation. If I have, in any small way, inspired other women to pursue their goals, I am proud of that.

My newest passion project is the resurrection of WOW (Women of Wrestling). I am assisting my friend, David McLane, who created two of the most successful women's professional wrestling events: GLOW (Gorgeous Ladies of Wrestling) in the 1980s and WOW a few years ago.

When David first invited me to attend one of the WOW matches at the Forum, I thought it would be women wrestling in mud or Jell-O, a format I had absolutely no interest in.

Finally, after weeks of prodding, I accepted his invitation. When I saw the event, I went wild. It wasn't what I thought at all. Instead, it was a spot-on depiction of female empowerment.

David's vision was to have female superheroes engaged in the age-old battle of good against evil. Some wrestlers like Caged Heat's Delta Lotta Pain and Loca were cast as villains, while American sweetheart Terri Gold (a Mary Lou Retton–type character) would fight for what was right.

It was a stark contrast to other professional wrestling events that showed women either as frail and needing a man to save them, or as conniving witches manipulating men to the point where their subsequent punishment was justified.

WOW has been on hiatus for the last few years, but I would love to see it brought back to life to inspire a new generation of young women.

WHEN PEOPLE ASK ME for career advice, I tell them:

- You should truly love what you do, because no amount of money is worth laboring at a job you don't like. You will never find happiness at a job like that because happiness is not all about money.

- You should always be prepared, because when opportunity comes your way, it won't do you any good if you are not ready to take advantage of it. Yes, I was given a privileged position at a young age, but if I had not been willing to work hard and prepare myself for all the challenges I would face, I would not have held on to my position all these years, regardless of my family ties.

- Don't be intimidated. In business, you are either a revenue producer or a revenue spender. If you can produce revenue, it doesn't matter who you are. You are golden to your employer.

When my dad made me general manager of the Strings at the age of 19, he told me not to doubt myself.

A few years into my career in the family business, he said, "I'm glad you finally figured out what I always knew: that you were capable of doing this job. You finally see yourself as I've always seen you."

It is a compliment I have treasured all these years, giving me a level of confidence that has enabled me to succeed as a woman in what was, for so long, a man's world.

18

JUNE–AUGUST

June 2

Be careful what you wish for.

I was rooting for the Celtics to beat the Magic in the Eastern Conference Finals because that gives us home-court advantage against Boston.

The Lakers remember the 2008 NBA Finals all too clearly, and still painfully carry the memory of being humiliated and eliminated in Boston in Game 6. It will be nice for the players to have the opportunity to go back there and redeem themselves.

Anytime these two teams meet for the championship, fans across the country get involved, picking one side or the other. This is truly a national rivalry.

There is, however, a risk in playing the Celtics. If they win, they add another NBA championship to their legacy. In trying to achieve my dad's goal of having the Lakers exceed the number of titles owned by Boston, the hill would be even steeper to climb. The Celtics would have 18 championships to our 15. If the Lakers win, it's 17–16. Big difference.

The Celtics are crafty enough and experienced enough to be victorious.

And they're focused on the ultimate goal. When Boston beat the Magic, none of the Celtics would touch the conference trophy. They know it isn't about that. It's about holding the championship trophy.

Lakers-Celtics has a completely different vibe than any other matchup. My stomach is already churning.

About two weeks ago, actor Rob Lowe told me, "If the Lakers play Boston in the Finals, I have to be there. I was there in the '80s and I want to feel that energy again."

He is not alone. The demand for seats is already ridiculous. People are begging for tickets, leaving messages on my voice mail devoid of pride and reason. One person, who installed my satellite dish three years ago, demanded I respond to his request.

How do we handle it? We prioritize. Business comes first. If I have to turn down some people who don't have a business connection with the organization, I will do that. It is important to make hay while the sun shines, and the sun is shining on this franchise right now.

One individual called several people in the organization and insisted that I promised him floor seats for the Finals.

I don't even know this person.

He told Tim Harris, "Jeanie told me that over the weekend when I saw her."

Either the person was making it up or there's a Jeanie Buss impersonator out there giving away floor seats to the Finals.

This is what we have to deal with.

Rob Lowe, on the other hand, is never demanding. That's why he has done well in the entertainment business. He would never complain about where I put him. He's just happy to be anywhere in the building, so I'll take care of him.

We follow tradition, so more than likely Jeffrey Osborne will sing the national anthem the first night.

All anthem singers must be approved by the NBA because league officials want an anthem that sets the tone for the series, but it won't be a problem getting them to sign off on Jeffrey.

The NBA takes control of many of the production elements at the Finals. In some ways, that's a relief because our staff is already being stretched to its limits.

But in some ways, it can be difficult because league officials tend to make the arena more of a neutral site, like a Super Bowl. Our fans have waited an entire season to have the privilege of seeing the NBA Finals in their building. The league wants to brand it as the NBA championship; to our fans, it's still the Lakers. They want the Lakers' flavor, the Lakers' style, and the Lakers' home-court advantage.

League personnel run the player introductions. They bring in a gigantic blowup of the Larry O'Brien NBA Championship Trophy that the players have to jog through with smoke swirling around them. That would be a little over the top for most games, but this is the NBA Finals.

We accommodate the league, but are given total freedom when it comes to the game format. That includes the Laker Girls and our video presentations.

We used to broadcast the game on the big screen outside STAPLES Center, but are now prohibited from doing so. It would be a huge draw for fans who don't have tickets, but we can't control the crowd because we don't know how many people are going to show up. Do we prepare for 10,000 or 100,000?

We cooperate fully with the Los Angeles Police Department and take their advice on security.

Who can forget the craziness that ensued after we won the 2000 championship, with vandals roaming the streets and cars set on fire?

Fortunately, much has changed for the better now in the surrounding area. There used to be many parking lots around STAPLES Center, areas where crowds could gather. Now, with L.A. Live fully functioning with its restaurants, theaters, and hotels, there are many events going on nightly, so people don't go down there just to loiter.

With an enormous series like Lakers vs. Celtics, it's peak season for ticket brokers and ticket scalpers.

There is a big difference between the two. Ticket brokers are individuals working for established, reputable companies. They have legitimate jobs and pay taxes.

Our problem is with the scalpers who are on our property selling tickets illegally. And too often, they are selling counterfeit tickets.

The duped fan will try to use that ticket only to learn it's not valid. The person has spent a lot of money and has no way to find the scalper who sold the ticket.

That fan wants justice, or at least to see the game, but because that person is not our customer, his or her complaint is out of our control.

Hopefully, a strong police presence will keep scalpers from the public, preventing them from marring what should otherwise be an incredible series.

June 3

LAKERS 102, CELTICS 89

"Did you have any dreams last night?" I asked Phil when he woke up this morning.

"Yeah," he said. "Paul Pierce was an unwelcome visitor in my dreams."

Phil should have sweet dreams tonight after the Lakers opened the NBA Finals with a victory over the Celtics.

When we lost to Boston two years ago in the Finals, it was a shock to the Lakers' collective system. Pau Gasol had only been on the team for four months and had never been past the first round of the playoffs. He didn't know what to expect.

Now, with Pau and many of his teammates having been in the Finals the past two seasons, they are savvy and confident. They know how to function effectively in the NBA's ultimate spotlight.

Phil was certainly satisfied with today's result, but now he awaits the next move in his chess match with Doc Rivers. What adjustments will Doc make, and how will Phil counter those moves?

Boston guard Rajon Rondo wasn't as effective today as he was previously in the playoffs, so the Celtics will try to get him more involved to see if he can again become the dominating force he was in the earlier rounds.

I SAW A RUMOR on the Internet and let Phil know about it right away. The story being circulated is that Khloe Kardashian is pregnant.

Phil asked Lamar Odom about it and Lamar said it's not true.

If it were true, Phil wouldn't see it as a distraction. Just the opposite. If someone is expecting a child, it's exciting. Teammates should acknowledge important milestones in each other's lives. That's what being on a team and being a family is all about.

I WOULDN'T WANT THIS INFORMATION to get out because it could be used by Doc Rivers to fire up his players, but we have been having meetings with city officials about a Lakers victory parade.

This is not in any way an indication we are overconfident or arrogant. It's an uncomfortable subject to discuss because we know that even though the Lakers were victorious in Game 1, we haven't won anything yet.

But parades don't happen overnight. The team doesn't just hop on a bus and start waving. We have to prepare, and if we don't win, the plans can be easily canceled.

There have been talks for the last two weeks among the city, the police department, the fire department, and the Lakers. We don't want to put any undue burden on a city that is already struggling financially. But there is a realization by all concerned that this would be a good thing for L.A., a chance to get away for one day from the economic crisis that has hit so many and enjoy a celebration.

We just have to figure out the right way to do this. We understand that city officials must put a limit on their parade expenditure at a time of layoffs and debt. And the Lakers organization, in deciding how much we can afford, has to be aware of a possible work stoppage after next season if there isn't a new collective bargaining agreement.

So the question is, how do we satisfy our fans without breaking the bank?

We will create a realistic budget that both the Lakers and the city can live with.

The celebration cannot be of the same scope as it was last year when we finished the parade at the Coliseum because this is a different economic environment. Using the Coliseum was very, very expensive, almost doubling the cost of the parade.

Besides, I don't think we should do the same thing over and over again. Each championship should have its own unique signature.

There are a lot of things we can do to lower the cost, like altering the length of the route.

Once the plan is established, all we have to do is win. That's no small task against a team like the Celtics.

June 7

Phil sent me a text message from his Boston hotel room that read, "I'm here in my prison cell for the next week."

The Lakers stay in a nice hotel with no reason to complain about the accommodations. Phil just means he's isolated and can't roam the streets of Boston without being mobbed, mostly by Celtics fans.

He has all of his children and grandchildren joining him there. That will make him feel less isolated over the next week as the Lakers play Games 3, 4, and 5 of the Finals.

There's more pressure now that the Lakers lost Game 2 at STAPLES Center yesterday, 103–94. They have to win at least one game in Boston in order to bring the series back to Los Angeles.

While Phil isn't about to criticize the officials again—it has already cost him a lot of money to do that—there is no question the high number of calls against the Lakers took some of the team's intensity and aggression away because nobody wanted to foul out. Kobe got out of his rhythm when he got into early foul trouble.

After Lamar picked up his second foul, Phil turned to his coaches to ask, "Think I should pull him out now?" Almost as the words were coming out of Phil's mouth, Lamar added his third foul. End of debate.

Ray Allen was incredibly accurate, hitting 11 of 20 from the floor including eight of 11 three-point attempts. Phil blames the Lakers' defense. What weakness did the Celtics exploit to free Allen up that much?

One positive Phil took out of Game 2 was the 39 minutes of solid effort by Andrew Bynum, who continues to play through the pain of the torn cartilage in his right knee.

Last Friday, I attended the dedication of a Chick Hearn Reading Room at the Los Angeles Red Shield Youth & Community Center.

Andrew's mother Janet was there and I told her, "You must be so proud of your son because we know how much pain he is in. And he has not complained one time. I admire him, so I can't imagine what you must feel."

She said it's hard for her to see her baby in pain, but she's thrilled by his effort and determination, as well as the support of his teammates.

I HAVE NO DESIRE to go to Boston for the series and hear people cheering for the Celtics and booing the Lakers. There will be a lot of energy in TD Garden tomorrow night. I wouldn't handle that well because it hurts my feelings when our team is booed, or when a Laker gets mocked for shooting an airball.

My gut reaction would be to tell them to stop, but of course that's not my place. Not that anybody would pay the slightest attention to me.

Cheering their team and booing the other team is what fans do. That's what our fans do. That's the way it should be. I just don't want to be there to hear it.

The last time the Lakers faced the Celtics in the Finals, a few Celtics fans got out of control. It was after the Lakers were eliminated in Game 6 in Boston. Our team bus apparently lacked the proper security. Fans surrounded it and started rocking the bus. That was a little bit scary.

I remember when I went to the NBA Finals in Boston one year in the 1980s and the fans kept setting off the fire alarm in our hotel. We had to evacuate several times in the middle of the night. We were told the problem stemmed from the fact that it was a new hotel and the bugs hadn't all been worked out. We figured all those "bugs" wore green.

My dad also chose not to go to Boston this time. He's at the World Series of Poker in Las Vegas.

YESTERDAY, I WAS with my Pilates instructor, Elizabeth, who is not a big sports fan.

"This might be a dumb question," she said, "but what do you guys win if you win the Finals?"

"Wow," I replied, "I don't think you realize the depth of what you've asked me. And I don't really know how to answer you. We get a trophy. We make more money as an organization because we are in the Finals, meaning more games. And we get rings.

"But it's not about any of that. Not the trophy or the ring or the money. You just want to win. It's an intangible reward."

It was such a simple question, and yet it really made me think about what is at stake and how important this all is, not just in the moment but for the rest of my life.

Phil says you have to live in the moment and realize what life is about. It's pursuing something that is motivating. The trophy is not a motivator. It's a symbol of what motivates us all in this organization.

"Probably," I told Elizabeth, "a good way to answer you is to explain what happens if we lose. It ruins the entire summer because Phil doesn't take losing well."

"Then I hope you win," she said, "because I want you to have a good summer."

June 8

LAKERS 91, CELTICS 84

I thought I had heard it all from Phil, but this is the first time I've ever heard him say his team was facing a "must-win" game.

He really wanted this one to regain home-court advantage.

The fact that Derek Fisher was the star—with 11 fourth-quarter points and a key rebound and subsequent three-point play—made it all the sweeter.

Phil is often asked, "Why are you so loyal to Fisher? It's time to move on. Try Shannon Brown. Try Jordan Farmar."

Phil isn't about to heed that advice because he has complete confidence in Derek. When it comes down to needing a big play, this is the guy Phil can count on. It takes many years to develop that kind of confidence. He has stuck with Derek and it has paid off.

Phil has also made Derek co-captain with Kobe. As a coach, you know there has to be a certain level of peer leadership. A coach can only do so much. You also need players in the locker room to set the example, especially for the younger players. And nobody is respected more than Derek and Kobe.

When Phil came back to the Lakers for the 2004–05 season, Derek wasn't here, having opted out of his contract and signed with Golden State.

Smush Parker was the starting point guard. Phil made the most of it, but there was a striking difference when Derek came back to the team after three seasons.

Unfortunately, his return was due to distressing circumstances. His daughter Tatum, 11 months old at the time, had cancer in her left eye. Derek had been traded to Utah, but because he needed to be near specialists familiar with this rare form of the disease, Derek wanted to leave Salt Lake City and Jazz owner Larry Miller let him out of his contract. That was very considerate of Larry, who has since passed away.

It all worked out well. Tatum has recovered, which is the most important thing. And Derek wound up back with the Lakers. People forget now that he was ever gone. Why he left in the first place I don't know, but his return was a turning point for this team.

Derek is also president of the NBA Players Association, and I think it's an advantage for that group to have somebody like him, a calm and intelligent leader who can explain things in an articulate manner to the public and has the respect of the players. Everybody in the NBA—league officials, owners, players, fans, and media—benefits from his presence as we work toward a new collective bargaining agreement.

Derek's Lakers contract is up after this season, but I don't want him to retire and neither does Phil.

AFTER GAME 2, Paul Pierce said the Celtics "ain't coming back to L.A." Asked about the comment, Phil said, "It's our job to make him a liar."

With a 2–1 lead in the series, if the Lakers win Games 4 and 5 the Finals will be over and Paul Pierce will be right. He won't be coming back to L.A.

EVEN THOUGH THE LAKERS are on the road, I love being reminded of their championship run by the abundance of Lakers flags on cars. To me, it's always the first sign summer is around the corner.

June 10
CELTICS 96, LAKERS 89
When Phil called me after the game, I could tell his energy level was down. He sounded the way the team looked.

It was a winnable game in the last few minutes, but the Lakers weren't able to come up with the plays, the Celtics did, and the result was a huge missed opportunity. Instead of the Lakers leading the series 3–1, it's now tied at 2–2.

Phil is particularly concerned about how many minutes he can get out of Andrew Bynum, a key to this series. The torn cartilage has robbed

Andrew of strength in his right leg. As a result, he played less than two minutes in the second half tonight

The Lakers also don't have a lot of firepower coming off the bench. Jordan hurt his hand tonight when he fell. That's another worry.

Phil is looking for someone to hit a big shot, make a big defensive stop, or grab a key rebound. He is in search of a player who can step up like Derek Fisher did in Game 3. No one answered that call tonight.

The crowd at TD Garden is loud, but Phil sees that as a positive for the Lakers. The us-against-the-world feeling helps them focus on one another and form a tighter unit.

Kobe is tired. You can see it on his face. He had 33 points but played 43 minutes, and he hasn't gotten much rest in any game in this series.

The Lakers exited the arena tonight bruised and tired. Phil is giving them tomorrow off. That's going to be helpful for treating all these nagging injuries and giving the players some rest.

It's a series. It isn't one game. You can't wallow in the bad. You can't rest on the good.

June 13

CELTICS 92, LAKERS 86

I waited hour after hour to talk to Phil after the game. I was so anxious that I was pacing back and forth. I was afraid to take my dog out for a walk because I didn't want to miss Phil's call. I wanted to connect with him.

Normally, he'll call around 30 minutes after a game. This time, it was three hours before I finally heard his voice.

He had been out to dinner with his kids.

Even though the Lakers are now down 3–2 in this series, Phil said it's not surprising because this is the way it's supposed to be. A team is supposed to win its home games.

Watching the game on TV tonight, I heard a comment by Phil in a fourth-quarter huddle during a timeout that made my hair stand on end.

With the Lakers trailing, Phil was overheard saying Boston "lost more games in the fourth quarter than anybody in the NBA. They know how to lose in the fourth quarter, all right? They're just showing us that right now."

The comment was picked up by a microphone the network had placed on Phil.

What he said is exactly what a coach should say when his team is down and he's doing everything he can to give his players hope.

But was that comment too private for national TV? Yes.

Phil is not sorry he made the remark. But the understanding between the league and the network is that when a coach is wired for sound, his remarks are *never* heard live. If there is swearing or a coach is chewing out a specific player, which might be humiliating to the player, that won't be aired. No disparaging, negative speeches are to be used. It should only be about Xs and Os.

But Phil's comment was aired, and now it will be around forever on YouTube.

I told Phil what happened when I talked to him, but he said the NBA and network people had already alerted him after the game that his remark had gotten on the air.

He's not upset, but that wasn't the agreement. In the future, maybe Phil will purposely turn off his mike when he has something sensitive to say. He does have a kill switch. But when you are coaching a game, the last thing you want to worry about is whether your microphone is on or off.

June 16

Phil has got a spring in his step. Despite all he has experienced and accomplished in his illustrious career, tomorrow will be a first for him: a Game 7 in the NBA Finals. He can't sit still, so he's been cooking.

And talking basketball incessantly. I asked him a question about the game last night and he diagrammed a play and gave me the seven principles of an offense. One question and his answer took 30 minutes.

I wouldn't say Phil is nervous, but rather full of anticipation. He wants to finish the job. He can taste victory.

It's kind of bittersweet for me because this could be the last game he ever coaches for the Lakers. We'll make the most of it, however it turns out.

SO MANY PLAYERS CONTRIBUTED to our win in Game 6, an 89–67 victory that set up Game 7. From Kobe to Pau to our bench, everybody was heard from.

I love watching Kobe in big games. He is so inspiring when he puts his game face on. When Magic would get in that mode, you knew he wasn't going to be denied.

Kobe and Magic are not the same player, but they are the same in their approach, attitude, and unyielding drive.

Jimmy Connors and John McEnroe were like that. They weren't playing for the money. The winner's purse could have been a dime sitting on the court. They were going to do anything they could to win.

Those are the kind of athletes who only come around once in a generation, and Kobe certainly belongs in that group. Knowing how beat up and tired he is, I am in awe watching him take over a game at this elite level. If the Lakers need a rebound, Kobe gets a rebound. If they need a big shot, he hits a big shot. If they need someone to calm Sasha down, he does that, too.

Sometimes, Kobe will make an incredible shot and you'll say, "Did he really just do that?" When he spreads his arms out after a big play and sails around the court, I think that must be what it feels like to fly. When he is in the zone, the basket must look as big as the ocean. We are so privileged to be able to watch him.

You cannot teach what Kobe has. You have to be born with it. He was, and so was Magic.

I think Kobe is going to be a coach someday because he is so good at being in the moment.

IF WE ARE FORTUNATE ENOUGH to win Game 7, the decision must be made as to who will accept the trophy on behalf of the Buss family. My dad will make the choice. The options have run the gamut from my father to my brother Joey to me. When they asked me, I suggested perhaps Magic would be the best representative.

The fans want to hear what Kobe, Derek, and the other players have to say. When a team wins a championship, it is the players' time. They are the ones who worked so hard to get it. Since Magic is part owner of the team, and considering we are playing the Celtics, I think it would be a special moment for him. And he knows how to defer to the players. Nobody wants to hear me talk.

That said, I do think if my dad were to agree to accept the trophy, STAPLES Center would go wild.

June 17

LAKERS 83, CELTICS 79

Phil was in a great mood driving to STAPLES Center. We were having such a good time. He was very talkative, discussing Los Angeles, the traffic, and what a beautiful day it was.

I asked him if one of the players will make a pregame speech tonight. He said that wouldn't be appropriate. It's really important that the players keep doing the same thing they have been doing all year. This isn't a time to be changing anything.

Upon arriving at the arena, we always part at the door to the locker room. We kiss and then Phil walks in.

Tonight, he just turned to walk away.

"You are not going to kiss me?" I said.

I think he felt funny because there were so many more people around than usual. But he walked back and gave me the kiss.

"You are going to stay and be here for me afterward, aren't you?" he asked.

"Absolutely," I replied. "I'll be here no matter what happens."

AS THE LAKERS FELL 13 points behind Boston in the third quarter, I thought, *This can't be happening. This isn't the way it's supposed to be. I don't think I'll recover if we don't win.*

It seemed like every basket took so much effort. There was just no flow to the game. It was ugly.

The Lakers had only 14 points in the first quarter and 34 at the half. It didn't seem like this game was going to end well. Game 6 was such a work of art, so well executed that I wasn't prepared for the Lakers to struggle as much as they did.

But they kept crawling back.

Some of my friends who weren't at the game were encouraging me by text message, saying, "They'll make a run. They'll get back in it."

I was uptight, but I looked over at Phil and he didn't seem worried at all. There is something reassuring about seeing that confidence. It spread to the players. There was no panic on the bench. Phil was determined to stick to the game plan.

I didn't realize Derek Fisher hurt his knee in the second half. He went to the locker room and Phil didn't know how bad the injury was. But Derek came out and finished the game.

There were big shots by Ron Artest and big free throws by Sasha, two players who have struggled this year. But they came through tonight when Kobe was struggling. Instead of him putting the team on his back like he usually does, it was the team putting Kobe on its collective back.

It was a draining but exciting game. I don't think I've ever heard our fans as loud as they were tonight. They had been going strong all evening because everybody got there on time even though the game started a little after 6:00 PM.

I didn't exhale until the very end when Lamar tossed the ball down to the other end to let the clock run out.

Finally, the buzzer sounded and the confetti started falling. It had been so tense that I still wasn't sure we had won. Joy and relief overwhelmed me.

I stayed in my seat rather than going out onto the court. Phil's kids were all there to be with him, and there were so many other people on the court, so I hung with my girlfriends.

Phil fought through the crowd to get over to my seat and give me a hug, and that meant a lot to me.

I thought the trophy presentation was perfect, my dad accepting it with Magic by his side. It was very special to our fans to have Magic there since he had played such a key role on the first Lakers team to beat the Celtics after being dominated by them for so many years.

I was hugging everybody: Kobe's parents, our assistant coaches, Phil's kids.

It's all kind of a blur, but I'll never forget it.

June 21

For the championship parade, I rode on the truck with the players because Phil asked me to represent him.

Phil doesn't do parades. He doesn't like crowds. Even if he had not had medical appointments today, he wouldn't have been there.

I, on the other hand, love the parade. You can imagine the energy of thousands of fans, but there's nothing like actually feeling it. The positive vibes from the fans were magical. It's a unique experience, one not to be missed.

It doesn't get old to me and you never know if you'll have another one, so I want to take advantage of them while we have a team capable of winning a championship.

It's really hard to read Phil right now. Is he going to come back to coach? The offer is on the table, but I can't tell what he's going to do.

I told him, "This is really stressing me out. I stand behind you in whatever decision you make. You have to do what's right for you. But whatever you decide affects me. I need you to understand that."

I don't know if I can give him a sympathetic ear right now. I'm too nervous over the possibility of him leaving.

June 25

Phil left for Montana without announcing his decision.

He has a house there on Flathead Lake. He bought the property while playing for the Knicks. It was really important for Phil to provide his kids with some roots.

Coaches are vagabonds. They have to go where the jobs are. But Phil's kids always knew that wherever their dad was coaching, they always had Montana in the summertime. That was the family home. That's why it is still so special to him more than 30 years later.

When most people in L.A. think about Montana, they think of sprawling ranches and big-sky country, but that is the southeastern part of the state. Phil lives next to the largest freshwater lake west of the Mississippi in northwestern Montana, a gorgeous area that looks a lot like Oregon.

He has a boat, he fishes, and his kids love to water ski. They all spend a lot of time on the water.

I visited there for the first time in the summer of 2000 after Phil and I had been together for a year. That was a meaningful honor because it meant I was Montana-worthy in his eyes.

I was excited that he wanted to share his retreat with me, but as we drove there, I was also afraid of what it was going to be like. I had never been to Montana and I have a tendency to get homesick, maybe because I never went to summer camp.

The lake turned out to be extremely beautiful and totally peaceful. I immediately understood why he liked it so much.

I stayed for two weeks on that first trip, but I have to admit I got bored. I could get used to the slower pace there, but the problem for me is that I'm busy with work during the summer. July is the month we finalize the upcoming Lakers schedule. Things come up and I have to be available. It's hard for me to be in the middle of nowhere, taking it easy while thinking about all the things I have to do back home.

Huckleberries are the pride and joy of Montana, a prized possession if you can find them. Phil got me all pumped up by talking about how we were going to pick them.

I put on my best hiking gear and we went out to find huckleberries. We drove to a spot and then hiked for about 10 minutes. It was quite an adventure to reach an isolated area where Phil knew few others would have gone. In the public areas, most of the huckleberries have already been picked.

Phil showed me how to find them by softly lifting the leaves and how to gently pick them. If you are too rough, the berries get bruised.

Phil decided we should spread out, so he went in one direction and sent me in another. When we were about 60 yards apart, he yelled, "I told you what to do if you see a bear, right?"

I said, "A *what*? Are we going to see bears?"

"They really like huckleberries," he said.

"Well, what am I supposed to do?"

"If it's a grizzly," Phil said, "then you need to climb a tree. But if it's a brown bear, you need to play dead."

"How do I tell the difference?" I yelled back. "That's it. That's enough huckleberry picking. I've had it."

Like I said, I'm a city girl.

July 1

Phil was tired when he left for Montana. I could understand that. I was so tired that I felt like retiring, too.

It made me anxious that he left town without a commitment to coach the Lakers again. He was stalling for some reason. I even privately theorized that he wanted to wait until the beginning of the free-agency period so that he could have a conversation with LeBron James. Since Phil would not be under contract with the Lakers, he would be free to communicate with LeBron's agent.

But I talked myself out of that idea by realizing Phil just needed to process everything, to get in touch with his feelings, take a break from L.A., and just rest. Once he reached Montana, he sounded so much happier. Being in his home resets his brain.

Phil's medical reports all look good. His sore knee won't inhibit his ability to coach. So his health isn't an issue.

Because Brian Shaw was a candidate for the Cavaliers' coaching job, Cleveland officials called Phil to get his opinion on Brian's qualifications. Once Phil began speaking to them, he was back in basketball mode. For the first time, he started talking to me about next season's Lakers after focusing solely on this season for so long.

Yesterday during a phone conversation, Phil asked me if Doc Rivers had decided to remain the Celtics' coach. I told Phil that Doc had announced his return several days earlier. The fact that Phil was thinking about Doc's future and perhaps a rematch in the Finals was another indication he was leaning toward signing up for one more season.

I was growing more and more optimistic.

I knew Phil's agent, Todd Musburger, was negotiating with the Lakers. I was not involved in any of those discussions.

Finally, John Black came into my office today and dropped a press release on my desk.

"Congratulations," John said.

It was the announcement that Phil has agreed to a one-year deal with the Lakers.

He's made it clear this is his last stand, so we won't have to go through all the speculation again next year. The organization will have plenty of time to figure out who the next coach will be. There won't be any distractions during next season.

When Phil called me 15 minutes after I heard the news, he sounded enthusiastic about his decision. He was already talking about his plans for next season, the Lakers' roster, and the team's preseason games in London and Barcelona.

And beyond next season?

I'm 48 years old, I don't have children, and I have no desire to multitask. Becoming a parent would have meant either cutting back on my level of commitment to my job or not being the mother I would want to be. It is not in my nature to make that compromise, but I admire those who can find that balance.

I know Phil and I are never going to be married. I don't think I'll ever be married again.

Phil is planning to leave the Lakers at the end of next season and that means he will probably have to leave me as well. I know I cannot move to his retirement home in Montana, nor do I see him staying in a big city like Los Angeles.

I am a working girl and the Lakers are my employer, which means my life is here.

It's been a good life, and I do not regret a minute of it.

August 13

Today was the perfect end to a perfect season. In front of family and friends, NBA greats, and Lakers legends, my father was inducted into the Naismith Memorial Basketball Hall of Fame in Springfield, Massachusetts.

Listening to my dad's speech really touched me. He nailed it, his warmth, charm, and humor coming through loud and clear as he spoke.

My mom, my sister, and I were all crying. It was such a meaningful occasion, one I'll never forget.

I observed my dad taking it all in as well, savoring the moment.

He and I walked the red carpet together, holding hands. I told him how proud I was of him. Karl Malone and Scottie Pippen stopped to hug him. It was surreal.

This was an event with a guaranteed happy ending for Lakers fans. There was no game to win or lose. It was all just love and joy.

My dad being enshrined in the Hall of Fame is the ultimate reward for an unrivaled career.

I think about him as a shivering kid in a Depression-era bread line and as the beaming recipient of a Hall of Fame plaque. He has made an incredible journey in his lifetime, from the grip of poverty to the embrace of a league, a city, and a legendary team.

ACKNOWLEDGMENTS

UNDERTAKING THE TASK OF WRITING A JOURNAL WAS INTIMIDATING. Without the encouragement and support of my agent, Lon Rosen of Lagardère Unlimited, I would have avoided it completely. He matched me with my co-author, Steve Springer, and a book was born. Thank you to both gentlemen.

Thank you to Triumph Books for undertaking this project and guiding me through to completion. Special thanks to publisher Mitch Rogatz, editorial director Tom Bast, and developmental editor Adam Motin.

I would like to thank my mom and dad, my siblings, and my entire family for their unwavering support. I have been blessed to be surrounded by their loving embrace.

Thank you to Linda Rambis for being a sounding board for the duration of the process. Thank you to Stacy Kennedy for the inspiration for the book cover—you should be an art director in addition to your other titles. Thank you to Linda, Stacy, and Danielle Robb for sharing Lakers games with me.

A debt of professional and personal gratitude to my friends at the Anschutz Entertainment Group (AEG): Phil Anschutz, Tim Leiweke, Lee Zeidman, Dan Beckerman, Ted Fickre, Michael Roth, and Christy Castillo Butcher. Thank you for the support and always making the Lakers look good.

To Andy Bernstein, thank you for taking the photo for the cover and for contributing many more photos for this book, as well as for being there for all the momentous occasions in Lakers history. Thanks to Michael

Harris for coordinating the shoot and to Rodney Webb and Ray Reese for serving as the cover models.

Thank you to my mentors and role models: Jerry Fine, Billie Jean King, Mr. Wakeman, Earvin "Magic" Johnson, Linda and Kurt Rambis, Claire Rothman, Marge and Chick Hearn, Paul Tobias, and Carolyn Williams. You all contributed to making me who I am as a person and as a professional.

To my friends who have shared their time with me along the journey: Ellen Idelson, Megan Black, Lauren Piper MacPherson, John Carrabino, Chip Engelland, Jon Berger, Hermina, Ilana Kloss, Jerry and Karen West, Bob Steiner, John Black, Debbie Zafrani Fogel, Kathryn Schloessman, Sharon Chew, Tim Harris, Robin White, Lee Zeidman, Mardi and Bobby Hull Jr., David McLane, Rick Adams, Marcel Chagnon, Tim and Bernadette Leiweke, Joe and Sharon Hernandez, Joyce and Bill Sharman, Ed and Eydie Desser, Laurie and Lon Rosen, Laurent Saint-Circq, Garry Simmons, and Dr. Paul Drew.

Thank you to my Twitter family. You rock, and I look forward to many more DMs and convos with you all.

With deepest gratitude, I would like to thank the Jackson family and extended family and friends for being the coolest folks I've ever had the pleasure to meet and share time with.

Finally, to my sweetheart, Philip D. Jackson, thank you for understanding the sacrifices I made to meet the deadlines for this book and also for contributing the foreword, which was perfect.